Powerful Places
in Wales

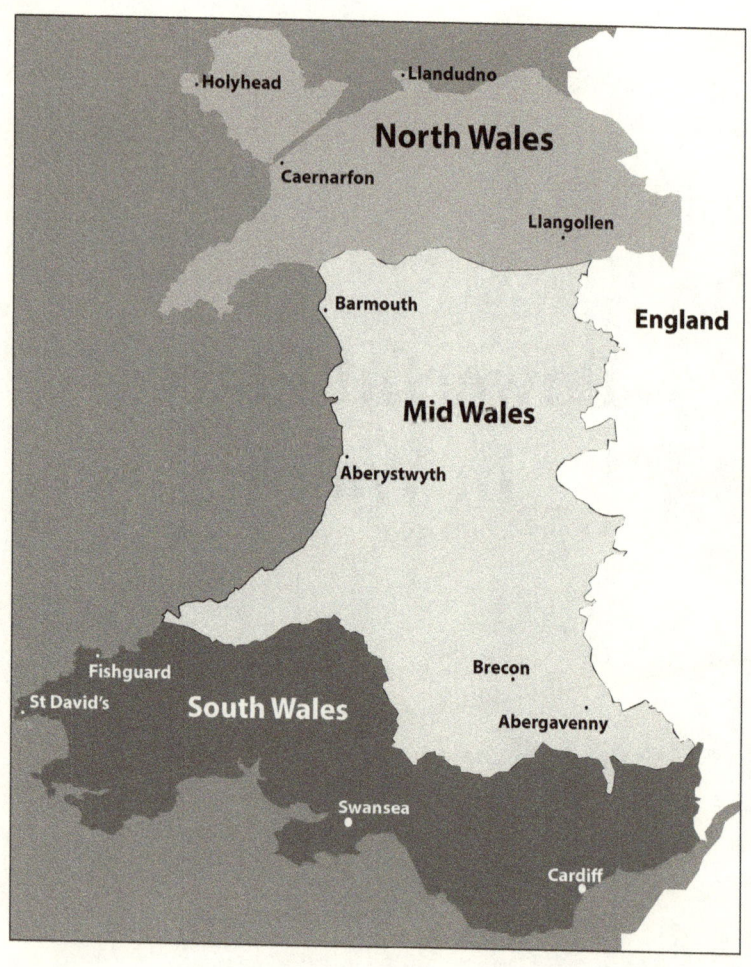

Powerful Places
in Wales

Elyn Aviva &
Gary White

Powerful Places in Wales

by

Elyn Aviva & Gary White

Copyright © 2012 by Pilgrims Process, Inc.

http://www.PowerfulPlaces.com

All rights reserved. No part of this publication, including illustrations, may be reproduced in any form or by any means, electronic or mechanical, including photocopy, recording, or any information storage and retrieval system, without permission in writing from the publisher.

The authors and publisher have made every effort to ensure the accuracy of the information in this book at the time of publication. However, they cannot accept any responsibility for any loss, injury, or inconvenience resulting from the use of information contained in this book.

ISBN: 978-0-9835516-7-6

Library of Congress Control Number:

2012915666

Set in Minon Pro 10 pt. and Gil Sans Light 10 pt., with display in Minon Pro in various sizes. Cover and title set in Reliq Std and Briso Pro.

Cover photo: Carreg Samson cromlech, Pembrokeshire. Photo by Gary White. All interior photos by Elyn Aviva or Gary White unless otherwise noted.

Photo on p. 120 courtesy of Brian John

Contents

A Note About QR Codes viii
Acknowledgments 1
Introduction to Powerful Places Guidebooks 3
   Powerful Places 4
   What Makes a Place Powerful? 5
   Experiencing a Powerful Place 7
Powerful Places in Wales 11
   Kinds of Powerful Places 15
      Location, Location, Location... 15
      Holy Islands, Mountains, and Caves... 18
      Holy Springs, Lakes, Rivers, and Sea... 21
      Trees.. 23
      Stones.. 24
Some Historical Background 26
Traveling in Wales 35
   Language – A Few Suggestions 39
   Names and Numbers.. 41
   Additional Resources 42
South Wales (Cardiff, Newport, Monmouthshire, the Gower, Carmarthenshire, Pembrokeshire) 45
   Llandaff Cathedral (Eglwys Gadeiriol Llandaf), Cardiff 47
      More to Experience... 50
   Tinkinswood Burial Chamber, Vale of Glamorgan 56
   Carreg Cennen and Dinefwr Castles, Llandeilo, Carmarthenshire..... 59
      Carreg Cennen Castle, Carmarthenshire 60
      Dinefwr Castle and Park, Carmarthenshire 64
   Parc le Breos Cwm Burial Cairn, Cat Hole Cave, Gower Peninsula (West Glamorgan) 68
      More to Experience...72
   Gumfreston Church and Holy Wells (Ffynhonnau Eglwys Gumfreston), Pembrokeshire 75
      More to Experience... 80
   St Davids (St David's), Pembrokeshire 87
      St Davids Cathedral and Bishop's Palace, Pembrokeshire 90
      St Non's Well and Chapels, Pembrokeshire 93
      More to Experience... 96
   Llanwnda: Ffynnon Wnda (Wnda's Well), the Church of St Gwyndaf, and Garn Wnda, Pembrokeshire 98
      More to Experience... 102
   The Gwaun Valley, Pembrokeshire 105
      Llanllawer Church and Holy Well, Pembrokeshire 107
      Parc y Merw (Parc y Meirw), Pembrokeshire 109
      St Brynach's Church, Pontfaen, Pembrokeshire 110
      More to Experience... 112

Mynydd Preseli – The Preseli Hills I, Pembrokeshire 114
  Carn Ingli (Carningli), Pembrokeshire 118
  Carn Enoch, Pembrokeshire 122
Mynydd Preseli – The Preseli Hills II, Pembrokeshire 124
  Maenclochog Church, Pembrokeshire 124
  St Teilo's Well, Pembrokeshire 126
  Gors Fawr Stone Circle, Pembrokeshire 129
Mynydd Preseli – The Preseli Hills III, Pembrokeshire.. 132
  Pentre Ifan, Pembrokeshire 133
  Tycanol (Tŷ Canol) Wood, Pembrokeshire 138
  More to Experience... 139
St Brynach's Church, Nevern (Eglwys St Brynach, Nanhyfer), Pembrokeshire 144
  More to Experience... 152
Ffynone Waterfall (Ffynone Cwm Cych), near Abercych, Pembrokeshire 152
  More to Experience... 156

Mid Wales (Ceredigion, Cambrian Coast, Powys, part of Gwynedd, and the Brecon Beacons) 160

Strata Florida Abbey (Abaty Ystrad Fflur), Ceredigion 162
  More to Experience... 169
Cadair (anglicized as Cader) Idris, Snowdonia National Park, Gwynedd................. 171
  More to Experience... 176
The Cambrian Coast 181
  Harlech (Harddlech), Gwynedd... 181
  Ardudwy Megaliths, Gwynedd.. 182
  Two Waterfall Walks, Gwynedd... 183
  Aberdovey (Aberdyfi) and Tre Taliesin, Gwynedd... 187
  More to Experience 190
Brecon Beacons National Park (extending through several counties)...................... 194
  Myddfai and Llyn y Fan Fach, Carmarthenshire.. 197
  Sarn (H)elen, Brecon Beacons.. 200
  More to Experience... 203
Patrisio (Partrishow) Church and Holy Well, Powys.. 206
Llanthony Priory, Monmouthshire 212
Radnor Forest, Cascob Church, and St Michael's Church in Discoed, Powys.......... 216
  St Michael's Church, Cascob, Powys... 218
  St Michael's Church, Discoed, Powys... 222
  More to Experience:.. 225
St Melangell Church, Pennant Melangell, Powys 227
  More to Experience... 234

North Wales (Snowdonia, the Isle of Anglesey, the Llŷn Peninsula, the North Coast, Denbighshire, Flintshire) 239

Dinas Emrys, Snowdonia National Park 243
  More to Experience... 251
Anglesey (Ynys Môn), county of Anglesey 257
  Bryn Celli Ddu, Anglesey.. 259
  Bryn Gwyn Standing Stones and Castell Bryn Gwyn, Anglesey...................................... 264
  Barclodiad y Gawres, Anglesey.. 267
  Lligwy Complex 271
  Penmon Priory and St Seiriol's Holy Well, Anglesey... 277
  More to Experience 282

Driving toward the Llŷn Peninsula, Gwynedd 292
   Llanfaglan Church, Gwynedd 292
   Dinas Dinlle, Gwynedd 294
Llŷn Peninsula, Gwynedd.. 298
   St Beuno's Church, Clynnog Fawr, Gwynedd... 299
   Nant Gwrtheyrn, Llŷn Peninsula, Gwynedd 302
   N52 58 32 W4 27 29.. 302
   St Beuno's Church, Pistyll, Llŷn Peninsula, Gwynedd 306
   Garnfadryn (Carn Fadrun), Llŷn Peninsula, Gwynedd... 309
   St Cybi's Well, Llangybi, Llŷn Peninsula, Gwynedd 310
   More to Experience.. 313
Gop, the North Coast (Denbighshire) 317
   More to Experience.. 321
Castell Dinas Brân, Llangollan, Denbighshire... 326
   More to Experience.. 329

Afterword 331
Pronunciation Guide... 333
Glossary 340
Bibliography 351
Index 358

A Note About QR Codes

Throughout this book you will notice square boxes filled with tiny rectangles of various sizes. These boxes are QR codes (quick response codes) that link to websites. To read these codes you need to have a QR code reader installed on your smart phone or tablet and you need an internet connection. You can find the app in the app store for your device if one is not already installed.

When you have the app installed, start it up and aim the camera at this QR code:

You should see the Powerful Places website appear on the device. You can move about that website and see what we have to offer and how to order our books in various formats.

Every URL reference in this book has a QR code near it to allow you to go easily and quickly to the websites we recommend. These provide additional information, photos, videos, and other resources to enrich your reading experience. Let us know if the QR codes make a positive contribution to your experience in *Powerful Places in Wales*.

The URLs were active when this book went to press. However, the internet changes every day and it is inevitable that some of the references will be out of date or no longer active when you view them.

Acknowledgments

Gratitude to our mentors and teachers, including Ferran Blasco Aguasca, Mara Freeman, Sig Lonegren, Anne Parker, R. J. Stewart, and Dominique Susani. Gratitude to all the earth-mystery writers and researchers, including Paul Devereux, Tom Graves, and Nigel Pennick, who have opened the way for so many others. Gratitude to our friends and manuscript readers, especially Sandra Chris, Ros Briagha Foskett, Jane de Rougemont, Paul and Lesley Juckes, and Hilary Wylde. Many thanks to Gwen Saunders Jones and Huw Tegid, formerly at Menter Iaith Môn, for their painstaking work on the pronunciation guide. Gratitude to each other for patience, tolerance, and enthusiasm. Gratitude to the land, the stones, the trees, the water, the temples, and the people of Wales—especially the people, who have been ongoing sources of inspiration.

For those interested in following up with our mentors we offer the following websites:

Ferran Blasco Aguasca: http://www.acupunturabarcelona.com/zahoriart/

Mara Freeman: http://www.chalicecentre.net/

Sig Lonegren: http://www.geomancy.org/

Anne Parker: http://www.latitudewithattitude.com/

R. J. Stewart: http://www.rjstewart.org/

Dominique Susani: http://www.sacredgeometryarts.com/

Introduction to Powerful Places Guidebooks

Over the years we have traveled to a number of unusual places, drawn by curiosity, lured by possibility. Gradually we realized that although many of these sites were interesting, some of them x much more—they were powerful. These were places where we felt something out of the ordinary, ranging from a shiver up the spine to an unexpected sense of serenity. Sometimes we had a strong intimation that we had entered a "thin place" where the veil between this world and the "other realm" was more easily parted.

In this guidebook we describe some of the powerful places we have found in Wales and invite you to experience them for yourself. We don't know what you will feel when visiting these sites. We have observed that one person may bask in the energy of a particular site; another may feel nothing at all; and a third may want to leave as quickly as possible.

> "There is a Celtic saying that heaven and earth are only three feet apart, but in the thin places that distance is even smaller." Sylvia Maddox

How did we (Gary and Elyn) choose these particular locations? We talked with people; we did research to discover powerful places that were not likely to be on every tourist's itinerary; we made extended and repeated visits to Wales; and we paid attention to what we experienced at different sites. We traveled with and consulted with expert guides. We then chose a variety of powerful places to include in this guidebook. We make no claims to be exhaustive; instead, we are selective.

Each chapter includes at least one brief, personal account by Elyn of a visit to a particular powerful place. This is followed by a description of the site, along with suggestions for experiencing the place, additional information in grey boxes, and numerous photos and graphics. There are directions on how to get there and other places to experience. The guidebook concludes with an afterword, a pronounciation guide, a glossary, a bibliography, and an index.

We hope that *Powerful Places in Wales* is the beginning of a relationship between you and Wales—and with our guidebook series. We look forward to hearing from you.

> "Why do I go to powerful places? And why do I return again and again? The experiences I have in powerful places remind me that there is much more to reality than I normally encounter—that the universe is a much grander place than I can imagine. These experiences reaffirm the mystery of creation, that 'everything is, but nobody knows exactly what it is,' to quote Terry Patten. I find this very reassuring." Elyn.

Powerful Places

The way a powerful place feels can take many forms, and it can be subtle or very strong, positive or otherwise. For example, during one visit inside a large, earth-covered passage grave in Ireland, Elyn felt increasingly uncomfortable and shaky but, against her better judgment, she stayed to listen to our guide. Afterwards, Elyn learned that several people had left immediately because they felt so ill at ease—but others thought the cairn was a wonderful place. A friend who visited the site at another time remarked on the exquisite rose fragrance that permeated the chamber during her meditation.

Fourknocks passage grave in Ireland

In an isolated monastery in the mountains of Spain, we were shown into an abandoned chapel. Instantly, we both felt an unconditionally loving presence. Our companion, a sensitive, intuitive woman, looked at us in puzzlement. She thought the energy in the room was nothing special.

Our experiences have differed on subsequent visits to the same site. Sometimes the explanation is simple: a large, noisy tour group has just trampled through the site, oblivious to what was there. Other times the answer is not so obvious. Perhaps it has something to do with being there at a different time of year or during a different phase of the moon—or in a different state of mind.

Experiences can never be repeated, whether it's your first bite into a chocolate gelato cone on a sunny day in Rome, or your first kiss, or your first visit to the Grand Canyon. To paraphrase the Greek philosopher Heraclitus, "No one ever steps into the same river twice, for it's not the same river and the person is not the same person." This is equally true of powerful places.

What Makes a Place Powerful?

In powerful places, we experience an interaction between the energies of the place itself, the human activities at that location (offerings, ceremonies, constructions such as stone circles or temples), and our own openness to experience what is happening at that moment. The land itself has underground water lines and faults or cracks in the earth (sometimes called fire lines), energy vortices, "blind" springs, and so on, which our ancestors were able to sense and utilize. An old Gaulish word, *wouivre*, refers to snakes that glide, to rivers that snake through the landscape, and to telluric currents that snake underground from the depths of the terrestrial strata.

Experienced dowsers using rods or pendulums can locate these underground features with great accuracy. If they couldn't, oil exploration and well-digging companies wouldn't waste their money on hiring them.

Powerful places are often located on what are called ley lines, which can be plotted on maps. The Englishman Alfred Watkins first wrote about "leys" in 1925 in his book *The Old Straight Track*. Watkins considered them a kind of "line of sight" guide for traveling across the country, and the ley lines he discovered intersected numerous Iron Age forts, holy wells, megalithic sites, notches in hills, and medieval churches.

> Sergio Berti, an Italian geobiophysical analyst, says "powerful places" produce a measurable effect on the body. They affect the sympathetic component of the autonomous nervous system. An increase in sympathetic activity is linked to action, optimism, and readiness to fight; a decrease is linked to relaxation, slower breathing, and the predominance of the mind over body. An underground fault may reduce sympathetic activity; granite may stimulate sympathetic activity; and metallic minerals may stimulate activity or not, depending on the type. (More information at http://www.architettura-geobiologia.it/Sito_architetturageobiologia/home.html)

More recently, some researchers have described ley lines as lines of energy that flow across the earth—meridians of Mother Earth, so to speak, "lines of light," or "paths" (the latter term used by Laurence Main). Some of them twist and spiral, and they usually must be dowsed "in situ" on location.

Experienced dowsers follow these lines for long distances. Some of them have been given names, like the Michael and Mary lines across England. Whether ley lines or spirit lines are "ener-

> Elizabeth Brown says the following: "Dowsing is 'a way of finding out by accessing information, with directed intent, using a means outside the five recognized senses and culminating in a physical response within the human body.' ... "Dowsing has existed in various forms around the planet for as long as humankind has been aware of a field of information or believed that an organized intelligence is at work, existing outside the individual conscious mind." ... "Dowsing is a tangible manifestation of our profound connection, on every level, to each other, to all forms of life and to the universe." (pp. 7-8, 288)

> "It is a theory held by many occultists, and confirmed by many others, that ley lines are actually the lines of power in the aura of the earth and that along those ley lines the power flows." Butler, p. 94.

getic" pathways, and whether sacred sites were built upon the ley lines to draw upon their energy, is a discussion beyond the scope of this book.

Our ancestors utilized these energies and their knowledge of geometry (circles, triangles, pyramid shapes, etc.) to construct sacred places. For example, an alignment of standing stones may have been placed to draw off energy from a destabilizing underground fault; a circle of stones may have been built to utilize the energy of an underground ("blind") spring or a vortex. The altar of a twelfth-century church may have been carefully placed over the crossing of under-

> "What is meant by a ley, or spirit path, is very much open to individual interpretation. Significantly, it is a straight path or track that is identified in one's subconscious and is consequently traced by a process of dowsing and connecting sightlines ... suggesting a divine or mystical significance." Main, p. 8.

ground water and fire lines, to take advantage of the "energetic steam" they generate. In addition, the ancient Master Builders used their knowledge of astronomy to orient some of these powerful places toward important seasonal events like the winter solstice.

Experiencing a Powerful Place

How do you experience a powerful place? The brief answer is: by centering, grounding, and being present to a site in whatever way works for you. Feeling the subtle energies that are present in a place requires practice, sensitivity, and intuition. It is a bit like tuning a radio dial to a particular frequency. Although some people are naturally gifted in sensing these energies, others need to be taught. We didn't feel much at powerful places until we started studying with geomancers and dowsers. Detailed instruction in dowsing and sensing earth energies is outside the scope of this guidebook, but we will give suggestions for how you can "attune" yourself to the powerful places we describe.

Crop-circle expert and sacred-sites researcher Freddy Silva lists seven principles of sacred space: water, electromagnetics, sacred measure, stone, sacred geometry, orientation, and "the human key." This latter principle refers to the interaction between the human energy field and its surroundings; for example, the awareness and intention we bring with us to a site. Intent is "the key that allows access into the invisible temple—its subtle energy field" (p. 231).

We encourage you to listen carefully to your own inner guidance as you open yourself to what may be available to you at a powerful place on a particular day, at a particular time of day, with the particular predisposition you bring to that moment. Use your own judgment to determine what is good or not good for you. Trust your feelings—and enjoy the mystery!

> "Beneath everything we know—or think we know—there is a web of energy that holds our reality together and exists beyond the visible world." Heaven, p. 217.

Much of the time we humans operate "on automatic," hardly registering where we are or what we feel. Visiting a powerful place is an opportunity to be intentional and alert. In order to experience fully a powerful place, it is important to be present. Be aware of your surroundings and of changes in yourself in response to the environment.

> "There is a sane and balanced ground for a thoughtful and rational agnostic to be open to the idea that consciousness and awareness pervades the universe, that it may be as or even more fundamental than material physicality, that there's no such thing as dead, unconscious matter, that we live in a psychophysical universe with interiority and exteriority, with an innerness, an inner life as well as its outer manifestation." Terry Patten, Lesson 4, Evolving Wisdom, spring 2011.

We suggest an acronym, **BLESSING**, to help remember how to prepare to enter

> "The nature of sacred art is to connect us directly to our highest being, our purest potential. And that is the purpose of working with the Earth energies. The 'art of the stones' or the art of working with the Earth energies as I understand it, is not just about dowsing rods or pendulums, not about water veins or underground faults. Those are the external aspects. The art of the Master Builders is a spiritual art: it enables us to experience that sacredness that we are, that infinite space of bliss." Ferran Blasco Aguasca.

a powerful place—whether it is a forest, a church, or a stone circle. **BLESSING** stands for: Breathe slowly and regularly, paying attention to your breath moving in and out. If you have a breathing practice, now is the time to do it. Look and Listen within: what are you sensing internally? How do you feel? Establish yourself in your location, perhaps by orienting to the seven directions (east, south, west, north, above, below, and the center within; or, before you, behind you, to your right, to your left, above, below, and the center within). Sense your surroundings, opening your five (or six) senses to what is around you. State your **IN**tention to respect this place, to experience what is present. Give Gratitude for this opportunity.

Mara Freeman's acronym **ECOLOGY** helps us remember how to approach a stone circle. It can, of course, be modified to apply to powerful places in general. "**E**" stands for Entry, which means enter by first circling the site in a clockwise (sunwise) direction. "**C**" is for Centering yourself. This is often best accomplished by touching one of the stones or an entryway. "**O**"

> "When approaching a human-constructed site: 1. Remember the site puts us in contact with the people who built it—not directly, but through the monuments themselves. People constructed them 5000, 4000, 3000, 1000 years ago. That's amazing. It's a kind of time travel. 2. Explore the uniqueness of the site. Our ancestors expended a great deal of effort constructing it. Pay attention to the stones, the sacred geometry, and the underground energies. 3. Experience the place itself—enter into relationship with it, communicate with it, connect with it. And 4. Notice the Mystery: nobody knows what any thing *really* is. (Gary)

stands for **O**ffering, which can be a bit of grain, milk, a strand of hair, saliva, etc. This shows that you come in good faith. The best offerings are biodegradable so they don't linger in the environment or build up over time. "**L**" is for Listening. Listen to the sounds around you: birds, wind, wild creatures, and other sounds of nature. "**O**" stands for **O**pening up your inner and outer senses. "**G**" is for **G**ratitude to the place, the Earth, all of life, and Nature. "**Y**" is for **Y**ou: you should leave a place just as you found it. Take nothing and leave nothing. You can see the result of people not observing this injunction at many popular sacred sites: trees damaged by people taking pieces of their bark or carving on them; sites littered with paper wrappers and trash; melted wax dripped over ancient stones. Observe **ECOLOGY** at sacred sites: the Earth and future visitors will thank you.

> "In the universe, there are things that are known, and things that are unknown, and in between, there are doors." William Blake

Before entering a church, temple, or tumulus, ask permission from the spirits, the ancestors, or the guardians of the place. Imagine that you are entering someone's home or place of worship: you wouldn't simply barge in without asking, and you would want to be polite. If you sense a positive response, place your hand lightly on the column or stone to the right of the entryway. Pause a moment to attune yourself (come

> "Even elements of the environmental movement approach the earth as an object to be preserved, rather than as a spiritual reality to be respected. This misconception may prove to be fateful, for, as Tony Gonnela Frichner of the Onondoga Nation has pointed out, 'How can you "save the Earth" if you have no spiritual relationship with the Earth? There is an intellectual abstraction about the environment but no visceral participation with the Earth. Non-Indians can't change the current course of destruction without this connection.'" Joseph Epes Brown, quoted in *Parabola* email newsletter, 3 Feb. 2012).

into energetic harmony) with the place. Then step over (not on) the threshold.

You might want to bring some narrow silk or cotton ribbons that will biodegrade and perhaps some oatcakes to leave as offerings at particular sacred sites. You also might want to have some empty bottles for collecting water at holy wells.

Powerful Places in Wales

"Croeso i Gymru (pronounced "kroyso ee gumree")— Welcome to Wales!

Welsh tourism promotes the outstanding beauty of the land, its scenic railroads, its impressive waterfalls, and its numerous well-preserved castles: 641 in all, more than in any other European country. Wales is visually stunning, with inviting beaches, extensive hiking trails in the hills and along the coast, and impressive historic buildings, lovely formal gardens, and charming market towns.

But there is much more to Wales. Wales is a very powerful place, a place that reveals itself slowly and gradually—if you are patient, attentive, and respectful. It has much to offer, but it does so without a lot of fanfare and with little show. If you take the time to engage it, to establish a relationship with the land and people, it will slowly blossom.

For starters, Wales is the only country in the world that has a red dragon *(y ddraig goch)* as its national symbol, affirming the ongoing vitality of mythic memory in modern Welsh life. The dragon evokes legends of Merlin (in Welsh, Myrddin), who prophesized about the battling red and white dragons, respectively representing the Welsh/Britons and the Anglo/Saxons, in the lake beneath Vortigern's falling tower. It also recalls

The flag of Wales

King Arthur, who supposedly used the red dragon on his battle standard. Other lands, including Brittany and England, claim Merlin and Arthur, but Wales claims them both with more probable cause.

Only Wales has the *eisteddfod*, a festival honoring Welsh music, performance, visual arts, and literature, which dates back to the twelfth century. The power of the word, of recitation, and of music (solo voice, choir, and harp) has a long and honored history in Wales, which has been aptly nicknamed "the land of song." Welsh choirs, encouraged by the nineteenth-century Nonconformist chapel movement and the Temperance Movement, are famous throughout the world.

And only Wales has the official post of Archdruid, elected every three years as the head of the Welsh-language Gorsedd of the Bards society. The Gorsedd is responsible for providing ritual and pageantry for the national *eisteddfodau*, and many ceremonies take place within a circle of standing stones erected for that purpose.

As you can tell, the Welsh take their traditions, their history, and their language seriously.

To be accurate, we should refer to Wales as Cymru (pronounced "KUM-ree" or "KOOM-ree," depending on the dialect). Cymru is Welsh for "Land of the Cymry" or "fellow countrymen." The name "Wales" comes from the Anglo-Saxon word for stranger or foreigner, and it was used by them to refer to Celtic Britons or anything else that they considered foreign.

"It be deep here," was the silent message Gary kept getting during our visits to Cymru, and deep it is in Wales. The land is deep here, the dragons battling beneath the surface, the myths embedded in the earth and mountains, in the lakes and sea—as well as in the minds and hearts of the "fellow country folk." The Welsh we met "be deep," just like the land.

The countryside, like the people, resonates with stories and legends. The poems of Taliesin and Aneirin, written down in the late sixth or early seventh century, are the earliest surviving examples of Welsh literature. They are older than any European literature in a language other than Greek or Latin. Wales claims one of the oldest unbroken literary traditions in Europe.

The medieval Welsh masterpiece, the *Mabinogi* (also, somewhat inaccurately, called the *Mabinogion*), was first written down in the late eleventh or early twelfth century, but it had circulated in oral form for hundreds of years. The earliest surviving texts are found in manuscripts from the thirteenth and fourteenth century (Bollard and Griffiths, p. 9). Composed of the Four Branches of interrelated stories and a group of seven additional stories, the *Mabinogi* contains valuable information about the beliefs, rituals, and social mores of pre-Christian Britain. Five of the additional stories recount the fantastic adventures of King Arthur and his knights.

> Many powerful places in Wales are not signposted. It's almost as if the Welsh don't want to publicize them. Several times local people told us that they knew of some powerful places, but they didn't want us to tell too many people about them. "We like these places to stay quiet and peaceful, so we can visit in solitude."

Many of the tales of the *Mabinogi* can be superimposed on the Welsh landscape. As you read the stories, you can imagine the gods and goddesses, and the demi-gods and demi-goddesses, journeying across Wales. There is Rhiannon on her white horse, riding across the southern fields near Arbeth (now Narbeth); Pwyll encountering the entrance to Annwn, the Celtic Underworld, in Cwm Cych (perhaps at nearby Ffynone Falls); Brân the Blessed and

Branwen, children of Llŷr—god of the sea—living at Harddlech (now Harlech Castle) until Branwen was given in marriage to Matholwch, King of Ireland; Arianrhod in her spinning castle off the coast of the Llŷn Peninsula; the wizards Math, son of Mathonwy (said by some to be a creatrix goddess), and his nephew, Gwydion, son of Dôn (the Welsh mother goddess), creating Blodeuedd, a flower-woman, in Snowdonia; Arthur pursuing a gigantic magical boar through the Preseli Mountains to Cornwall—and more, much more. It's as if the entire country, not just a few isolated locations, shimmers with archetypal connections and mythic images. See http://en.wikipedia.org/wiki/Welsh_mythology for a useful summary of the most important characters in the *Mabinogi*.

Rhiannon

> "What the *Mabinogi* as a whole maps out is the gradual transition of geo-political power between these various groupings, charting the archaic tribal history of the island through a complex sequence of hegemonic events – including marriages, wars, alliances and swindlings." http://www.mabinogion.info/four-branches.htm, retrieved 22 Jan. 2012.

We humans experience reality through a filter. At any moment, there is so much possible sensory input that we selectively pay attention to some things and exclude others. For example, we notice someone has had a haircut; we don't hear someone talking to us; we don't see a stop sign; we don't taste our food. Myths and legends provide another kind of filter. They shift our attention to something other than the geological, historic, or astronomical status

> To say "Here is where Rhiannon rode on her white horse" is not the same as saying "Here is where the Bill of Rights was signed." The first statement has a mythic reality; the second has an historical one.

of a particular location. In doing so, they evoke the archetypal images and energies that contribute to making that place powerful. This enriches our experience. Of course, some places are powerful regardless of the stories told about them—but that's no reason not to tell the stories when they are known.

"It be deep here." Wales is a powerful place that needs to be experienced through the double vision of mythic memory and creative re-imagination. There is an interaction, an interplay, between the stories and the sites, between the land and its people, between the see-er and the seen, as if each increases the resonance of the other.

Kinds of Powerful Places

> "Many of the tribal peoples of the world recognize that there are four places in nature where you can find deep peace and remember who you really are. One is in the deep woods; one is in the desert; one in the mountains and one near the ocean." (Angeles Arrien, "The Second Half of Life" transcript.) Wales lacks the desert but makes up for it in the power of its land.

Location, Location, Location

A powerful place does not exist in isolation from its surroundings. Ancient people often constructed several (or numerous) sites within a relatively close distance from each other. These sites often have a visual, and probably energetic, relationship to each other and to prominent natural features such as hilltops, gaps between hills, etc. This phenomenon is called intervisibility, and the landscapes themselves are called ritual landscapes.

Examples of prominent ritual landscapes occur around the Calanais Stones in Scotland, the megaliths at Carnac in Brittany, and Stonehenge in England, to name a few. In Ireland, dolmens dot the ridges around northern Co. Sligo and the Bricklieve Mountains in the south. Regions of the Isle of Anglesey in northwest Wales (see pp. 257-291) appear to have once been massive ritual landscapes, including dolmens, standing stones, processional walks, and sacred lakes. Pentre Ifan dolmen in Pembrokeshire (see pp. 133-137) looks toward the holy mountain, Carn Ingli, in one direction and toward dense, ancient woods in the other. There is much speculation about the purpose of these landscapes, but it is clear that they were created intentionally.

Not only were sacred sites constructed with an awareness of the energies of the earth and in relationship to each other and to surrounding natural features, they were also often built to interact with solar, lunar, or stellar events. Just as churches used to be constructed so that the altar was in the east, facing the rising sun and signifying the resurrected Christ, so were many megalithic sites designed to take advantage of recurring astronomical events.

Pentre Ifan in a 1613 drawing

For example, the light of the setting winter solstice sun shines into the entry passageway of Maeshowe, a site described in *Powerful Places in Scotland*. The Newgrange passage mound in Co. Meath is the location of a spectacular winter solstice event, de-

"A sacred space is a *temenos*, a Greek word meaning an enclosure that makes it possible to enter into a relationship with a greater reality. Entering into sacred space, one crosses a threshold and moves from *chronos*, human time and space, into *kairos*, eternal time." Hale, p. xiii.

scribed in *Powerful Places in Ireland*. On a clear morning the light from the rising sun enters through the roof box and pierces the 62-ft-long corridor, reaching toward the rear interior wall. Bryn Celli Ddu dolmen on the Isle of Anglesey in northwestern Wales is oriented toward the rising summer solstice sun (see pp. 259-263). At stone circles it may be more difficult to prove which, or how many, astronomical events were being marked, but often some alignments are obvious.

In Wales, another kind of location is equally important: the placement of churches. Perched on top of a windswept hill, located behind a protecting outcrop, built into the side of a cliff, nestled at the end of a narrow valley—notice where the churches, the sacred enclosures, are constructed. Often a church was built on top of the remains of an Iron Age fort or in the middle of a 4000-year-old circle of standing stones. It may be surrounded by ancient yew trees that predate the Christian building. Perhaps there is a view of a holy mountain, or of the setting sun over the sea, or of some

Patrisio (Partrishow) Church, Powys

other significant landscape feature, such as proximity to the ebbing and flowing tides.

Holy Islands, Mountains, and Caves

"No man is an island," but living on one can give you the sense that you are set apart, isolated from the mainstream of life by the ebb and flow of tides. Combine these bits of land with early Welsh Christianity, and you have a match made, if not in Heaven, at least in the minds of hermits and pilgrims seeking to escape from the mundane world.

> "According to traditional thinking, islands are inherently sacred, being places cut off by water from unwanted physical and psychic influences." Pennick, p. 105.

Wales has an extensive coastline (750 mi); only its eastern boundary is connected to England. Several important islands are just off-shore: Anglesey (known as Ynys Môn or Holy Island), where the last of the Celtic Britons made their final, unsuccessful stand against the invading Romans; Bardsey Island (Ynys Enlli), a magical place purported to be the burial place of 20,000 saints (i.e., holy men and pilgrims) and a candidate for the Isle of Avalon, where the wounded King Arthur was taken or perhaps where Merlin lies asleep in a glass castle; and Caldey Island, site of an important medieval monastery.

Mountains are often the focus of folklore and legends, probably because their hard-to-access peaks are that much closer to the heavens. They provide panoramic views, making humans feel less important but paradoxically more brave and powerful because they have reached the summit. The gods are often

> "To our civilized view, places are just commodities, to be bought and sold like any other commodity; but in the pagan view, probably best typified by that of the American Indians [and the Celts], places can have a sacredness, a spiritual importance, that seems to bear no relation to the more physical characteristics of the place." Graves, p. 5-6. [Interpolation added by Elyn Aviva]

reported to have appeared on mountains, and many mountaintop altars are dedicated to deities. Dangerous to climb, places where the weather is fierce, the winds strong, mountains are often sacred not only to the Sky God but also to the Earth Mother.

Snowdonia National Park, in northwest Wales, is associated with Merlin and Arthur, as well as with other mythic or half-mythic beings. Legend claims Arthur killed a giant called Rita Gawr on the top of Mt Snowdon. Along the north coast, Gop, the second-largest human-made hill in Britain, is constructed on top of a natural hill. It has a commanding location, perched between hills and water, and can be seen from great distances.

On the nearby Llŷn Peninsula, Garnfadryn mountain is named after Madron, the ancient Mother Goddess of the region. In the southwest, Mynydd Preseli (the Preseli Hills) are covered with megalithic sites, ancient trackways, and upthrusting summits, known as carns. Angels reportedly visited St Brynach on the top of Carn Ingli, one of Wales'

Cadair Idris in Snowdonia National Park

holiest mountains. Some see a reclining pregnant goddess, a face, or a giant in its silhouetted shape.

A cave is an opening into the earth, an entrance into the Underworld, a journey into the womb of the Great Mother. Caves offer us darkness, mystery, danger, death, rebirth, initiation, and transformation. What lurks within? The ancient goddess of the land? A sleeping hero? Is it a place of oracular wisdom, of healing dreams or nightmares? A subterranean, otherworldly kingdom, filled with treasures and guarded by dragons? In Wales, a number of caves are associated with King Arthur and his knights, who retired within and rest in suspended animation until awakened. Some say Merlin/Myrddin lies trapped by the Lady of the Lake in a cave on Bryn Myrddin, near Carmarthen, where he was supposedly born. Limestone caves beneath

> "If the cave is the deepest, most resonant archetype conjured by a natural sacred place, then the mountain must closely follow. We know its attributes: stillness and permanence." Devereux, p. 96.

Limestone caves beneath Gop

Gop held burials and were perhaps linked in ritual with the human-made hill above.

Holy Springs, Lakes, Rivers, and Sea

Our bodies are approximately 60-70% water: it is literally life giving. We also use water for cleansing, purification, and transformation. Water is a central part of baptismal rites around the world. Rivers and streams, and the lands they nourish, are vital for life and important for transportation of goods—and raiders. Lakes are repositories of water and provide a source of food, both aquatic and avian.

Water is also associated with healing, especially when it flows up from the ground or out of the side of a hill. Spring water comes from the realm of the unseen and brings some of that mysterious realm up into the light. Some holy wells (natural springs with buildings over or walls surrounding them) are believed to heal eye problems, others address "female" issues, still others are purported to ameliorate skin diseases or nervous conditions. Some holy wells may grant wishes of other kinds or impart wisdom. Visiting a holy well is an opportunity to interact directly with the sacred by taking it into your mouth and swallowing, or by dipping your hands in the flowing waters.

> "Celtic sacred waters are associated with the three archetypes of light: the sun, the eye and consciousness. When we use sacred waters, we commune with these archetypes, which manifest themselves to us as deities, legends, traditions and folk practices." Pennick, p. 63.

Miraculous wells are numerous in Wales and have been in use continuously for millennia. At one time, these wells may have had resident *anima loci* or were dedicated to particular pagan deities. Now Christianized, many sacred

> "The attributes of the holy wells of Wales, beyond their naming, are equally diverse. ... Most never freeze or run dry, while some are said to ebb and flow, make strange noises, or seem to be bottomless." Cope, p. 11.

springs are associated with local saints or the Virgin Mary. People continue to visit them, seeking healing that they have not found through more conventional means. Some are architecturally grand, like Ffynnon Gwenffrewi (St Winefride's Well) at

> "Most [holy wells] are believed to predict the future, grant wishes, and offer cures and sometimes curses. Some have the ability to turn objects into stone, others to erupt with milk or blood. Some were said to be haunted by ghosts and guarded by monsters, to be home to fairies and doorways into their underground dwellings, 'borderland places' where, in the words of Janet and Colin Bord, 'this world and the hidden Otherworld meet.'" Cope, p. 11.

Treffynon, the Lourdes of Wales; others are places of local devotion, decorated with handmade twig-and-twine crosses. Some are in soul-stirring locations: Ffynnon Fair (St Mary's Well) near Aberdaron is at the bottom of a cliff, submerged at high tide. Others, like St Teilo's Well near Maenclochog, are hidden in a dark, wooded valley.

Lakes were considered sacred by the Celts. Numerous votive offerings have been discovered at Llyn Carreg Bach and

St Teilo's Well

Llyn Fawr. Welsh lakes are also associated with deities and faeries. Local legends link Bala Lake with the Welsh mother goddess/wise woman/sorceress Ceridwen (Cerridwen) and her cauldron. Llyn y Fan Fach is purported to be the home of a beautiful faery, a "lady of the lake," who taught her half-human children the "herbal healing methods that were subsequently practiced for centuries by the Physicians of Myddfai. Wales is surrounded on three sides by water, and the seashore and estuaries have their own mythic resonances, including stories of submerged castles and towns.

Trees

Trees provide humans with fruits and nuts, with fuel, with wood for boats, shelter, furniture, weapons, and coffins. But trees are much more than objects for human use. Trees are vital to the wellbeing of the planet, helping to maintain the stability of the climate. They "inhale" carbon dioxide and "exhale" much-needed oxygen into the environment. They hold the soil in place and exchange nutrients with it. They provide home and haven for animals, insects, and birds.

Symbolically, a tree is an *axis mundi* (a cosmic axis) uniting the underworld, this world, and the heavens. Its roots are in the earth, its trunk in the air, and its branches reach toward the sky. Different trees have different mythic associations. Yggdrasil is the ancient ash tree that Norse mythology describes as an immense "world tree," complete with dragons entwining in its roots. Other examples of symbol-laden trees include the Trees of Life and Knowledge in the Garden of Eden, the Christmas evergreen, and the Yule log.

> "The tree that moves some to tears of joy Is in the Eyes of the others only a Green thing that stands in the way. Some See Nature all Ridicule & Deformity, & by these I shall not regulate my proportions; & Some Scarce see Nature at all. But to the Eyes of the Man of Imagination, Nature is Imagination itself. As a man is, So he Sees. As the Eye is formed, such are its Powers." William Blake, Letter to Dr. Trustler [23 August 1799]

Trees were often linked with particular deities, but they were also thought to have their own resident spirits. Individual trees might be the source of great wisdom or inspiration. Living for hundreds of years, they become imbued with a kind of "personality."

> Mara Freeman writes that in Celtic times, "trees not only provided earthly sustenance: they were regarded as living, magical beings who bestowed blessings from the Otherworld. Wood from the nine sacred trees kindled the need-fire that brought back the sun to earth on May Eve; tree names formed the letters of the Ogham alphabet which made potent spells when carved on staves of yew; rowan protected the byre; ash lent power to the spear's flight." http://www.chalicecentre.net/celtictreeoflife.htm

Greeks and Celts worshipped in sacred groves called *nemetoi*. The sacred yew and oak trees are found at many sites in Wales. A number of churchyards have at least one yew tree, and many are encircled by a ring of yew trees, some dating back over 2000 years. These ancient trees were planted before Christianity arrived and are believed to mark earlier Bronze Age sites.

> "The real Druids were the priests and scholars of the Celts… They combined the roles of healers, seers, and holy men….To Druids, all of nature is alive—and more than this, divine. It presents us with omens…." Heaven, p. 150.

Stones

Stone: enduring, eternal—or at least closer to ageless than frail human flesh. Meditate on a stone and eons of geological time unfold before you. Perhaps part of the allure of megaliths is contact with what seems eternal. It is also contact with a part of ourselves, for we, too, are composed of minerals. Dust to dust, rock of ages,

> Nigel Pennick (p. 24) asserts "The wild wood is the place in which we can restore our conscious link with our inner instincts by contacting the 'wild man' within all of us. When we are supported by the elemental powers of the wood, a rediscovery of forgotten things can take place."

> According to Freddy Silva, "The ancients did not regard stone as ... nothing more than lifeless matter. To them, each stone held specific properties because, and quite rightly, every stone is made under different conditions. In the world of correspondences, the appropriate type of stone enhances the purpose for which the temple was created" (p. 204). For example, volcanic rock vectors "masculine" sun energy; sedimentary stone vectors "feminine" moon energy.

we come from the earth and return to it.

But there's more to our attraction to the megaliths than like recognizing like. We have often found that the stones are not just inert building blocks used in sacred constructions. They seem to have their own energies, their own "personalities." Perhaps we are anthropomorphizing the stones, seeing faces and meaningful shapes in the random wear patterns of millennia. Perhaps not. Perhaps the stones were selected precisely because of their appearance. Some stones definitely have a "masculine" feel, others a "feminine" sensibility. Some seem to be standing guard or to hold a particular mystery.

We ponder about the meaning of a standing stone found inside a passage chamber or stones carved with swirls and spirals, discovered inside a large burial mound. We puzzle over the purpose of these constructions, often called tombs because of the human remains found within. But calling such places tombs is like calling Westminster Cathedral a grave, just because people are buried inside.

A number of researchers report strange electro-magnetic phenomena and higher-than-background levels of radiation at megalithic sites. Dowsers often discover underground lines of energy or water flowing beneath the

> "Singing brings a holy place into vibration, as if it were a tuning fork being struck. In these journeys the tuning fork was also my body, set into motion in a new way. I discovered that the ancients built their temples according to ratios of sacred geometry, universal principles that exist in numbers, shapes, and musical intervals and in the proportions that compose our bodies." Hale, p. xvii.

stones. Psychics may experience strange guardian-like figures or shadowy reenactments of ancient rites. Modern researchers have discovered that many chambers appear to have a particular resonance that enhances the sound of the voice and drumming, making it both louder and more mysterious. The enigmatic stones reveal and hide their purpose with the changing of the day, the turning of the seasons.

> "We believe that places are alive. We suggest that when human beings believe that, and act in ways that respect and value what places bring, the partnership becomes a powerful force toward great good in the world" http://www.powersofplace.com/about.htm.

> Stone circles, table-like dolmens, immense earth-covered cairns, their interior walls covered with mysterious symbols—when you find one that calls to you, draw near, breathing slowly, contemplating "the slow breath of stone" (Petro). Perhaps sing to it, or hum, or chant, and see if it replies. See what you discover as the minerals in your bones and skin and hair respond to the minerals that make up these silent monoliths. Take your time. Slow down. They've been there for millennia. They don't divulge their secrets quickly—and never to the casual tourist.

Some Historical Background

Powerful places occur in a context, and that context includes the land, the location, and the people who have erected or sanctified the site over the centuries. Thus it is helpful to know something about the social-historical environment of Wales. The following is a brief summary.

In the 1970s, a popular Welsh slogan was "We are still here." And indeed the Welsh are still here, despite centuries of conquest and invasion by the Romans, Vikings, Anglo-Saxons, and Normans. The worst insult you can give the Welsh is to call their country England or to call them English. It isn't and they aren't. Defiant, Celtic, separate—they have struggled for centuries to maintain or reestablish their cultural and political independence from their powerful and assertive English neighbor.

Wales is a rugged country, much of it covered by the Cambrian Mountain range. The highest mountains are in the north and central areas. Deep valleys radiate out from the center of the uplands. The lowland is mostly found along the coast and in the valley floors. Because the soil is not very fertile, Wales is a land better suited for cattle and sheep grazing than for agriculture. Coal, copper, and slate mines have all been important in its history. Today, approximately 2/3 of the 3,000,000 inhabitants of Wales live in the south, most of them in Swansea, Cardiff (the capital), Newport, and the nearby Valleys.

The oldest human remains known in Wales have been discovered in excavations at Pontnewydd Cave, Denbighshire, North Wales; these Neanderthal remains date back to 230,000 BCE. But it wasn't until the Upper Paleolithic (around 24,000 BCE) that significant communities began to form. By 10,000-8000 BCE, the end of the last Ice Age, continuous human habitation had been established in Wales. Sea levels were much lower then, and Great Britain was a kind of peninsula attached to Europe. By 8000 BCE, Wales was free of glaciers and covered with thick forests of oak, elm, lime, and ash. Population was sparse, and people lived by hunting wild animals, fishing, and gathering nuts, fruits, roots, and seeds.

Gradually, melting glaciers separated Wales and Ireland, forming the Irish Sea. By 6500 BCE, melting glaciers had also separated Britain from the rest of Europe and raised the sea level, although the Bristol Channel was still 33 ft lower than today.

Most megalithic sites date back to the Neolithic Revolution, which began in Wales around 4000 BCE. The Neolithic settlers integrated with the nomadic, hunting-and-gathering natives. The new inhabitants knew how to work stone and flint, and they built numerous megalithic tombs. They also began to clear the thick forests of Wales, establish pastures and plant crops, produce pottery, weave cloth, and construct defensive ditches around their villages. They built the early stone circles.

> It's possible that some of the Welsh legends that describe the sea between Ireland and Wales as being narrower and shallower, or of drowned cities in the sea, are mythologized memories of these ancient times.

The Bronze Age in Wales began around 2000 BCE. By this time, there had been much assimilation and exchange with other cultures. The Welsh now knew how to use metal and engaged in small-scale copper mining and smelting activities. They had established extensive trade networks and engaged in tribal warfare—hence the large number of earthwork forts.

Around 600 BCE, Celtic people began arriving from central Europe, bringing with them the roots of the Welsh language, cultural traditions, and a social hierarchy that included Druid priests. These new settlers knew how to use iron and work gold, and they had extensive maritime trading networks.

Julius Caesar invaded Britain in 55 BCE. In mid-first-century CE, the Roman forces reached Wales, where they met stiff resistance from the Celtic-speaking tribes. The Isle of Anglesey, the center of Druidic power, was the site of a fierce battle in 60 CE, which the Welsh lost.

For the next 300 years, Romans built fortified outposts and roads. They mined Welsh land for gold, lead, and silver. Remains of Roman settlements can still be found in Wales, but although the Romans controlled Wales until 390 CE, they never really conquered it. The natives simply fled inland, where few roads existed, and managed to maintain an independent existence. After the fall of Rome, numerous

> "It was they [the Celtic saints] who built monasteries, hospices and churches, became the councilors of princes, and were accredited with miraculous healing powers. Each became a cult in his own right with dedications over a wide area and the veneration of places connected with them and their relics." Watney, p. 17.

kingdoms developed in Wales—including one perhaps led by a British leader named Arthur.

Irish tribes invaded with more or less success; one Irish dynasty established itself in the southwest and ruled until the tenth century. Irish missionaries also came, spreading Christianity along with Irish myths and legends. Early Welsh Christianity owed much to Ireland but was different. Following an eremitical tradition adapted from the Egyptian Desert Fathers, ascetic missionaries in the fifth and sixth centuries established simple churches in sacred enclosures called *llan*. Hence the frequent appearance of *llan* in Welsh place names (Llangollen, Llandudno, Llandeilo, etc.).

The Welsh "Age of Saints" lasted from about 400–700 CE. Many churches were dedicated to a local or regional holy person, usually male, who had developed a following. Saint David, patron saint of Wales, was a native-born miracle worker who lived in the sixth century and established an important religious community at St David's in southwest Wales. For centuries, the church in Wales maintained its independence from Rome, considering itself superior. However, in 768, the church submitted to papal authority with regard to the date of Easter. The first bishop to swear an oath of allegiance to the archbishop of Canterbury was Urban of Llandaf in 1107.

By the late sixth century, Welsh language and literature had begun to develop, linking together a diverse people through shared legends, customs, and religion. Welsh identity was developing. Territorial fights continued between the Germanic tribes (Angles and Saxons) and the Welsh, who were often fighting amongst themselves. The Saxons, like the Romans, never succeeded in conquering Wales. In acknowledgement of that, Offa's Dyke, a linear earthwork, was built in 770 by the powerful Saxon king Offa to mark the boundary between Wales and Mercia. People beyond the Dyke in Wales called themselves *Y Cymry* (fellow countrymen) and they called their land Cymru. On the Saxon side of the Dyke, Cymru was called Wales, from Old English *wealas* (foreign land).

> *Llan* means "enclosed piece of land." Chiefs would donate land for a sacred enclosure in which Christians could be buried. Often, a hermit or monk would build a cell on the site, and later a church would be built. Some of these enclosures were established over already existing sacred sites, such as pre-Christian burial mounds, or inside ancient stone circles.

Cymru/Wales was divided into a number of small kingdoms, including Gwynedd in the north, Powys in the center, Gwent in the east, and Dyfed (and later Deheubarth) in the south. These names are still in use. In the ninth and tenth centuries, Danish and Norse pirates attacked the southern coast. In 1066 the Norman William the Conqueror conquered England and then began raiding Wales. He established the Marcher Lords, three powerful barons, along the border. Soon they managed to control most of the lowlands. Gradually the warring and disorganized Welsh were pushed further back into the mountainous northwest.

In 1267 the Welsh leader Llywelyn ap Gruffydd emerged and gained control of most of Wales. He called himself Prince of Wales and was acknowledged so by Henry III. But within ten years he had lost power. In 1272 Edward I set up a ring of castles to prevent further Welsh revolt, and he soon proclaimed his son Prince of Wales.

Resentment against the English grew during the next century. In 1400 the renegade nationalist Owain ap Gruffydd (also known as Owain Glyndwr or, anglicized, Owen Glendower), a descendent of the royal house of Powys, led an uprising. Fighting against Henry IV, Glyndwr managed to control most of Wales by 1404 and found allies in Scotland, Ireland, Northumbria, and France. He formed a parliament in Machynlleth. But by 1406 he had suffered numerous defeats and the English regained control. Glyndwr, the last native Welsh Prince of Wales, disappeared. His fame lives on, however, and he is commemorated in everything from statues to pub names.

Gradually the Welsh and English learned to coexist. Henry VII removed many restrictions on land ownership and promoted Welshmen to high office, but Wales was still controlled by England. Under Henry VIII, the Tudor Acts of Union in 1536 and 1543 established English sovereignty over Wales. The Welsh became equal citizens and were given parliamentary representation, and the Marcher Lords were abolished. But Wales was no longer independent. The Acts of Union included the abolition of Welsh law, and English became the language of the courts and administration.

The Cistercian abbeys at Valle Crucis and Strata Florida had been centers of learning and culture, but in 1536 Henry VIII disestablished Catholicism in favor of Protestantism, making himself the head of the Anglican Church. In the process, abbeys throughout Britain—including Wales—were dissolved. The Anglican Church in Wales became known as the Church in Wales. Ironically, it was due in part to this Protestant church and Anglican Bishop William Morgan that the Welsh language continued to be used. Bishop Morgan translated the Bible into Welsh in 1588, which resulted in strengthening the Welsh language and the national commitment to Protestantism. Welsh became the language of religious ceremony and literature.

The late seventeenth and early eighteenth centuries saw the rise of Methodism and the growth of other Nonconformist (non-Anglican) religious groups, including Congregationalists, Baptists, and Calvinists. Part of the reformist movement included emphasis on literacy, and in 1699 the Anglican Society for Promoting Christian Knowledge established schools where the Bible was taught, along with other subjects, in Welsh as well as in English. By the mid-eighteenth century, Wales was in the midst of the Methodist Revival, linked to Welsh nationalism. By the 1800s, most Christian worshippers in Wales were Nonconformist, not Anglican, and they attended chapel, not church. By 1851, 80% of the population was Methodist.

The Welsh economy had been based on agriculture, mostly livestock grazing. The iron industry began growing in the mid-eighteenth century, along with coal mining. The coalfield in Mid-Glamorgan in South Wales was opened in the nineteenth century and for a time was the largest in the world. Coal mining, copper mining, iron smelting, and slate quarrying became major economic activities.

> In the 2001 census, two-thirds of the population identified as Christian, though only about 10% attended church or chapel regularly. It is likely that the leading nature of the census question led to an erroneously large number of Welsh Christians. The largest denominations were the Church in Wales, the Roman Catholic Church, and the Presbyterian Church in Wales, which was born out of the Methodist revival. Conflicting statistics make it difficult to be more precise about religious affiliation.

With industrialization came mass migration from the countryside and from outside Wales. Gradually, inequalities between the predominantly Welsh-speaking, chapel-going workers and the English-speaking, Church-in-Wales-attending industrial barons grew unsupportable. The abominable working conditions and pay that came with the Industrial Revolution led to massive riots and to the rise of trade unions and liberal political parties.

The radical reformist movement became entwined with Nonconformist religion, in part because of the disparity of rights in comparison to the Anglican (the Church in Wales) church. Nonconformity came to stand for land reform, disestablishment of the Church in Wales as the official religion, and preservation of the Welsh language—which had essentially been banned in schools in the mid 1800s.

Gradually reform acts were passed that supported Nonconformism, including the disestablishment of the Church in Wales in 1920.

> The infamous "Welsh Not" was instituted in the mid 1800s. It was a piece of wood hung around the neck of a schoolchild caught speaking Welsh; the child could pass it on to another caught speaking Welsh. Whoever wore it at the end of the day was whipped.

In the late nineteenth century, the Romantic Movement inspired the Welsh to rediscover their heritage, albeit romantically. The *Mabinogi* tales were translated into English as the *Mabinogion*; the Welsh Language Society was founded; the *eisteddfodau* were reintroduced; and the *Gorsedd* was reinvented.

World War I resulted in a revitalized agricultural sector. In the 1920s the coal industry boomed. Subsequent economic depression and decline led to much unemployment and despair. Welsh nationalism emerged again, but most people were more concerned with working conditions, health care, and welfare services.

In the 1960s, the Plaid Cymru (the Welsh Nationalist Party, founded in 1925) gradually gained power, and Welsh nationalism soared. In the 1970s people began to think about self-government. Enthusiasm for Welsh language also grew, along with government funding, resulting in Welsh-speaking educational opportunities. In 1982 a Welsh-language TV channel was established, which has had a marked impact on encouraging Welsh cultural pride and language. In 1997 the establishment of the National Assembly was approved. It was the first all-Welsh assembly in

600 years. It is located in a stunning contemporary building in Cardiff.

Modern Wales still struggles with rural poverty and high unemployment, the decline of manufacturing, and the loss of population—but it is also a bright, thriving country, proud of its language and culture. Like the Welsh people, many powerful places have managed to survive the centuries of conquest and revolution. New industries, many of them "green" and "high tech," are finding a home in Wales, as have a number of alternative-lifestyle individuals. Tourism is a growing source of income. The red Welsh dragon, which has fought against the white Anglo-Saxon dragon for so long, appears at last to be closer to winning the war.

Traveling in Wales

> "Lovely the woods, water, meadows, combes, vales,/ All the air things wear that build this world of Wales." Gerard Manley Hopkins, "In the Valley of the Elwy."

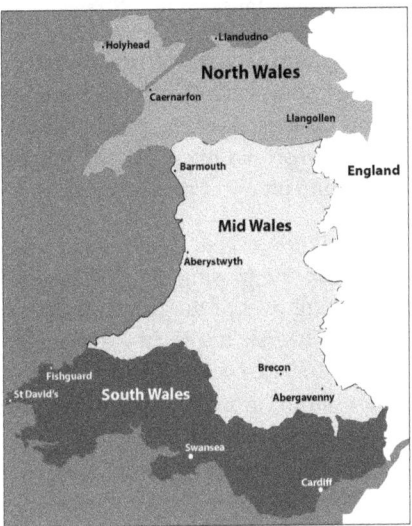

We have divided Wales into three areas, based on the way the Welsh divide their land: north, south, and "mid." There are significant differences between the south and north, not only geographically but also linguistically and culturally. The public transportation system, which runs mainly east to west across the north and across the south, helps maintain these differences.

Wales is much smaller than England or Scotland. It is 160 miles long by about 60 miles wide, depending on where you measure. Traveling by train or bus, you can reach a number of the towns in Wales, but it will take you a long time to get there if you have to rely on public transportation schedules.

We recommend that you either hire a car (**remember: drive on the left**) or hire a car and driver. Or walk. May 2012 was the launch date of the 870-mi-long Wales Coast Path. Following it, you can walk around all of Wales, from the Dee Estuary in the northeast to Chepstow in the south (see http://http://www.walescoastpath.gov.uk for details).

Wales teaches you to slow down. The distances between places aren't large, but many of the roads are narrow and driving tends to be slow. Average speed is about 35 mph, and high, dense hedgerows often line the narrow country lanes, making it difficult to see around corners.

Many rural roads are 1-½ car-widths wide, with frequent pullouts to facilitate the passing of vehicles, one of which must back up or pull over. If the driver in the car coming toward you flashes his/her headlights, that means "You go ahead, I'll stop"—and vice versa. The person closest to the pullout is supposed to make way, which may mean backing up. Obviously, this dance-like maneuver slows travel. Sometimes the road through a town is narrow because parking is allowed on both sides of the street; as a result, only one car can go through the bottleneck at a time.

Cadw (also CADW; pro. "KA-doo"), the Welsh equivalent to the English National Trust, manages some sites in Wales, but many others are minimally signposted or even unmarked. Detailed maps such as the OS Explorer or Landranger series are quite useful, as is a more general road atlas (e.g., *Wales AZ,* available from http://www.a-zmaps.co.uk). Kittiwake publishes an inexpensive series of small guidebooks with detailed descriptions and drawings of walks suitable for all abilities (http://www.kittiwake-books.com).

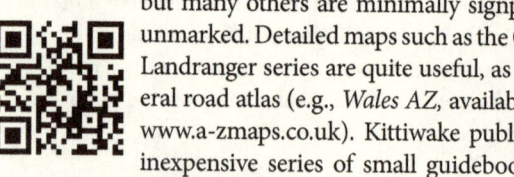

In this guidebook we provide "degrees, minutes, and seconds" Sat-Nav coordinates, which can be translated into GPS or decimal format using online converters. The scannable

QR codes link directly to a conversion page. It is very helpful to bring or rent a Sat-Nav (GPS) device, although it may not have up-to-date maps, or it may fail to indicate that a bridge is out or a road is under construction. Remember: it is a useful but fallible tool. Our Garmin Nüvi once led us out of the Brecon Beacons down a vertiginous one-lane country lane with closed, though not locked, livestock gates. "Nüvi" had decided the route was shorter (and therefore faster) than the two-lane highway we should have taken.

Bring a flashlight for peering into caves and megalithic sites. A candle with a protective sleeve so it doesn't drip is excellent for exploring caves, since it illuminates more fully, but bring a flashlight as well. A compass is useful for orienting yourself in ritual landscapes. Some trails are steep and/or slippery, so hiking sticks are useful.

Stinging nettle

In summer and fall, be careful of stinging nettles in the undergrowth. The leaves and stems have fine hollow hairs that can "sting" through jeans, so it is best to avoid them. If you get stung, look for dock usually found growing nearby; it produces a natural antidote. Bruise the dock leaf and rub the liquid on your skin immediately; this will greatly reduce pain and inflammation.

Broadleaf dock

Broadleaf dock (detail)

Wales is often damp and rainy, so be prepared with a large umbrella, an impermeable and warm rain jacket, and "wellies" (high rubber boots). You will be grateful for the protection to your feet and pant legs when slogging through a damp meadow. When in doubt, first put on your wellies.

Bryn Celli Ddu in 1847, before reconstruction

A few megalithic sites in Wales, including Bryn Celli Ddu, Gors Fawr, and Coetan Arthur in Newport, are oriented toward specific astronomical events. Your journey will be enriched if you plan to experience some of these sites at those times.

The stories and legends that enliven the Welsh countryside are a vital part of the experience. Many places may not look like much, but if you know the associated stories they take on a deeper significance. Because of this, we tell many stories in this guidebook, and we suggest several guides whom we know from personal experience to be "in resonance" with powerful places. We also suggest that you read the *Mabinogi* collection and stories of Merlin in advance, so you will have some prior knowledge of the mythic landscape. The three volumes by John Bollard and Anthony Griffiths (see bibliography) are an excellent introduction, complete with modern translations and stunning photographs of locations associated with the stories.

Traveling in Wales is not just about visiting powerful places. The Welsh people contribute to the power of place that we experienced, as well as to the pleasure we have had exploring their country. It is always dangerous to stereotype people or the people of a particular nation. However, drawing on our limited experience, we can say that the Welsh we were fortunate enough to meet were polite, friendly, curious, and often had a dry sense of humor. They were passionate about their language and culture, rooted in the landscape and the stories of the land. Take time to "be present" not only to powerful places but also to the people who inhabit Wales and whose character is formed by a symbiosis of sacred landscape, history, and myth.

Language – A Few Suggestions

Wales is officially a bilingual nation: people speak English and an increasing number—over 500,000 (20% of the population) at last count—speak Welsh (Cymraeg). Welsh is growing in importance in Wales, and it is possible to attend Welsh-medium schools from nursery school through university.

The Welsh language is descended from the British language and belongs to the Celtic branch of the Indo-European language family; it is related to Breton and Cornish, not to Old Irish. (Scots and Irish Gaelic, and now-extinct Manx, are Celtic languages that descended from Old Irish.) Although everyone in Wales speaks English, you will hear English more in the border counties and in the anglicized regions of Gwent and around Cardiff. Welsh is more predominant in northern Pembrokeshire and the west, and in the northwestern corner of Wales.

> "I have long known the deep beauty and mystery embedded in the landscape, the warm hospitality of the people, and the lovely lilt of their accent which '... goes up and down like the valleys of South Wales, doesn't it, lovely?'" Edie Stone, personal communication, Nov. 6, 2011.

Road signs are usually bilingual, but many locations, businesses, and public services have Welsh names. We provide a pronunciation guide for place and character names at the back of this guidebook (see pp. 333-339). In addition, http://www.forvo.com/languages-pronunciations/cy/alphabetically/ provides pronunciation for 1500 words.

At first glance—and first listen—the Welsh language seems a bit intimidating and lacking vowels, but, in fact, "w" ("double-u") and "y" often function as vowels. All letters are pronounced and usually the second-to-last syllable is accented. Its alphabet is similar to English but not identical, and there are regional variations in pronunciation. Northern Welsh (North Walian or Gog) and Southern Welsh (South Walian or Hwntw) used to be quite different in vocabulary, pronunciation, and grammar, but time and mass media have blurred many of the distinctions.

The distinctive "ll" sound takes practice to produce and to recognize when heard. It's a bit like the "tl" in "Bentley." Place the tongue behind the top row of teeth and breathe through the sides of your mouth, as if whispering—or blow air out the sides of the mouth while keeping the tongue in place. It sounds a bit like "hl" or "tl" depending on the dialect. We refer to it as a "voiceless, blown "l" in the pronunciation guide (see pp. 333-339). The Llŷn Peninsula sounds something like "**Thl**een," and the frequently occurring "llan" is pronounced something like "**thl**an."

Most vowels and consonants are pronounced the way they would be in European languages, but there are exceptions. "C" is always a hard sound, as in "**c**at," never a soft sound as in "nice." "Ch" is like the Scottish "lo**ch**." "Dd" is the hard "th" in "**th**ee" or "lea**th**er," never soft "th" as in "smith." "G" is always a hard sound, as in "**g**o," never a soft sound as in "gentle." "Ff" and "ph" are pronounced as in "**f**un"; 'f' is pronounced like the "v" in "**v**ine." "Ng" is as in "si**ng**." "Si" is pronounced as in "**sh**oe." "Th" is a soft "th" as in "**th**in."

"U" and "y" are pronounced roughly like a Welsh "i," either "t**i**n" or "s**ea**," depending on the context. A "ŷ" is pronounced like "**ee**" or "t**ea**." "W" can sound like the consonant "w" in "**w**in" or like the vowel sound "oo" in "p**oo**l."

In addition, certain sounds mutate according to particular rules.

Bryn Celli Ddu is pronounced like "brin KEll-ee thee"—the "ll" is a voiceless, blown "l"; the "th" is hard, as in "**th**is". Mynydd Preseli (the Preseli Hills) sounds like "muhn-ith preseli"—"dd" pro. like a hard "th," as in "**th**is)—if you have a northern Welsh accent. Myddfai is pronounced "muth-veye"—"dd" pro. like a hard "th," as in "**th**is"). Pwyll, a character in the *Mabinogi*, is pronounced "poo-ell"— the "ll" is a voiceless, blown "l". The Welsh cultural festival, the *eisteddfod*, is pronounced "aye-STETH-vot"; the plural, *eisteddfodau*, is pronounced "aye-STETH-vuh-dye"—"dd" pro. like a hard "th," as in "**th**en." The Afon Dyfi (River Dyfi) is pronounced "AV-on Duv-ee"—like the English "Dovey".

St David's and St Bride's may also be spelled St Davids and St Brides, without the apostrophe.

A few place-names that recur in this guidebook are: "aber" means the mouth of a river or stream; "cairn" means a pile of stone; "carreg" means stone; "cwm" means bowl-shaped valley or glen; "ffynnon" means (holy) well or spring; "llan" means enclosure, parish; "llyn" means lake; "mynydd" means mountain; "rhaeadr" means waterfall; and "ynys" means island. (A book like *Welsh Place-Names Unzipped* provides extensive information for decoding the meanings of place-names.)

Names and Numbers

In this book, place-names are given first in English, then in Welsh. Welsh place-names may have several different spellings. We have tried to provide alternatives often in parentheses after the more common spelling to facilitate Internet searches and Sat-Nav entries.

Determining the age of megalithic sites is not an exact science, and sources sometimes give different dates. Even determining the number of stones or the size of a megalithic site can be difficult. We have done our best to resolve such differences, but some are irresolvable.

Wales uses miles on official road signs, so we provide distances in miles, not kilometers. We use the following abbreviations: feet = ft; yards = yd; miles = mi.

To call Wales from outside the country, dial your own country's international access numbers, followed by 44 (British country code). For example, the Brecon Beacons Mountain Center's telephone is (0)1874 623 366. From the US, dial 011 44 1874 623 366; do not dial the initial (0). When dialing from within Wales, dial 01874 623 366.

 In general, sites managed by Cadw have opening and closing hours as well as entry fees, unless listed as "unrestricted access." If you plan to visit many Cadw sites, it may be beneficial to purchase an annual pass (http://www.cadw.wales.gov.uk).

Additional Resources

Although we don't usually recommend guides or people to contact, we have found the following people extremely helpful, knowledgeable, and attuned to powerful places. Check their websites for areas of expertise. They are listed in alphabetical order.

Ros Briagha Foskett at http://www.rosbriagha.org

Mara Freeman at http://www.celticspiritjourneys.com

Hilary Wylde at hilarywylde@btinternet.com

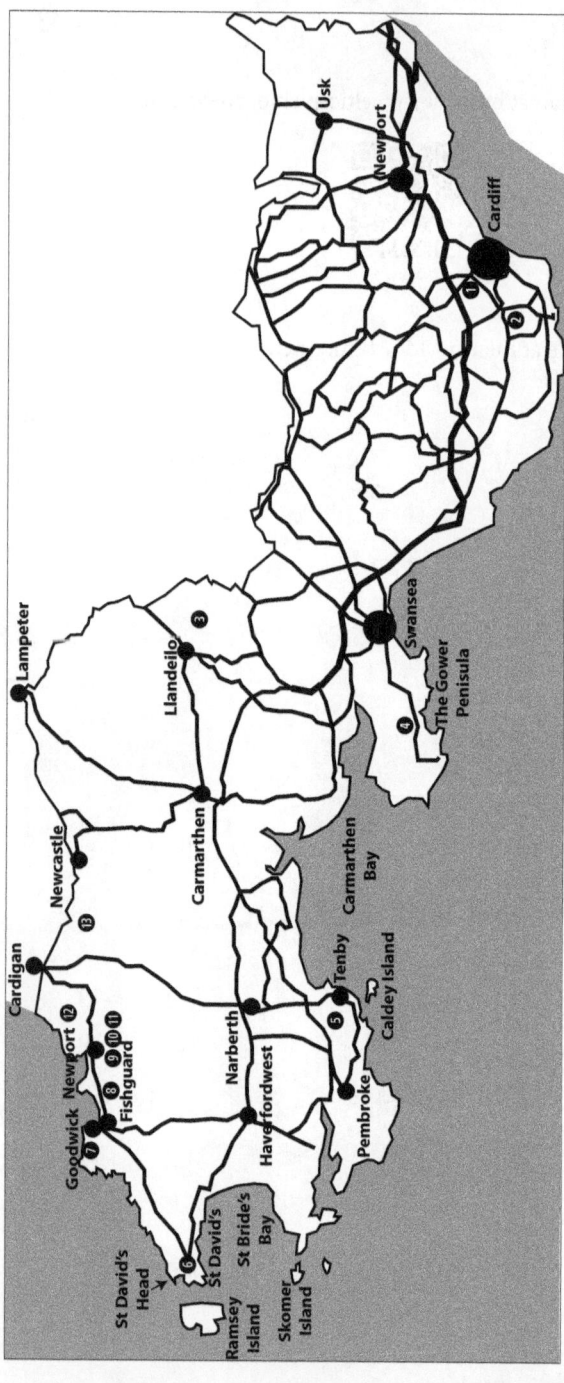

South Wales

1. Llandaff Cathedral (Eglwys Gadeiriol Llandaf), Cardiff
2. Tinkinswood Burial Chamber, Vale of Glamorgan
3. Carreg Cennen and Dinefwr Castles, Llandeilo, Carmarthenshire
4. Parc le Breos Cwm Burial Cairn, Cat Hole Cave, Gower Peninsula
5. Gumfreston Church and Holy Wells, Pembrokeshire
6. St Davids (St David's), Pembrokeshire
7. Ffynnon Wnda, the Church of St Gwyndaf, Pembrokeshire
8. The Gwaun Valley, Pembrokeshire
9-11. Mynydd Preseli – The Preseli Hills, Pembrokeshire
12. St Brynach's Church, Nevern (Eglwys St Brynach, Nanhyfer), Pembrokeshire
13. Ffynnone Waterfall, Abercych, Pembrokeshire

South Wales (Cardiff, Newport, Monmouthshire, the Gower, Carmarthenshire, Pembrokeshire)

Most of the population of Wales reside in the southeast corner of the country. Settled for millennia, it includes Neolithic sites, Iron Age ruins, Roman fortifications, Arthurian locales, Norman castles—and much more. It is the most anglicized region of Wales, as well as the most industrialized. The further west you go from the English border, the more Welsh the culture and people become, except for an English language-and-culture enclave in southern Pembrokeshire. This region, defined by what is known as the Landsker Line, stretches from St Bride's Bay to Carmarthen Bay; it is also known as "Little England Beyond Wales."

The southeast was once Britain's coal-mining and iron-working heartland, but it also includes the pastoral Wye and Usk Valleys. The iconic Welsh coal-mining towns are in "the Valleys," north and west of Cardiff, the capital of Wales. Rhondda Valley is the most famous.

Located west of Cardiff, the Gower is a compact peninsula famous for sandy beaches and surfing, designated an Area of Outstanding Natural Beauty. It also includes important megalithic sites and was an inspiration for Dylan Thomas' poetry. This famous Welshman was born in Swansea. Carmarthenshire is famous for its gardens, including the National Botanic Garden of Wales. Carmarthen is quite old, settled by Celtic tribes (if not long earlier), then by Romans; its name and surroundings are linked to Merlin.

Pembrokeshire (Sir Benfro in Welsh), in the southwest, is noted for its magnificent scenery and the alluring Pembrokeshire National Park and Coast Path, with beautiful beaches, stunning sea cliffs, nature reserves, hills, and islands. The southwest includes the so-called birthplace of Welsh Christianity at St Davids and the magical Preseli Hills, which include a bluestone quarry, a holy mountain, and numerous megalithic sites.

> On his first visit to Wales, Will, the young protagonist in Susan Cooper's *The Dark is Rising* sequence, "felt that he was in a part of Britain like none he had ever known before: a secret, enclosed place, with powers hidden in its shrouded centuries at which he could not begin to guess" (p. 438).

Many legends are written upon the land of southern Wales. The First Branch of the *Mabinogi*, "Pwyll, Prince of Dyfed," tells of Pwyll; his wife, Rhiannon, associated with the Romano-Gaulish horse-goddess Epona and the British queen/goddess Rigantona; and their son, Pryderi. The ancient region of Dyfed included Pembrokeshire, parts of Carmarthen and Cardiganshire, and the ruins of "Pwyll's castle," which can still be seen in Narberth. The meeting of Pwyll with the Lord of the Underworld may have taken place at a clearing near Glyn Cuch (Cwm Cych), possibly by Ffynone Falls (see pp. 152-156).

Much of the action in the Third Branch of the *Mabinogi*, "Manawydan, Son of Llŷr," takes place around Narberth. The protagonists travel into Hereford (England) and then return to the kingdom of Dyfed.

Llandaff Cathedral (Eglwys Gadeiriol Llandaf), Cardiff
N51 29 45, W3 13 5

We approached the cathedral from the south, walking through the woods to the atmospheric cemetery. At last we found an open door and friendly greeters welcomed us. A modern Christ in Majesty hangs suspended on a circular organ case on top of a concrete parabola that soars across the nave. Tattered regimental banners flutter in a side aisle and in the Welsh Regimental Chapel. A medieval memento mori *tomb, featuring a stone-sculpted armless and legless skeleton, ribs arched in agony, proclaims the inevitability of death. Goosebumps spread up my arms. In this cathedral, religion and patriotism, heroism and death, march hand in hand. (Elyn)*

Two miles northwest of Cardiff's city center is the Church of Wales' Llandaff Cathedral (Eglwys Gadeiriol Llandaf), seat of the bishop of Llandaff and built on one of the oldest Christian sites in Britain. The church was apparently founded in the sixth century by St Dyfrig, who was soon followed by St Teilo. St Teilo's purported skullcap is enshrined in the cathedral. The present church dates from 1120,

Exterior of Llandaff Cathedral

when it was expanded at the orders of Bishop Urban, the first bishop appointed by the Normans. In the twelfth and thirteenth centuries, it was expanded again.

By the late fourteenth century, however, the cathedral had fallen into disrepair. According to Llandaff Cathedral archivists, during the Civil War (mid-seventeenth century) the cathedral was converted into an alehouse, the choir became a calf pen, part of the building was used as a stable and another as a post office, and the font became a hog trough. Major restoration work began in the early 1840s and again after severe bomb damage during World War II.

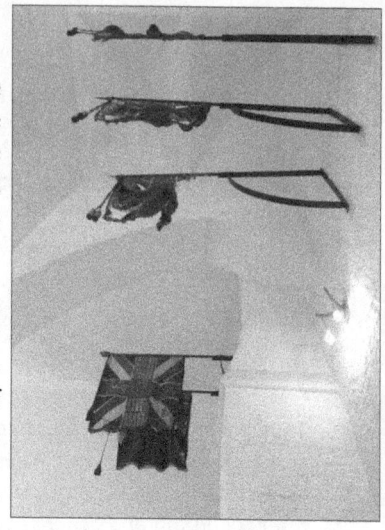

Looking up at tattered regimental banners

The medieval memento mori *tomb*

An impressive triptych called "The Seed of David," by pre-Raphaelite artist Dante Gabriel Rossetti, is displayed in St Illtyd's Chapel. Jacob Epstein's controversial suspended Christ in Majesty is a contemporary—and stunning—addition. Llandaff has the only surviving Cathedral Choir School in Wales. Be sure to attend a service when the Cathedral Parish Choir is singing; you will be able to experience the church come alive with the vibration of sacred chant. Go to the website, http://www.llandaff-cathedral.org.uk/, for opening hours and the choir schedule. Go early, pick up a descriptive brochure, ask the friendly greeters for suggestions, and explore the cathedral. Although over the centuries the building has been much abused, today it has a warm and comforting feeling.

Getting There

Llandaff is on the outskirts of Cardiff and can be reached by walking or by public transportation. Walk northwest up Cathedral Road and follow the signs.

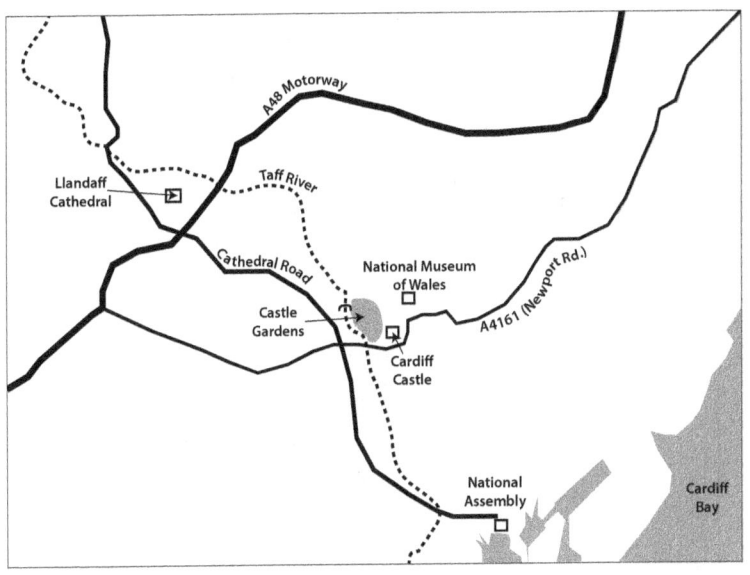

Cardiff area map

More to Experience

Cardiff has much to see, including the kitsch Cardiff Castle (entry free; opening hours; http://www.cardiffcastle.com), the lovely and tranquil Cardiff Castle Gardens, the Victorian shopping arcades, the contemporary National Assembly building in Cardiff Bay, and the National Museum of Wales. The museum exhibits are an excellent introduction to a number of sites in this guidebook. Take a ride on the hop-on, hop-off tourist bus to familiarize yourself with the city. If you want to stay in an urban environment, Cardiff is not a bad place to base yourself for day-trips out.

Cardiff Castle

Getting There

Arrive in Cardiff by air (Cardiff International Airport), by train (from London), or by car via M4 from England (Cardiff exits 29-32). Public transportation to Llandaff Cathedral is available from the city center (near Cardiff Castle) or you can walk. If you walk we suggest that you begin in the beautiful Cardiff Castle Gardens taking the bridge over the Taff River at the end of the gardens and find your way to Cathedral Road. It will take about a half hour to reach the cathedral on foot (see map on p. 49).

Caerleon, Newport County

Northeast of Cardiff is Caerleon (Caerllion, "City of the Legion"), located near the River Usk. It contains the remnants of a major Roman administrative center, headquarters of the elite Second Augustan Legion from 75 CE to the

> King Arthur is first mentioned—but as a warrior, not a king—around 830 CE by the Welsh monk Nennius in his *Historia Brittonum*. Geoffrey of Monmouth (another Welsh cleric) used Nennius' work as a source for his own *Historia Regum Britanniae*. Geoffrey describes Arthur as a sixth-century Celtic British King who defeated the Saxons. The legend was greatly amplified in subsequent years.

end of the third century. Caerleon is strongly associated with King Arthur, and many believe that Camelot was located here, rather than in England.

You can visit the Roman Legion Museum, the Roman Fortress Bath Museum (with an excellent high-tech, virtual-reality experience), and the ruined, 6000-seat Roman amphitheatre. Before being excavated, the amphitheater was hidden under a mound known as "King Arthur's Round Table." Don't miss the Ffwrrwm Center with its Celtic and Arthurian shops, large mythic-themed woodcarvings—including a 44-ft-long Welsh lovespoon in the shape of a dragon—and pleasant cafe. Cadw manages some sites; check for opening hours. http://www.caerleon.net/; http://web.me.com/alessandrovolpides/The_Ffwrwm/Welcome.html.

Getting There

Caerleon is located 4 mi north of Newport and 18 mi from Cardiff.

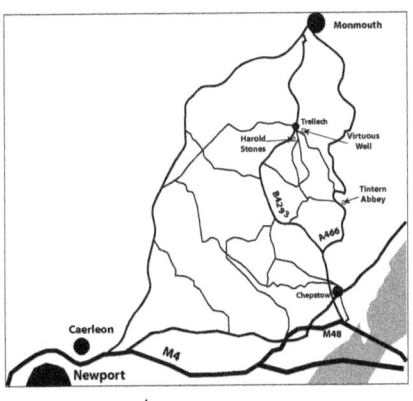

Area map

Tintern Abbey, Monmouthshire

Tintern Abbey (from Dyn Teryn, "King's Fort"), one of the most intact medieval abbeys in Britain, is on the banks of the River Wye. This romantic, ruined Cistercian abbey has inspired numerous artists and poets. William Wordsworth wrote "Lines Composed a Few Miles Above Tintern Abbey" during a visit in 1798. The abbey was founded in 1131, and the huge abbey church was built between 1269 and 1301. It was abandoned in 1536 after King Henry VIII's dissolution of the monasteries.

> "Tears, idle tears, I know not what they mean,/Tears from the depth of some divine despair/ Rise in the heart, and gather to the eyes,/ In looking on the happy autumn-fields,/ And thinking of the days that are no more." "Tears, Idle Tears," by Alfred, Lord Tennyson, inspired by Tintern Abbey.

Evidence of earlier settlements at the site dates back to the Bronze Age, and King Tewdrig lived here as a hermit in the sixth century be-

Tintern Abbey

fore defeating the Saxons. The abbey was built on the ruins of his hermitage.

Try to avoid Tintern Abbey during high season in summer when it is filled with tourists. Allow several hours to explore the ruins and experience the atmosphere. Managed by Cadw; entrance fee.

Getting There

Six mi north of Chepstow on A466 (see map on p. 51).

The Harold Stones, Trellech, Monmouthshire

Trellech ("Three Stones" or "Town of Stones") village is located 4 mi northwest of Tintern Abbey, about 4.5 mi south of Monmouth on B4293. Just southwest of the village are the Harold Stones. The three large upright puddingstone (local brown conglomerate) megaliths are in the middle of a field. The stones date to 3300 BCE and are oriented 72 degrees east of true north. They may be aligned to the holy Skirrid Mountain, 12 mi away. The central stone has two cupmarks. Legend says that Jack o' Kent had a contest with the Devil; he hurled the stones from the summit of The Skirrid, and they landed in this field.

Harold Stones

The Virtuous Well, Monmouthshire

To the east of Trellech is Ffynnon Rhinweddol, the Virtuous Well, also known as St Anne's Well. This holy spring is reputed to have powerful healing properties for eye ailments, colic, scurvy, other "distempers," and "female ailments." The word "virtuous" refers to its positive medicinal qualities. When we were there, candles and offerings adorned the horseshoe-shaped stone housing that encircles the waters. The waters are chalybeate—heavy in iron—as are the waters of Chalice Well in Glastonbury.

> "A visitor would take a small pebble and dropping it quietly into the water [in the central well], make a wish. If plenty of bubbles appeared the wish would be granted; if moderately few, there would be a delay…; and if there were no bubbles at all, the wish would not be realized." Barber, p. 103.

Apparently, once there were nine wells, but now only four remain, supposedly fed by separate springs. Each well was believed to cure a different ailment. The central well was and still is used for wishing.

Although St Anne is the mother of Mary, the name "Anne" associated with Virtuous Well may have come from Annis, Celtic goddess of rivers, waters, wells, magic, and wisdom. Virtuous Well is also associated with faeries, es-

The Virtuous Well

Another view

pecially on Beltaine, summer solstice, and Samhain. The faeries are believed to drink from the well at night from harebells (bluebells), often found there the following morning and collected by local folk to cure certain ailments. For an interesting account of a visit to the well, go to http://www.legendarydartmoor.co.uk/vir_well.htm.

Getting There

The Virtuous Well is just southeast of Trellech on the road toward Tintern Abbey (see map on p. 51).

Tinkinswood Burial Chamber, Vale of Glamorgan
N51 27 04 W3 18 26

Silhouetted against a background of hawthorn trees, the partly reconstructed, partly ruined dolmen rests. And waits. Incomplete, timeworn, it doesn't look like much. But we climbed inside its three-sided chamber (the fourth wall is gone) and chanted an ancient Welsh word, Awen (A-oo-en), meaning poetic or spiritual inspiration. Slowly the stones began to vibrate and the sound of our voices reverberated, as if we were in a sealed vessel. It felt as if the chamber was still charged with ancient energy—and recharged by modern ceremony. (Elyn)

The 4300-year-old Tinkinswood Burial Chamber (Siambr Gladdu Tinkinswood) is reached down a grassy trail. It is a huge, stone-capped burial chamber, also called a long cairn, which appears to be half-submerged in—or half-emerging from—the ground. Its 50-ton, lichen-covered capstone is impressive, partly supported by modern reconstructed pillars. The capstone, said to be the largest in Britain, is 28 ft long by 18 ft wide, and nearly 3 ft thick. The chamber itself is 18 ft by 15 ft and 6 ft high. It opens off a forecourt and is a type known as a Cotswold-Severn type tomb. It is oriented ENE-WSW,

> A contemporary use of *Awen* can be seen at The Wales Millennium Centre (in Cardiff, Wales). Engraved on the front of the building are two lines of poetry by Gwyneth Lewis. The Welsh line is, "Creu gwir fel gwydr o ffwrnais Awen," meaning "creating truth like glass from inspiration's furnace." The English line is, "In these stones horizons sing." See http://en.wikipedia.org/wiki/Wales_Millennium_Centre, retrieved March 1, 2012.

> "Hi. My name is Ginny, and I come to Tinkinswood on a very regular basis. In fact I call Tinkinswood my spiritual home. I feel at ease here, and I suspect that this feeling comes from the thousands of years of occupation and the coming together of people and ideas at this one very special site. ... Living human activity has continued within sight of the ancients at Tinkinswood: we continue to visit and practice our own commemorative acts and rituals, culminating with our own Handfasting (a Pagan marriage). We also perform our rituals throughout the seasons. A communal group of people share food, drinks and gifts and do so at every seasonal ritual or Full Moon celebration. These are done in a respectful way in which we believe our ancestors would approve." http://tinkinswoodarchaeology.wordpress.com/2011/11/09/the-community-at-tinkinswood/

with the forecourt and entrance at the ENE end. A number of other stones lie to the east and south. The woodland behind the burial chamber is worth wandering through and meditating within.

One story says that the stones scattered around the cairn are women who danced on Sunday and turned to stone—a common cautionary tale found in other Catholic countries, including Ireland and Brittany. Another story says that fa-

Stone-lined entrance to Tinkinswood Burial Chamber

eries lived inside; another, that anyone who sleeps inside the cairn will either die, go mad, or become a poet—a legend repeated at other Welsh sites, including Carn Ingli and Cadair Idris.

Artifacts prove that Tinkinswood was a place of reverence for thousands of years. It is still in use: local neo-pagans gather regularly to hold ceremonies and celebrations at the site.

Interior of Tinkinswood showing modern reconstruction

Tinkinswood is located north of the magnificent Dyffryn House and Gardens, beside a wooded lane between Dyffryn and St Nicholas. Managed by Cadw; opening hours.

Area map

Nearby is the not-as-impressive but still powerful St Lythan's Cromlech, half a mile SE of Dyffryn House. It has three upright stones and a capstone; its chamber is 7 ft 6 in by 6 ft; it is 6 ft high. Recent archeological excavations have uncovered lengthy use of the chamber, including medieval pottery and a modern crematorium tag (http://tinkinswoodarchaeology.wordpress.com/2011/11/25/st-lythans-

dig-diary-first-weeks-round-up/). It is said that "On Midsummer Eve the capstone is supposed to spin around three times, and if you make a wish there on Hallowe'en it will come true" (Barber, p. 46).

Getting There

Take A48 west from Cardiff to St Nicholas. Turn left (south) in the town and after about 500 ft you will see a sign on the right for Tinkinswood. Park and follow the tree-lined path to the monument.

Carreg Cennen and Dinefwr Castles, Llandeilo, Carmarthenshire

The rough stone passageway at Carreg Cennen was dark and slippery. Our flashlights illuminated only a little of what lay before, what lay around. But there was no sense of threat or ill will. Rather, I felt surrounded by a loving, motherly embrace, welcomed by the darkness. Cautiously, we stumbled forward, eager to reach the subterranean spring at the end. At last we heard the drip-drip-drip of water, filtering down through the rocks above into a large stone basin. We turned off the light and breathed into the slow breath of water seeping for centuries to reach this place, breathed into the slow breath of minerals dissolving and gradually coating the stone with rhythmic ripples. Gary felt this was a tomb-like, not womb-like place. (Elyn)

Carreg Cennen Castle and Castell Dinefwr are located within a few miles of each other and Llandeilo, the ancient capital of West Wales. Llandeilo is a pleasant little market town with upscale aspirations, located in the Tywi Valley, on the far western edge of the Brecon Beacons National Park. The Church of St Teilo houses two eighth-century Celtic crosses. In the church tower is an interactive display of the Llandeilo Fawr Gospels, an eighth-century manuscript that contains the earliest known example of written Welsh. The original is in Lichfield Cathedral in England. Check opening hours for exhibit (http://www.llandeilofawr.org.uk/gosp.htm).

Carreg Cennen Castle, Carmarthenshire
N51 51 16 W3 56 8

As you drive up the narrow lane, you will see the ruins of Carreg Cennen Castle perched on a steep limestone crag, 300 ft above the Cennen River. The castle commands an impressive view over Carmarthenshire and is an intimidating sight, but the walk up is not as steep as it appears.

Carreg Cennen Castle

Archaeological evidence reveals that prehistoric people and Romans utilized the site. Perhaps at one time there was an Iron Age hillfort on this imposing crag. Some say that Sir Urien, a knight of King Arthur, built the first fortress on the site. Although never of much strategic use, the castle was important symbolically as a seat of power for the Welsh princes, beginning with Rhys ap Gruffydd in the twelfth century.

The current castle was built near the end of the thirteenth century. It was dismantled in 1462 during the War of the Roses. The castle has an inner ward, gate towers, the remains of cisterns, kitchens—what you would expect to find in an important medieval stronghold. Unless you are interested in military architecture, however, that's not the main reason to visit Carreg Cennen. The main reason is the cave.

Deep below the castle is a natural cave with a fresh-water spring. It is possible that a fissure in the bedrock was modified to form the cave as it now appears. Bring a flashlight (or rent one at the ticket office); you might also bring a candle with a protective sleeve.

The spring within the cave

Below the castle and along the top of the steep southern cliff is a covered gallery, a 200-ft-long passageway that leads down to the mouth of the cave. The entrance to the passageway is located in the SE corner of the inner ward. You descend a steep set of stairs to the sloping stone-lined, vaulted corridor, with window-like openings to the outside, then descend another set of uneven steps. You have reached the opening to the cave, a narrow, slippery, rocky fissure about 150 ft long that ends in a damp, limestone grotto. It takes about five minutes of careful walking to reach the spring at the end of the cave—a journey that seems much longer going in than coming out.

Vaulted corridor leading to the cave

Water drips through the limestone and fills a large natural stone basin, hollowed out by time (and human tools?) from the solid pedestal of rock below. From there it flows down a channel in the floor of the cave into a deep cavity, where a perforated horse tooth and the bones of two adults and a child were discovered. One source reports they were painted with red ochre. These date to the Upper Paleolithic (before the end of the last Ice Age) and are perhaps 30,000 years old. The walls beside the dripping water are coated with flowstone from the dissolved minerals in the limestone. Stalactites and stalagmites can be seen above the wall behind the spring. The grotto is large enough for three to four people to stand together.

Once you reach the end of the cave, turn off your flashlight and blow out your candle. Spend time in the dark. What do you see? What do you hear? What do you feel? Gary felt a sense of compression, aware of the weight of rock over his head; he left the cave in an altered state that lasted for some hours. Elyn felt a cozy, restful, welcoming darkness. She felt the cave had been used for important rituals—perhaps dream incubation or initiation.

Purchase tickets and, if needed, rent a flashlight ("torch") at the shop/tearoom at the bottom of the hill; opening hours. The tearoom serves snacks and light meals. Cadw manages Castle Carreg Cennen, but it is part of a privately owned farm. The farm includes pedigree Longhorn cattle, Welsh sheep breeds, and other animals (http://www.carreg-cennencastle.com/).

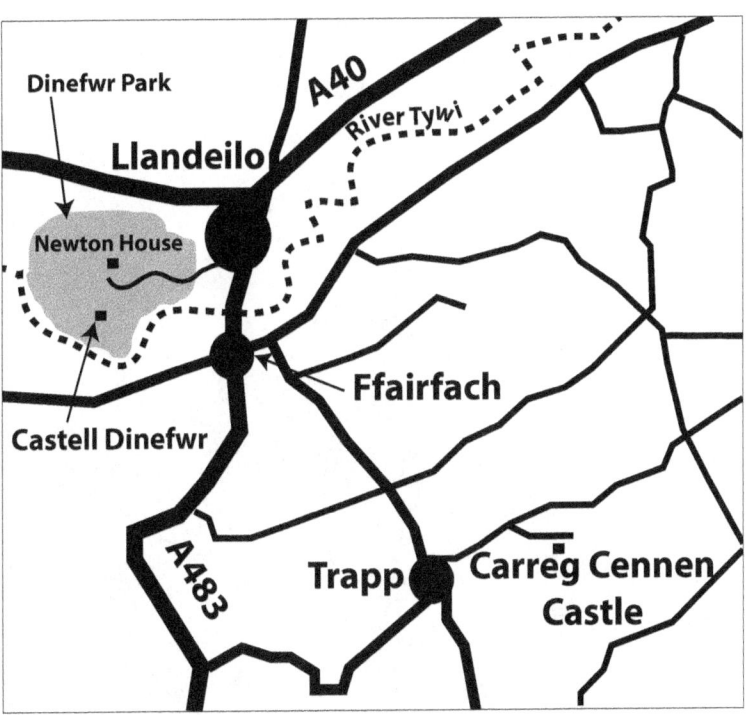

Area map

Getting There

Carreg Cennen Castle is east of Trapp on a minor road. Go south from Llandeilo on A483 to Ffairfach. Trapp can be reached on a minor road from Ffairfach or off of A483 south of Ffairfach (see map on p. 63).

Dinefwr Castle and Park, Carmarthenshire

N51 52 36 W4 1 6

Only a few miles northwest of Castle Carreg Cennen is another ruined castle, Castell Dinefwr (anglicized as Dinevore Castle), located in the midst of the extensive, 800-acre Dinefwr Park. For over 1000 years, the castle has loomed over the Tywi River, a great fortress in the posses-

Newton House

sion of important Welsh princes, including Rhys ap Gruffydd, the Lord Rhys (d. 1197), and his sons. He was prince of Deheubarth, one of the ancient kingdoms of Wales.

According to Dinefwr Park Warden, Wyn Davies, Dinefwr is a microcosm of Welsh history. At one time the site contained an Iron Age fort, and the remains of two Roman forts have recently been uncovered. What may be vestiges of the Carmarthen-Llandovery Roman road have also been discovered, along with traces of other roads and trackways that may be Roman and/or medieval. The park includes a medieval castle, two medieval towns (Welsh and English), a sixteenth-century deer park, a remodeled seventeenth-century mansion, Newton House, now a 1912 "living history" museum, and an eighteenth-century farm.

In addition, Dinefwr features the first designed naturalist landscape. In 1775 George and Cecil Rice, with a few suggestions from Capability Brown, organized the medieval castle, house, gardens, woods (some oak trees are over 700 years old), and deer park into a unified landscape. The park is currently home to more than 100 fallow deer and a small herd of rare Dinefwr White Park cattle.

Dinefwr is the only National Nature Reserve parkland in Wales and has been managed since 1987 by the National Trust. A scenic 3-mi circular wildlife walk leads through a variety of woodlands, bog woods, beech clumps, lakes, and the ruined castle.

Besides its natural attractiveness and historic resonances, there is a particularly compelling reason to visit Dinefwr: the herd of approximately 30 rare White Park cattle. The cattle have been important in Welsh myth and history for millennia. According to Warden Wyn Davies, the cattle are very primitive—some of the most primitive in the world—direct descendents of the huge wild aurochs that used to roam the region. This is their ancestral home. They are white with either red or black "points"; the coloration on

White Park cattle

their nose, ears, around the eyes, horn tips, socks on feet, and teats. In the twelfth century, some had red points, some black, but now all have black.

The white cattle have had an important place in medieval Welsh lawmaking and legend. Anglesey in northern Wales was the final refuge of the Druids fleeing the Romans, and white cattle were used in Druid sacrifices. In later centuries, the White Park cattle breed (perhaps descended from these original sacred cattle?) was an emblem of the power of Welsh princes. The cattle are first recorded in 856 CE when Rhodri Fawr established Dynevwr (Dinefwr) as the seat of political power in the kingdom of Deheubarth. "Rhodri's grandson, Hywel Dda, formulated the

> Millennia ago in Ireland, the white cattle lent their name to places such as Inishbofin (Island of the White Cow); the River Boyne is named after Boann or Boand, whose name means "White Cow." The Irish epic, The Cattle Raid of Cooley, takes place sometime in the first millennium BCE and mentions white cattle with red points. In it, Queen Maebh of Connacht invades Ulster because she is jealous of her husband's white horned bull.

famous codes of legislation in which the white cattle assume a special status as currency in the payment of fines." The laws were formulated approximately 942-950 CE (http://lawrencealderson.com/page3.htm). For example, tribute of white cattle with black points was to be paid for personal injury to the king of Deheubarth.

In the legend of the faery lady of the lake at Llyn y Fan Fach (see pp. 197-200) near Myddfai, the lady emerged from the lake with livestock of various kinds. When she later returns to the waters, she called her cattle—including "the white bull from the king's court"—to join her. The physicians of Myddfai, who were employed as physicians to Rhys Gryg, Lord of Dinefwr in the late twelfth century (see p. 163) were purported to be her descendants. Over the centuries, the legend of the faery cattle, including "the white bull from the king's court," the physicians of Myddfai, and the white cattle of Dinefwr became linked together in popular imagination (see Gwyndaf 197).

Today you can see descendants of the original Dinefwr herd grazing on the grounds of Dinefwr Park. They peacefully coexist with the fallow deer.

Merlin is also associated with Dinefwr, but this connection may simply be the result of artistic license. In Edmund Spenser's epic poem, The *Faerie Queen*, Merlin is reported to consort with spirits deep in a cave in the isolated, wooded bluff beneath the castle. However, no such cave has ever been found. Legend also claims Merlin's grave (one of many) is somewhere in the area, but our inquiries were met with polite negation. Wyn Davies

> "And if thou ever happen that same way/ To travel, go to see that dreadful place;/ It is a hideous hollow, cave-like bay,/ Under a rock that lies a little space/ From the swift Tyvi, tumbling down apace,/ Amongst the woody hills of Dynevwr:/ But dare thou not, I charge, in any case/ To enter into that same baleful bower/ For fear the cruel fiends should thee unawares devour." Spenser, *The Faerie Queen*, Book III, Canto 3.

told us that people come and ask, but as far as he knows there is no Merlin connection with Dinefwr.

Managed by National Trust and Cadw; fee for parking includes visiting Newton House and the grounds; opening hours (http://www.nationaltrust.org.uk/dinefwr/). Walkers enter the park free, and there is a free car park near the castle.

Getting There

Dinefwr Park is just west of Llandeilo (see map on p. 63).

Parc le Breos Cwm Burial Cairn, Cat Hole Cave, Gower Peninsula (West Glamorgan)
N51 35 10 W4 06 43

A smear of orange-red ochre stained a depression in the top of a boulder outside the Cat Hole Cave, a contemporary continuation of ancient practices. Perhaps the blood-like damp smear was evidence of modern initiation. Nothing was left except a stain; nothing remained except a mystery. We joined hands in a circle and asked permission to enter. Suddenly we smelled incense: sandalwood, with a hint of something indefinable, filled the air. Was this the "fragrance" of the Spirit of the Place? (Elyn)

Parc le Breos Cwm Cairn, named after a great medieval deer park, is located in a narrow, dry valley (in Welsh, *cwm* means valley; pro. "koom"). Like Tinkinswood, Parc le Breos is a Cotswold-Severn type burial cairn, a trapezoidal mound with an extensive "horned" forecourt. Mortu-

Parc le Breos Cwm Burial Cairn

ary and other ceremonies were conducted in the forecourt. Animal bones and human remains of approximately 40 individuals were found inside, indicative of long-term use during the millennia after the tomb was built.

Unlike Tinkinswood, Parc le Breos has four side chambers, two on each side, leading off the forecourt. It was constructed around 3800 BCE from upright limestone slabs with fine dry-stone walling filling in the gaps. What look like reconstructed dry-stone walls are actually (for the most part) the original construction. Originally Parc le Breos was probably covered with a mound of stones, but now neither the mound nor the capstones remain, and the walls are not very high. An upright stone marks the threshold boundary between the forecourt

Interior of Parc le Breos Cwm Burial Cairn

and the inner chambers. We noticed quartz in some of the stones, perhaps selected to generate "energy."

Although the cairn looks ruined, open to the sky, you still need to center yourself and ask permission before entering—especially before stepping over the threshold stone.

The burial cairn is overlooked by Cat Hole Cave, a karst cave that was occupied by Ice Age hunters thousands of years before the tomb was constructed. To reach the cave, follow the asphalt road about 100 yd past Parc le Breos. You'll pass a lime kiln on the right. Watch carefully for an overgrown path leading off to the right up the hill. As you walk along the road, you will pass a number of tall trees on the right, then shorter trees and bushes. The trail is unmarked, in the ferns, just after the tall trees, just before the road starts to curve left.

About three minutes up the stony trail, on your right, just before a wooden pole and before a boulder that blocks the trail, you'll come to the first cave, which is closed with a

Ros Briagha inside Cat Hole Cave

metal gate. Follow the path up to the right (be careful: it may be a bit slippery) and you'll come to a clearing with a large stone in front, perhaps still stained with ochre. Behind that is the triangular opening to Cat Hole Cave.

The cave is tall enough for people to stand up inside. It is composed of several different chambers. Two stone points, probably 28,000 years old, were found in the cave, but most of the finds are from the Late Ice Age (10,000 BCE). These include burins, scrapers, flint awls, and a needle and awl of bone. Animal remains were also found. Mesolithic hunters also used the cave, and during the Bronze Age it was used for burials; human remains and burial urn sherds have been found. Also found in the cave were a bronze socketed axe and two human skeletons. Clearly, ancient people found this a desirable location, and perhaps there was a mortuary association with the Parc le Breos cairn in the valley below.

> Our guide, Ros Briagha Foskett, has spent a number of years living in tepees. She was able to visualize how this cave would have been a very comfortable home, with separate sleeping, cooking, and living areas. It is dry and well ventilated, with natural light.

Spend time, letting your eyes adjust to the lack of light. Imagine how this cave would have made a spacious, well-organized home, nicely sheltered from the wind and rain. Sit on the flat-topped stone "seat of power" opposite the entrance and imagine yourself living here, staring out at the

Gary on the "seat of power" inside Cat Hole Cave

sky. Commune with the guardian spirit if you desire and it is willing.

Getting There

Parc le Breos is located near the Gower Heritage Center at Parkmill. Follow the road past the Gower Heritage Center to a small parking area. Bring a flashlight.

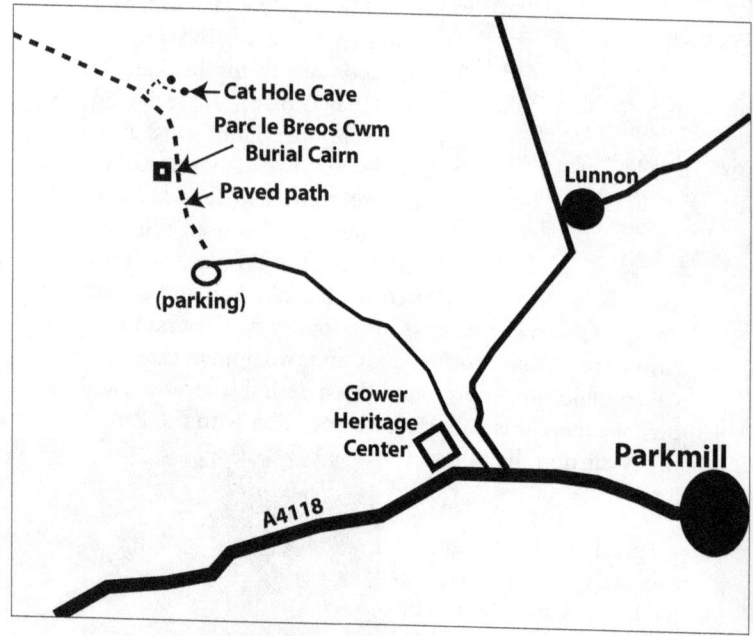

Site map

More to Experience

There is much to see on the Gower Peninsula, which is practically littered with prehistoric remains. A week could be spent exploring megalithic sites, caves, and sandy beaches. We have selected a few important sites to describe in depth.

Paviland Cave, the Gower Peninsula, West Glamorgan

Paviland Cave is where the ochre-stained skeleton of the "Red Lady of Paviland" and remains of jewelry were found in 1823 by a vicar. Being a devout Christian, he believed the skeleton was both female and post-Flood—a Roman prostitute, perhaps, painted red. Subsequent analysis determined that "she" was the 29,000 year-old skeleton of a 21-year-old male. The original is in the Pitt Rivers Museum, Oxford University; replicas of the skeleton and burial are in the Swansea Museum.

The red ochre undoubtedly had a ceremonial purpose. It is possible that this individual was much revered, perhaps a shaman. According to Ros Briagha, the red ochre may have symbolized blood, so covering the corpse with "blood" could link it to the womb and rebirth. The "Red Lady of Paviland" is powerful evidence of ceremonial usage of caves and of ancient mortuary rituals.

The "Red Lady of Paviland" may be the oldest-discovered ceremonial burial in Western Europe. At the time of burial, the sea level was 250 ft lower; instead of being on the shore, the cave would have looked out on a plain. Finds in the cave included perforated seashell necklaces, stone needles,

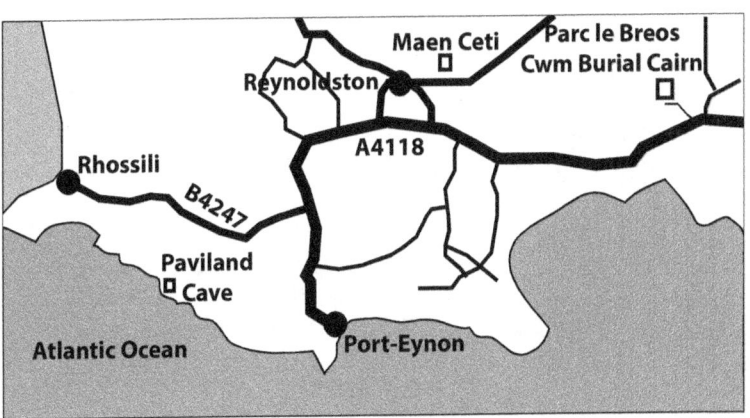

The Gower Peninsula

mammoth-ivory bracelets, and worked flint. See http://www.archaeology.co.uk/articles/welsh-skeleton-re-dated-even-older.htm; http://www.bradshawfoundation.com/british_isles_prehistory_archive/red_lady_paviland/index.php.

Getting There

The cave is located in southwest Gower, halfway between Port Eynon and Rhossili, accessible by coastal path (see map on p. 73).

Maen Ceti, the Gower Peninsula, West Glamorgan

Maen Ceti, Arthur's Stone in the Gower (NB: there are many other "Arthur's Stones" scattered around Wales), is a massive, isolated dolmen sitting on a ridge in the middle of open moorland. It is perhaps all that remains of a dispersed cairn that was originally 75 ft in diameter. What remains is a twin chamber formed by (possibly) 12 orthostats, though only 6 supporting stones remain. Maen Ceti is crowned by a massive, partly frost-shattered capstone that weighs over 25 tons. It is about 13 ft by 10 ft by 7 ft. In the "Welsh Triads," raising this capstone was called one of the "three mighty achievements of Britain," from which comes the proverb, "Mal gwaith Maen Cetti"—"Like the labor of the Stone of Cetti." It is possible that the capstone is a natural boulder deposited at the site by a glacier and that the chambers were dug out beneath.

Many legends surround the stone, including one about King Arthur. According to the story, the king was out walking and found a stone in his shoe. He removed it and threw it, and it landed on Cefn Bryn—seven mi away from where he stood. The pebble grew into an immense

> The "Welsh Triads" are a group of related medieval texts that preserve fragments of Welsh mythology, folklore, and traditional history in groups of three, perhaps as a mnemonic device.

quartz boulder, swelling with pride at having been touched by the king.

According to an antiquarian writing in the 1830s, there was supposed to be a spring known as Our Lady's Well that issued from beneath the dolmen, but when he went there, it was dry. See http://themodernantiquarian.com/site/111/maen_ceti.html for related folklore.

Getting There

Maen Ceti is located just east of Reynoldston in a field north of the road. Park near the main road and walk about 15 minutes to the site. See map on p. 73.

Gumfreston Church and Holy Wells (Ffynhonnau Eglwys Gumfreston), Pembrokeshire

N51 40 37 W4 44 11

Gumfreston church is a very old place, a medieval church erected over a sixth-century church, which was probably erected over something else. The building feels organic, like a living thing, rather than like an organized construction. You can feel the church's rootedness in the ground. It is ancient and strong. In the sloping ground behind the church, three holy wells flow together and downhill. A friend of ours swore the waters had helped her aching knees. I stood beside the holy wells, meditating, lost in the sound of moving water. The bubbling springs whispered of a time long before Christians claimed the site as their own. (Elyn)

Nestled on the side of a gently sloping hill in the verdant Ritec Valley, the first you see of Eglwys Gumfreston is its tall, square, crenellated French-Norman tower. Given the tower's size, you might expect the church to be an impressive building, but it's not. It is a small, simple sanctuary. But size isn't everything. Gumfreston Church, dedicated to St Lawrence, is a powerful place, built on a site that has been sacred for millennia. By the sixth century, Celtic saints had established themselves in the area, probably creating a *llan* (sacred enclosure) that included the three healing springs, undoubtedly sacred since pre-Christian times.

There is evidence that Carew Cheriton, 4 mi to the west, was an important Celtic royal and religious site. It is possible that pilgrims and other travelers made their way from Carew to the wells at Gumfreston before journeying on to the south of Wales. In the woods to the south are the remains of a village that was located beside the quay on the river estuary. This was on the pilgrimage route across south Wales to St Davids, as well as to the major seaside port of

Gumfreston Church

Interior of the church

Tenby, from where pilgrims embarked to Europe and the Holy Land.

According to the church brochure (dated 2007), it is possible that there was a connection between Gumfreston and the leper group in Tenby cared for by the Magdalenes, a group of lay and religious women. The brochure also says there was a Magdalene hospice at the bottom of Gumfreston Hill in an area now known as the Maudlins, a suburb of Tenby, and perhaps lepers were brought from there to the healing wells.

You enter the twelfth-century church through a moss-covered porch, perhaps all that is left of a more ancient sanctuary. Large, deep windows punctuate the thick white plaster walls, and old wooden pews line the nave. The interior has a somewhat haphazard layout. At some point, the originally detached tower was connected to the church and its ground floor turned into a small chapel. There is a shallow alcove on the west wall and a "passage squint" (an opening in the wall, so one could observe the action from the side) facing the altar. Perhaps an anchorite's cell was there at one time, or perhaps the "squint" enabled the aforementioned lepers to view Mass from the side. Modern, Celtic-themed stained-glass windows add color, as do the faded icon prints and hand-made twig crosses. It's a homey place, full of bric-a-brac and assorted candlesticks. The décor seems the result of accretion rather than of intentional design. Despite the crosses and icons, it's a place where even a pagan could feel at home.

Ffynhonnau Eglwys Gumfreston are the healing springs located on the grassy slope behind the church. They flow from an outcrop of limestone and are set in millstone grit. Each of the springs has a different mineral content and a different medicinal purpose. The spring closest to the church is shaped like a leg and is for legs; its water is pure. The chalybeate (iron-bearing) spring in the middle is said to heal arms and hands. The lower, circular pool, with its sulphurous water, is for eyes.

One of the holy wells

The modern Gumfreston community honors both its Christian present and its pre-Christian past. It has established a monthly healing service. On Easter Sunday the small congregation "throws Lent away" by tossing nails into the three wells. This bears a strong resemblance to the pagan tradition of offering crooked pins and metal objects to the Spirit of the Waters.

Rarely have we been in a church where the presence of ancient ritual and belief seemed to blend so seamlessly with modern theology. When we visited Gumfreston, Elyn didn't want to leave. She spent an inordinate amount of time sitting beside the wells, then back inside the welcoming little church, then back to the wells. She felt that this was a place of great serenity and longstanding, powerful sanctity.

Getting There

Drive west from Tenby on B4318 to Gumfreston. Take a minor road to the left to the church. There is a sign at the turning.

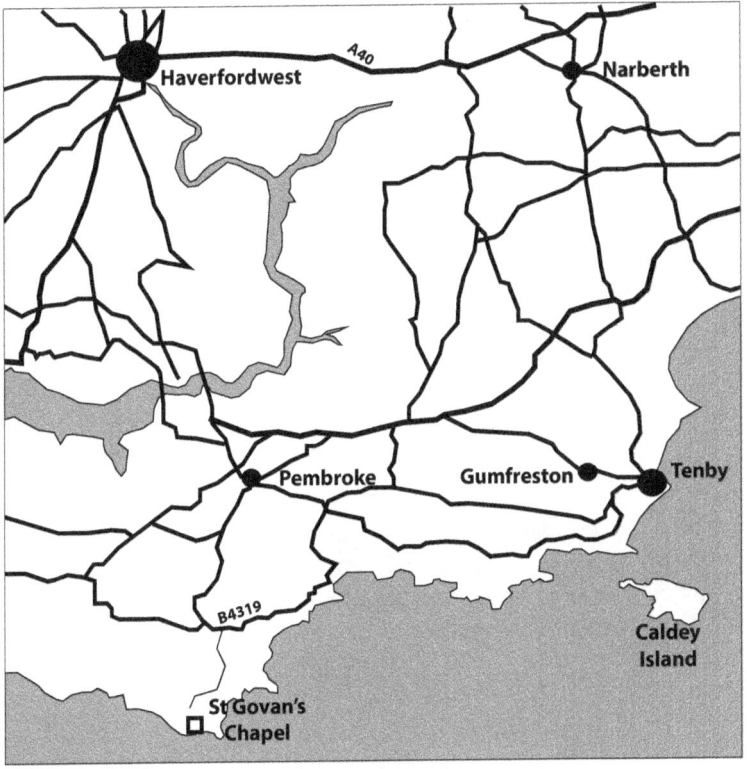

Area map

More to Experience
Caldey Island, Pembrokeshire

Caldey Island (Ynys Pyr), 3 mi from Tenby harbor, is home to numerous sea birds, grey seals, and a community of some 20 Cistercian monks. Domestic refuse found in caves suggests that people visited the island 50,000 years ago. Celtic monks settled on the island in the sixth century. In 1136, Benedictine monks founded a priory, but they left in 1536 with the dissolution of the monasteries. In 1906 the island was sold to a Benedictine monastic order and subsequently to Reformed Cistercians, who have lived there ever since. They support themselves by producing specialty perfumes, chocolate, and shortbread.

Footpaths lead to the Old Priory, restored in the twentieth century, and to twelfth-century St Illtud's Church, with its ancient stone walls and well-worn pebble floor. An important sixth-century stone, engraved in Ogham and Latin, is displayed in the church, which is part of the Old Priory. We've been told the stone has a strong presence and a sense of mystery—as does the Old Priory.

St Davids Parish Church, on the hill above the village, is built on a pre-Christian burial ground. The church was constructed in Norman times but may contain remnants of the earlier sixth-century chapel.

The island has a lovely feeling and is well worth a visit. Better yet, arrange to take a retreat, either in the retreat center or in self-catering accommodations (http://www.caldey-island.co.uk/).

Getting There

Boat trips depart from Tenby nearly every half hour from April to October for the twenty-minute ride. It is difficult if not impossible to visit during other months. See map on p. 79.

St Govan's Chapel, Pembrokeshire

St Govan's Chapel and Holy Well, near Bosherton, Pembrokeshire, are in a breathtaking location: wedged halfway down the side of a cliff, overlooking the pounding surf. Little is known about St Govan. Some claim that he may have been the sixth-century Irish abbot Gobhan of Wexford, others that he was Gawain of Arthurian fame. "He" may have been Cofen, wife of a fifth-century chief, who decided to become a recluse. (Gary "dowsed" that a female saint had retreated to this isolated place.)

The tiny chapel is at least 800 years old and may be much older. Legend recounts that pirates attacked St Govan but the cliff opened up in front of him and then closed around him, hiding him from view. Later, when the danger was gone, the cliff released him. Approximately 74 stone steps lead down to the chapel and a small cell hewn out of rock. There you can see the vertical cleft which, according to legend, opened to hide St Govan. The steps continue down to the rough and roaring sea.

St Govan's Chapel

The steps down to the chapel are uneven, but the metal hand railing and anti-slip treads on some of the steps make the descent relatively easy. It is said that the number of steps can't be counted accurately, possibly because the steps are so irregular that people often fail to count the half-steps. It is also said that if you make a wish while standing in the cleft and facing the rock, it will come true—providing you don't change your mind before turning around.

A large boulder known as the Bell Rock stands outside the chapel. Legend states that St Govan was given a silver bell but pirates stole it. Devastated at the loss, he prayed for its return. Angels returned the bell but placed it inside the rock for safekeeping. St Govan would "ring" the bell by striking the rock—and the sound was a thousand times stronger than the note of the original bell. Which boulder it is, is no longer known. There are "singing stones" in the Preseli Mountains as well; see pp. 124-125.

The chapel was built directly above a holy well, now dry, which attracted pilgrims to its miraculous healing waters, especially for curing lameness. This seems a bit counter-intuitive, given the difficult-to-reach location of the well. As late as 1811, people who had been miraculously healed had left numerous crutches there. Another smaller well, still filled with water, is found inside the chapel.

Getting There

St Govan's Chapel is located 5 mi south of Pembroke off B4319. It is under the care of the Pembrokeshire Coast National Park. Access to the cliff-top path leading down to the chapel is dependent upon the military Firing Range being open to the public, so watch out for a closed gate or flashing lights (see map on p. 79).

Narberth, Pembrokeshire

Narberth is small, but it is the best town in eastern Pembrokeshire for clothing boutiques, Spanish food, and contemporary music, art, and theater. There's a more mythic reason to visit the town, however. Narberth, once known as Arberth, plays a key role in both the First and Third Branches of the *Mabinogi*. It was the location of the court of Pwyll, legendary Prince of Dyfed. In the First Branch, it is while sitting on the mound outside his palace in Arberth that Pwyll sees the beautiful Rhiannon riding by on her white horse. He sets chase but is unable to catch her until she so chooses. In a humorous scene in the Third Branch, Manawydan, son of Llŷr, builds a tiny scaffold to hang a shape-changing mouse he has caught raiding his field near Arberth.

The ruined but picturesque castle (not open for visits) is in the southern part of town, built upon a steep hill. Whether Pwyll ever held court there or not, Narberth did grow up around an early fortification, burnt down by Norsemen in 994 CE. The current ruin was built in 1264.

Getting There

Narberth is south off A40, east of Haverfordwest (see map on p. 79).

St Anthony's Well, Llansteffan, Carmarthenshire

St Anthony's Well (Ffynnon Antwn) near Llansteffan, Carmarthenshire, is supposed to be a powerful healing well, also famous as a wishing well for lovers. It is linked to the sixth-century Welsh hermit Antwn, who took his name from the early ascetic Christian hermit, St Anthony of the Desert. Scallop shells, symbols of the pilgrimage to Santiago de Compostela in Spain, are scattered on the floor of the well house, a reminder that St Anthony is the patron saint of Welsh pilgrims. The location is attractive; the well house is spacious; and the modern sculpture of St Anthony, set on the wall, is quite impressive.

Gate to St Anthony's Well

Although we had been told that St Anthony's Well was a sweet place to visit, when we visited in June 2011 the energy felt horrible and the well was dry. We felt so uncomfortable that we quickly fled back down the path to the nearby beach, where we rinsed ourselves off in the stream flowing from below the well house. We've been told that, after dowsers "worked" on it, the well has returned to being a sweet, welcoming place.

Getting There

Our experiences at St Anthony's Well are an important reminder that not all powerful places feel good—and that what might feel good to one person might not feel good to another. In addition, the energy of a powerful place can shift, depending on the season of the year, the phase of the moon, the way the site has been used. In this case, perhaps underground disturbances blocked the energies of the place, stopping the flow of water—although water still flowed in the stream below.

St Anthony's Well is near the beach south of the village of Llansteffan. Park in the parking lot for the beach and walk to the outlet of the tiny stream issuing from the well. There is a paved path up to the well. See map on p. 86.

Carmarthen, Carmarthenshire

Carmarthen (Caerfyrddin) is a pleasant county town, located on the bank of the River Tywi (anglicized to Towy). Carmarthen has numerous services, including a train station, pharmacies, and car-lease offices.

The current town was founded as a Roman fort, but its name is thought to refer to the wizard Merlin, who was reputedly born there. Caerfyrddin means "Fort of Myrddin" (Merlin). Carmarthen makes as much as it can of the Merlin connection, including Merlin-themed shopping streets and stores. The town holds an annual Merlin festival, "Gwyl Myrddyn," a fun-filled family frolic with magicians, storytellers, crafts persons, street musicians, and a roaming dragon (http://www.carmarthenshire.gov.uk).

A local oak tree, planted in 1660, was linked to a prophecy Merlin made: "when Merlin's tree shall tumble down, then shall fall Carmarthen town." Fortunately, the prophecy failed to materialize when the tree died in the 1970s. Pieces of the tree can be seen in the Carmarthen County Museum.

Several miles to the east of Carmarthen is Bryn Myrddin, Merlin's Hill. One legend asserts that Merlin is buried there, but a differ-

Downtown Carmarthen

ent legend declares that he lives still under Merlin's Hill, where he will remain until King Arthur and his knights rise up to save Britain from great danger. Regardless of whether Merlin lies asleep or dead, we have been told that the hill is a very powerful place, and that strange things happen on its summit.

> Other legends assert that Merlin is buried or alive in Brittany, or in a glass castle on Bardsey Island, where he guards the Thirteen Treasures of Britain (see pp. 314-315).

Getting There

Carmarthen is at the junction of A40 and A48 (see map).

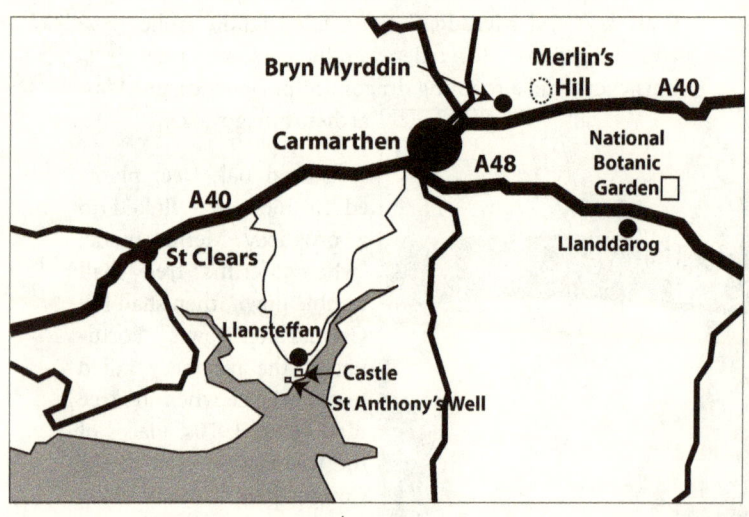

Area map

The National Botanic Garden of Wales, Carmarthenshire

The National Botanic Garden of Wales (Gardd Fotaneg Genediaethol Cymru) is just east of Carmarthen. Set in historic parkland dating back 400 years, it was only opened to the public in 2000 and is still in development. It has already become the centerpiece of the Tywi Valley. Lakes, sculpture, landscaped walks through different kinds of habitats, a Japanese garden, and an apothecary garden are some of the offerings. The vast oval-domed glasshouse designed by Norman Foster is the largest single-span glasshouse in the world. It is worth visiting the gardens for this alone. Inside are plants from various Mediterranean climate regions.

The garden is designed on environmentally sustainable principles, and some of the land surrounding the garden is being used for organic farming and for grazing Welsh breeds of cattle and sheep (http://www.gardenofwales.org.uk/). Entry fee; opening hours.

Getting There

The National Botanic Garden is just north of A48 near the village of Llandddarog (see map).

St Davids (St David's), Pembrokeshire

We walked across the wet fields to St Non's Well, covered with a vaulted stone well-house. I descended the steps to the spring, which issues forth below ground level. Sitting on the ledge, dipping my fingers in the water, I felt surrounded by sweet, dark, velvety-rich, maternal love. It must have been the Spirit of the Well, or maybe it was St Non. Or maybe those are different names for the same thing. (Elyn)

St Davids (Tyddewi; means "House of David") is the smallest city in the UK in terms of population. Although it is more like a village, it was given the title of city because of its grand cathedral and its importance in Welsh religious history. St Davids is the holiest Christian site in Wales, traditionally founded by Wales' patron saint, St David (Dewi Sant). Legend says he was born at nearby St Non's Well in the sixth century. He established a monastic community at St Davids and later died there.

> The author of the eleventh-century *Life of Saint David* states that St David traveled to Glastonbury, England, toward the end of his life, to found a church. Writing 40 years later, William of Malmsbury, the foremost English historian of the twelfth century, tells a slightly different story. He wrote that there already was a church in Glastonbury, which St David planned to rededicate. However, St David received a message from Jesus proclaiming He had already dedicated the church in honor of His mother. So instead, St David commissioned an extension of the Glastonbury church. He is also said to have brought a traveling altar with a large sapphire as a gift to the abbey.
>
> This story adds credence to the idea that Jesus came to England, and perhaps Wales, with Joseph of Arimathea, who was reportedly a tin merchant. This claim also gives priority to Glastonbury as the first church in England and should perhaps be taken with caution. It should also be treated with caution because it seems highly unlikely that Jesus, a Jew, would dedicate a church.

St Davids grew to become the ecclesiastical and spiritual center of medieval Wales. In the Middle Ages, two pilgrimages to St Davids were equivalent to one to Rome—and three were equivalent to one to Jerusalem. For centuries, hoards of pilgrims followed the Pilgrims' Ways across Wales to this distant southwestern tip of Pembrokeshire. They came to leave offerings and pay homage to St David's relics, displayed in an elaborate shrine in the cathedral.

For centuries this end of the peninsula was a busy place. It was at the junction of a major land route and numerous important sea routes between Ireland, Scotland, and northwest Britain, with access to Cornwall and then on to Brittany and the rest of Europe. Numerous ships landed and departed from the nearby harbor at Porthclais. In St David's time, it was a "front door" to Wales rather than a "back door," with exchange of ideas and commerce, and Viking raiding—taking place much easier by sea than by land. Instead of being an isolated "Land's End," as it seems today, it was a hub of activity.

There is much to explore in and around St Davids, including the cathedral, the Bishop's Palace, the art gallery and bookstore at the National Park Visitor Center, boutique shopping, delis and fine dining, and St Non's Well and chapels. You can also take boat rides to neighboring islands and walk short stretches of the Pembrokeshire Coast Path.

> St David (b. around 500 CE; d. either 589 or 602 CE) was a very down-to-earth man who lived simply and austerely. His symbol is the daffodil (*daff* = David, so "David's flower"). He was frugal and ascetic, living, it is said, on bread and water, hence his nickname, "Aquaticus" (Water Man). Or perhaps he was known as the Waterman "because of his fondness for the ritual purification of the sick and sinners using herbs and water" (Heaven, p. 125). On his deathbed, St David exhorted his followers to "Do the little things." He is the only official Welsh saint from the "Age of Saints." He was canonized in 1123.

This region of Pembrokeshire is a rugged and windswept land, where resistant earth meets surging sea and winds blow strong. The result of its complex geology is a mix of moors and stone-bounded fields, treeless hills, and stunning coastal scenery.

The National Park Visitor Center, east of the town square, provides extensive information and support for people walking the Pembrokeshire Coast Path. Helpful clerks provide weather reports and bus schedules for the Puffin Shuttle and Celtic Coaster that transport walkers and tourists back and forth along the coast. The 186-mi-long Pembrokeshire Coast National Park is Britain's only coastal national park; the stretch around St Davids Head and the Marloes peninsula, either side of St Bride's Bay, are the most

  popular and inspiring, with ever-changing views of scenery, wildlife, and vegetation. See http://www.pembrokeshirecoast.org.uk and http://www.nt.pcnpa.org.uk; also check the Coastal Bus Service schedule at http://www.pembrokeshiregreenways.co.uk.

St Davids Cathedral and Bishop's Palace, Pembrokeshire

N51 52 55 W5 16 4

Although churches are usually built on high ground, intended as spiritual and architectural beacons that are visible for miles, St Davids Cathedral is not so easy to find. Hoping to avoid the attention of Viking raiders, the twelfth-

St Davids Cathedral

> "I am David./ In the Vale of Roses/ I have built my house/ In a solitude of stones/ Crowded with daffodils/ In a cleft of sea-green hills. ... I am David./ Under my feet/ The rock of Dyfed/ Has raised me up/ To tower in time's March gales./ I am David. I am Wales." Poem by Raymond Garlick.

century builders situated the massive cathedral in a boggy hollow rather than on a high spot in the area. Since this was also the site of the sixth-century monastery built by St David, they were taking advantage of already sanctified ground. Unfortunately, their plan was unsuccessful. The cathedral was raided seven times, and the marshy ground has caused ongoing problems for the building, leading to much subsidence and stress. Numerous efforts have been made to stabilize the Cathedral and repair the damage.

St Davids Cathedral has been a major site of pilgrimage for nearly 1000 years, though pilgrims began coming to St Davids centuries earlier to visit the grounds hallowed by the saint. The cathedral is worth a lengthy visit to appreciate the various aisles, chapels, and the amusing sixteenth-century misericords in the choir. Carvings include a seasick pilgrim, Green Men, and fantastic and humorous animals. The sixteenth-century carved oak ceiling over the nave is impressive. Tours are available and worthwhile. Donation suggested; charge for photos; opening hours; religious services.

Lady Chapel

Although we felt the entire cathedral had a sweet, pleasant energy, we particularly enjoyed the Lady Chapel. Originally built in the late thirteenth century, it was left ruined and roofless for centuries until it was restored in the twentieth. Perhaps one of the other chapels will draw you in and you will find it to be a powerful place. English monarchs from William the Conqueror to Queen Elizabeth II have worshipped here, and you can, too, if you choose to stay for a service. If so, try to attend one in Welsh (http://www.stdavidscathedral.org.uk).

> Legend says that St David sited his monastery at the bend of the river near a spring that issued forth when he struck the ground with his staff on a dry summer's day. This sounds somewhat suspicious and probably indicates the site was sanctified in pre-Christian times. The spring is now concealed beneath the ground outside the Lady Chapel.

During the Middle Ages, the Diocese of St Davids was the largest and richest in Wales, and its bishops were po-

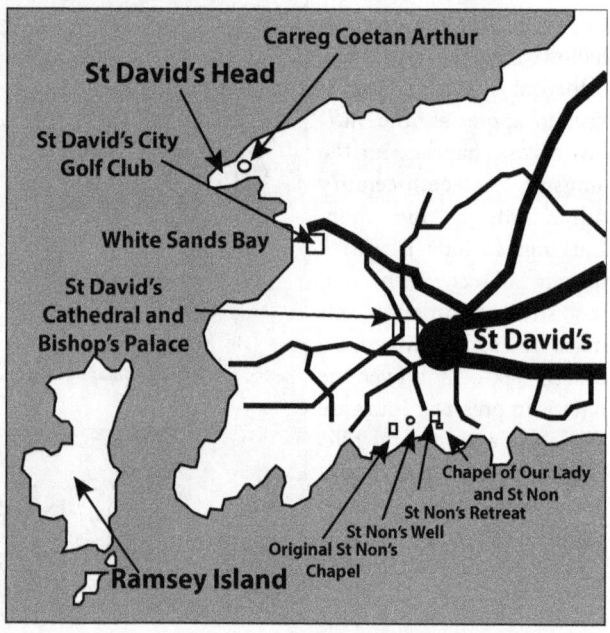

Area map

litically powerful. The fourteenth-century Bishop's Palace is just across the River Alun, which was diverted to build the cathedral. Its ruined grandeur is a display of wealth, power, ostentation, and, ultimately, arrogance, both of Bishops Beck and Gower who built it and of Bishop Barlow who destroyed it two centuries later. He stripped the lead roofs off the buildings to provide money for dowries for his five daughters. Managed by Cadw; admissions charge; http://cadw.wales.gov.uk/daysout/stdavidsbishopspalace/?lang=en.

St Non's Well and Chapels, Pembrokeshire
N51 52 20 W5 16 06

St Non's Well (Ffynnon Non) and chapels are a short walk from town (3/4 mi south), overlooking the sea. Named after St Non (also known as Nonnita, Nonna, Nun, and Nonni), mother of St David and perhaps niece to King Arthur, the well holds healing water and mystery. There are indications that it was probably a birthing place and sacred to the Goddess long before Christians came.

Conflicting biographies exist of St Non, including that she may have been related

> There may be a link between the islands off the coast—Ramsey, Skomer, and Grassholm—and the "Green Isles of the West," which are said to be home to one of the faery races of Pembrokeshire. According to Mara Freeman, "Caer Sidi, the 'Faery Castle,' one of the citadels of Annwn, has been associated with the small island of Gwales, the archaic name for Grassholm, which lies eight miles off the coast of Pembrokeshire. Well into the nineteenth century it was said to be populated by a host of faeries and to have an occasional habit of disappearing beneath the sea." http://marafreeman.blogspot.com/ retrieved 17 Dec. 2011.

to King Arthur. One story says that the noblewoman Non, granddaughter of a chieftain, lived as a nun until she was raped, and that St David's father is unknown. Another legend asserts that her husband, Sant, the King of Ceredigion, took her against her will. Either way, sexual violence is an integral part of the story.

St Non's Well

Legend says that St Non gave birth to St David either where the holy well now flows or else in the nearby ruined chapel/St Non's house during a torrential thunderstorm, sometime between 462-512 CE. The dates are uncertain. Storm clouds swirled around, rain lashed the land—but a beam of light shone down from Heaven to illuminate the place where St Non was giving birth. At that very moment another miracle occurred: a spring burst forth from solid ground. Although this makes a memorable story, it is more likely that there was a holy well there before St David's birth, and that it had been sacred long before Christianity co-opted the pagan sacred site.

Celtic-spirituality authority Mara Freeman suggests that these legends of St David's conception are distortions of earlier events, in which a (Celtic) priestess gave birth during a time when wedlock was unimportant—or perhaps that David was conceived in an act of "sacred sexuality," in which case his paternal line was not important. Perhaps the legends are indicative of changing times, or retrospective revision, in which the consecrated female (either priestess or nun) was no longer honored.

Ruins of St Non's Chapel

Whatever its origin, natural or miraculous, St Non's spring water is famous for healing women's issues, eye problems, and for helping children. Pilgrims still come and toss coins into the water, as they have for millennia.

Nearby, visible through a wooden fence, are the ruins of the thirteenth-century chapel dedicated to Non. It was built over earlier foundations—perhaps over St Non's house, where St David may have been born. It is thought to be one of the oldest Christian buildings in Wales. A large slab known as St Non's Cross is propped against a corner. Dating from the seventh to ninth centuries, it is inscribed with a cross within a circle. There is no way to know if it was originally located at the site. Note the standing stones nearby, indication of the lengthy sanctification of this place.

A very short walk uphill leads to the modern Chapel of Our Lady and St Non, the most westerly chapel in Wales. The location is superb. It overlooks the sea and provides shelter from the fierce storms that

"In the chapel field there are a number of standing stones which may be evidence of an Iron Age settlement. It is possible that the chapel was built within an original pagan circle of standing stones." http://en.wikipedia.org/wiki/Chapel_of_St_Non, retrieved 28 Nov, 2011.

buffet the region. Measuring only 12 ft by 25 ft, with walls 2.5 ft thick, it was constructed in 1934 from stones gathered from nearby ruined chapels, monasteries, and cottages.

It is a sweet and powerful place, with stained glass windows commemorating St Non, St David, St Bride, St Brynach, and St Winifred. A statue of the Virgin lovingly embracing her son stands to the left of the altar. The nurturing feminine energy in the chapel is palpable. This modern chapel is a good reminder that a sacred place doesn't have to be old to be powerful. The chapel is watched over by the Sisters of Mercy, who run the St Non's Retreat center next door (http://www.stnonsretreat.org.uk/).

Modern St Non's Chapel

Getting There

You can drive to St Non's Retreat from St Davids and walk to the Chapel of Our Lady, St Non's Well, and the Original St Non's Chapel ruins below the retreat center (see map on p. 92). Or you can walk.

More to Experience
St David's Head, Pembrokeshire

There are wonderful coastal walks from Caerfai Bay and St Non's, filled with wild coastal scenery, cliffs, seabirds, pounding sea, and megaliths. St David's Head has been called one of the most mysterious and magical places in Wales, filled with evidence of ancient habitation, including an impressive Iron Age (750 BCE-100 CE) defensive line known as the Warrior's Dyke (Clawdd-y-Milwyr) and the 6000-year-old burial chamber known as Carreg Coetan Arthur or Arthur's Quoit.

Legend states that King Arthur visited these shores—visiting relatives, perhaps? Visible from over a mile away, the burial chamber has a flat capstone measuring 13 ft by 10 ft, currently supported by a single 5-ft-tall pillar. Although it looks as if the capstone was levered out of the ground and supported at one end, several other uprights have been found. From Arthur's Quoit, continue walking steeply uphill to the rocky summit of Carn Llidi. South of Carn Llidi are two more cromlechs (covered burial chambers). This carn and others in the area are made of igneous intrusive rock, formed from solidified molten magma.

Getting There

Park at Whitesands Bay; follow the Pembrokeshire coastal path towards St David's Head for about 1 mi (1.75 km) (see map on p. 92).

Hilary Wylde describes the energy south of St Davids at St Non's and St Bride's Bay as gentle, womb-like, "moon" energy flowing inland up to the south slopes of the Preseli Mountains. She contrasts this with the powerful, masculine, "sun" energy sweeping down from the north slopes of the Preselis and around the coast through the various igneous outcroppings, including Carn Ingli, Carn Enoch, Garn Fawr, Garn Fechan, and the cluster on St David's Head. Mythologically, the feminine energy of St Non (and St Bride) come together with the masculine energy of St David—and King Arthur.

What Hilary describes in terms of energy circulation, Gary describes in geological terms. The harder, igneous, erosion-resistant material forms outcrops from the Preselis to St David's Head and out to the islands beyond, as well as a rougher, edgier coastline. This contrasts with the softer material in the south that has been worn away by water to create the gentler "crescent moon" of St Bride's Bay and the softer-appearing terrain to the south of the Preselis. These explanations are an intriguing synergy of geology, earth energy, and myth—and may in part explain why the area is considered so mystical and mysterious.

Ramsey Island, Pembrokeshire

Ramsey Island, also known as Ynys Dewi ("the Island of David"), lies off St David's Head. It is an RSPB (Royal Society for the Protection of Birds) reserve, famous for its large breeding populations of seabirds and grey seals. There is evidence of early human habitation on the island, as well as a sixth-century Christian settlement. It is said that 2000 saints (holy people) lie buried there. Tour operators run trips to the island from St Justinian's (2 mi from St Davids), but only Thousand Islands Expeditions, located at Cross Square, St Davids, is allowed to land (http://www.thousandislands.co.uk).

Llanwnda: Ffynnon Wnda (Wnda's Well), the Church of St Gwyndaf, and Garn Wnda, Pembrokeshire
N52 00 56 W5 00 55

Hidden behind the bushes, reached via an overgrown trail, Ffynnon Wnda was obviously neglected. Perhaps it had fallen out of fashion. Most in our small group quickly turned away from the murky spring, preferring the bright sun and sparkling sea. But I stayed, pondering this holy place that seemed abandoned, its stone cover overgrown with moss and ferns, its water stagnant. Did this make it any less holy? Any less a powerful place? I meditated beside the still, silent pool, and felt a slight movement, a gentle response. Even powerful places like to be remembered. (Elyn)

Entrance to the Church of St Gwyndaf

Ffynnon Wnda and Llanwnda Church are dedicated to the "irascible Breton" saint, Gwyndaf. Located on an ancient Roman road, the well and church were a major stop on the Pilgrims' Way to Saint Davids, especially for those arriving from Ireland. Giraldus Cambrensis (AKA Gerallt Cymro or Gerald of Wales), the famous twelfth-century Welsh cleric, historian, and writer, was rector here for a short while.

Five pre-Norman, seventh- to ninth-century, cross-incised stones are set into the exterior church walls. They were discovered during extensive Victorian renovations. It appears that the stones were carved for other buildings or for an earlier church that was once on this site.

Cross-incised stone

The most unusual of the inset stones has an incised face within four intercrossing lines; above it is an "X," perhaps representing the cross of St Andrew. According to *Saints and Stones* (p. 7), "the face may be that of a female, a monk or Christ-as-Pantocrator." The large, flat stone is located at the east end of the south transept. As you face the church, turn right; at the first corner of the building, step down and turn to face back toward the church. The stone is set into the wall in front of you. It may be hard to see because it is covered with lichen and sometimes ivy.

Llanwnda Holy Well

The base of a decorated cross can be seen in the northwest corner of the graveyard. Inside the tiny church, the third timber roof beam from the west end, facing the altar, has a fifteenth-century carving of a monk's head.

The church is pleasant enough, the setting strong, looking out to sea, but we found the ancient well, surrounded by ferns and moss and filled with stagnant water, a more powerful place. Two standing stones on the path form what appears to

Llanwnda Holy Well detail

be a gateway. Elyn "got" the following at the well: dark, neglected, sweet, deep, forgotten, but full of secrets and memories. Take time to attune yourself to the surroundings and see what you experience. As you drive up to the church, the well is located in the trees and bushes to the left of the road.

Llanwnda has a more modern claim to fame than its old church and holy well. It is 1.5 mi from Carregwastad Point, site of the ill-conceived 1797 "Last Invasion of Britain." This madcap, unsuccessful French invasion is commemorated in a charming 100-ft-long tapestry that is on display in nearby Fishguard's Last Invasion Gallery (http://www.fishguardartssociety.org.uk/The%20Last%20Invasion%20Tapestry.html).

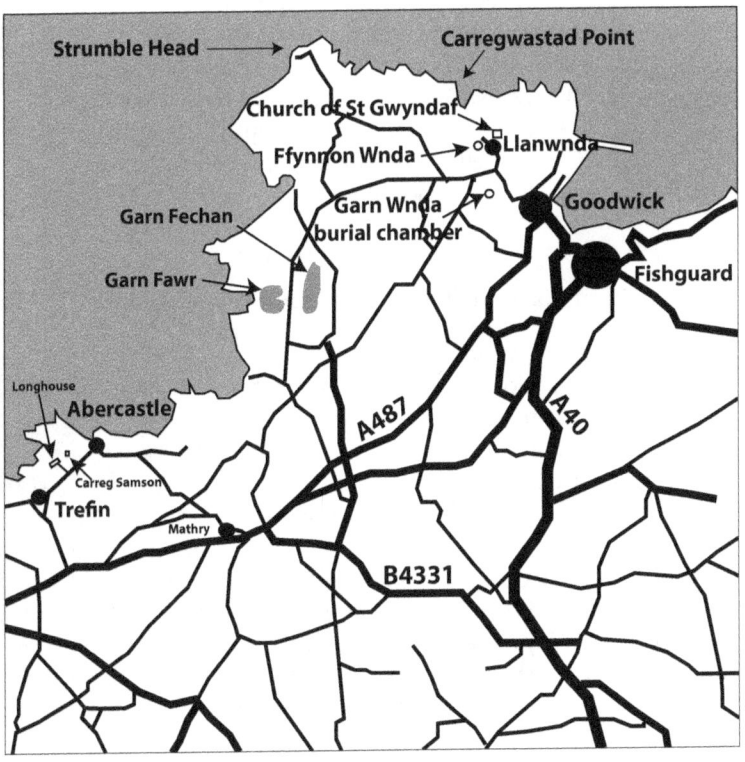

Area map

Garn Wnda burial chamber is located nearby, high on a hillside with excellent views over the Pembrokeshire countryside. Poking out below the rocky outcrop of Garnwnda, it faces northwest toward Strumble Head. The megalith resembles a human-built cave, since it is partly earth-fast (built into the ground). The capstone is held up on one edge by a single orthostat.

When we went there with a group, several people climbed into the chamber. One person said it felt peaceful, another that it was a gateway to faeryland. Elyn, on the other hand, refused to enter. It gave her the shivers. Bring hiking sticks to assist on the climb.

Getting There

Drive out of Goodwick in the direction of Llanwnda. At the village, drive through until the road ends. On your right will be the Church of St Gwyndaf and on the left, Ffynnon Wnda in a small grove of trees. Note that the well is not shown on OS maps (see map on p. 101). See http://www.themodernantiquarian.com/site/2365/garnwnda.html.

More to Experience

Carreg Samson (Carreg Sampson), Pembrokeshire

Carreg Samson cromlech is located near Longhouse farmhouse. The setting is outstanding: in the middle of a field looking down to the bay, with craggy carns visible in the distance. The 5000-year-old monument exudes a

> It's important both to ask permission and to check "inside" yourself before entering a powerful place. We have found on a number of occasions that some people will feel drawn to a particular site and others will feel repelled. This has to do with individual responses to different energies and with individual attunement. This is neither good nor bad. Certain music may be jarring to one person but enjoyable to someone else. Nonetheless, such feelings should not be ignored or overridden.

Carreg Samson

sense of power. Standing alone, impressive, serene, it is not trampled over by tourists. It is not even signposted.

Its huge capstone tilts toward Garn Fawr, Garn Gilfach, and Garn Wnda on Strumble Head. To the south are two other tombs: White Horse, Llanhowell, and Treffynnon, Llandeloy. Carreg Samson appears to be in line with Carn Menyn to the east, origin of many of the bluestones found at Stonehenge, 140 mi to the east in England (http://www.landscape-perception.com/visual_mapping/carreg_samson/, retrieved 11 March 2012).

The capstone is 15 ft long, 9 ft wide, and supported by 3 of the 6 or 7 (depending on how you count) remaining upright stones. The chamber is tall enough to stand up inside. The capstone and several of the supporting stones are unusual, with veins of rose quartz and black-matrixed minerals. They were obviously selected for their particular characteristics. It is likely that it was a portal dolmen, built over a pit, and originally covered with an earthen mound. Excavations revealed burnt human bones and an early Neolithic bowl.

According to local legend, Saint Samson created the monument by flicking stones with his little finger from the island in Abercastle harbor. Although this Samson is a Celtic saint, he still has much in common with the biblical strongman Samson.

Getting There

Drive between Trefin and Abercastle (see map on p. 101). Park at the green Longhouse sign or drive up into farmyard and ask permission to park in yard. Carreg Samson is in the middle of the field to the right, accessible down a (muddy) cement path. Or you can walk up the trail from nearby Abercastle.

While in the area, you might want to visit Garn Fawr (Big Hill), with its fine stone fort and magnificent views, and Garn Fechan (Small Hill) on Pen Caer headland (see map

A section of "The Last Invasion of Britain" tapestry

on p. 101) to experience the "masculine" volcanic energies of the area. Drive east of Trefassen and turn onto the road to Stumblehead. Keep driving to a parking lot on the left and a faded wooden signpost. Park. Across the road, on the right, you'll see an information panel for Garn Fechan. Climb over the stile and follow the trail to Garn Fechan and impressive views of the Preselis. Bring hiking sticks. The trail is not very long or steep, but it's rocky and does go up a bit.

Fishguard, Pembrokeshire

Fishguard (Abergwaun, meaning "Mouth of the River Gwaun") is a pleasant town for a break, perched on a headland between the modern port at Goodwick (pro. "GOOD-ick"), with ferry traffic to Ireland, and a former fishing village. The Lower Town was used as a setting for the 1971 film version of Dylan Thomas' *Under Milk Wood*. The town is within easy access to a number of powerful places, including St Davids to the south and the Gwaun Valley to the southeast. It has a number of services, art galleries, the Last Invasion Gallery, a post office, and a health-food store.

Getting There

Fishguard is on A40 north of Haverfordwest or on A487 from St Davids. There is ample parking in town (see map on p. 101).

The Gwaun Valley, Pembrokeshire

Cwm Gwaun is only a few miles from Fishguard and Newport, but it might as well be on another planet. The bucolic valley was formed around 200,000 years ago and is Europe's oldest glacial melt-water valley. Narrow, twisting roads wind through steep, heavily wooded hillsides. For centuries the inhabitants of the tiny hamlets maintained the "Old Ways," and faeries are said to be hiding in the hills. (Elyn)

> "The Mari Lwyd' (Grey Mary) consists of a horse's skull with false ears and eyes attached, along with reins and bells, covered with a white sheet and decorated with colored strips of cloth or bright ribbons and carried around on a pole. The horse's jaw is operated to open and close, usually by a young, agile man, disguised under the sheet, who carries the Mari Lwyd from door to door accompanied by his companions." (http://www.britannia.com/wales/culture2.html)
>
> "Hunting the wren" (a bird thought to embody the evils of winter) was a widespread Welsh tradition on Twelfth Night (either the eve of or Epiphany Day). The bird was captured and killed, then placed on a miniature "bier" in a beribboned wren house, which rested on four poles. Four men carried the "funeral bier" around town, groaning from the weight and singing of the hunt. They would be welcomed in homes and given money or drink (*Reader's Digest*, p. 397; Owen, pp. 44-45).

The River Gwaun (Afon Gwaun) rises in the foothills of the Preseli Hills, flowing eventually out to sea near Fishguard. It winds its way behind Mynydd Dinas, whose ample sides are dotted with standing stones and remnants of Iron Age forts and huts.

Located in the foothills of the Preseli Hills, Cwm Gwaun is a hidden, peculiar place, where time seems to stand still. Residents in Llanychaer and Pontfaen hamlets still use the Julian calendar, which was superseded by the Gregorian in 1752, to determine the date of the New Year. As a result, they celebrate it on January 13. Traditional Christmas season customs involve dead wrens and horses' skulls, and children collecting *calennig*, a New Year's gift. The horse-skull tradition is a remnant of the "Mari Lwyd" (Grey Mare) celebration and perhaps harkens back to the horse-goddess Rhiannon, who rode her magical white horse across Pembrokeshire in the First Branch of the *Mabinogi*.

Although the distances are short, allow a day to explore the narrow Gwaun Valley by car or foot. One can access the valley from several directions, but we suggest starting at the west end, at Fishguard. You'll soon arrive at Llanychaer, which has an Iron Age enclosure behind the village pub. The Bridge End Inn is a decent place to eat.

Llanllawer Church and Holy Well, Pembrokeshire

N51 59 8 W4 55 59

Cross over the bridge at Llanychaer and go steeply uphill for about half a mile to a T-junction. On the left is the Church of David at Llanllawer, a house, a gate, and a high wall. The large gate gives access to the church-

Llanllawer Church

yard and Llanllawer Holy Well. The well, also known as Ffynnon Gapan (the Lintel Well), Ffynnon Sanctaidd Llanllawer, and Llanychaer Holy Well, is across the field to the right of the church, behind a wall that blocks it from view from the road. The well is covered with a large, finely built stone and cement vault; a red wooden gate is adorned with ribbons, dried flowers, and other offerings. When we were there the well was fern-lined but dry—it was reported dry as long ago as 1966—but it had a pleasant, well-cared-for feeling.

> Llanllawer Holy Well "granted wishes both good and bad depending on whether the proffered pin was straight or bent. Richard Fenton described it as a healing well in 1810, especially efficacious for treating eyes." Cope, p. 73.

The church was "atmospheric," to say the least. Its overgrown cemetery was eerie and spooky. It is not a place to visit at night, and perhaps not even in the day. The churchyard is elliptical, suggesting it was built on a pre-Christian site.

Llanllawer Holy Well

Parc y Merw (Parc y Meirw), Pembrokeshire
N51 59 7 W4 54 51

The lane that forms a T-junction across from the church leads east into the Preseli Hills. A short distance down the lane, near Trellwyn Farm, are seven (or eight) large stones, four of which are still standing and are set into a hedge bank running NW-SE. Called Parc y Merw, which means "Field of the Dead," the alignment is 131 ft long. It is the longest megalithic alignment in Wales.

Why is it called the Field of the Dead? No one knows, but there are many stories. One is that the name refers to the nearby Battle of Mynydd Carn in 1081. A White Lady is said to wander in the field, visible on moonlit nights.

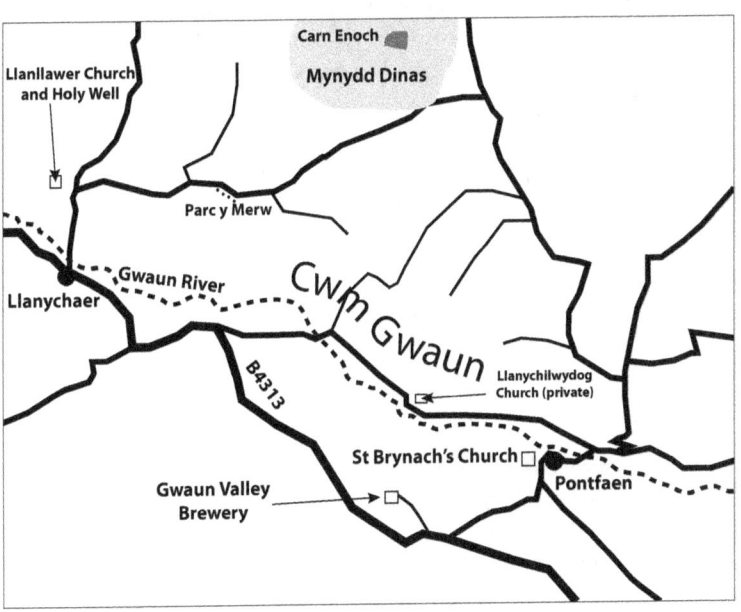

Western Gwaun Valley

Robin Health (2010, p. 101) says that the stone row is an observatory, aligned to the extreme minor standstill moonset in the north, and its distant foresight is Mount Leinster, 93 mi away in Ireland. This astronomical information would have been useful in predicting eclipses. Whatever the stones were used for, we are in a powerful landscape, sanctified for millennia, even if only incomplete traces remain.

One of the Parc y Meirw stones

The best way to see the stone alignment is to find a place to park and walk the fence line. Be careful of traffic: the country lane is very narrow. Two of the standing stones have been used as gateposts for a field entrance 300 yd to the west of the Trellwyn farm. To enter the field to explore further, it is essential to ask permission from the farmer (see map on p. 109).

St Brynach's Church, Pontfaen, Pembrokeshire

N51 58 9 W4 52 54

St Brynach's Church (Eglwys Pontfaen) in Pontfaen is worth a visit. A large metal plaque on a lichen-covered stone wall marks the driveway that leads to the church and to a private house. A small sign says "no cars please," so don't turn into the drive. Continue on the road and pull into the farmyard on your right, where you can park on the grass. Walk back to the driveway and up the path to another stone wall and a gate, which opens onto the well-restored church.

St Brynach was a peripatetic Irish saint who traveled widely. He founded the church in 540 CE. The church is set in a circular churchyard, indicative of pre-Christian origins, as may be the two seventh- to ninth-century cross-inscribed standing stones, usually described as pillar stones. The church foundations are several feet below the current surface of the churchyard, another indication of great age. A huge sycamore shades the church.

Inside the pleasant little church is an intriguing stained glass window of St Brynach. He is pictured surrounded by oak trees, acorns, and pigs: traditional Druidic symbols.

Many stories describe St Brynach's life, most of them probably inaccurately. He was born around 500 CE, an Irish nobleman who converted to Christianity. At some

St Brynach's Church, Pontfaen

time he became a good friend of St David. Then he went to Rome and to Brittany. Later he traveled to Milford Haven, "floating on a stone." This probably refers to his portable altar. Then he went to Pontfaen, where he cast out demons and founded the church. From there he traveled to Nevern, where he founded a monastic community (see pp. 144-151) from which he periodically escaped for retreats on Carn Ingli (see pp. 118-121), where he communed with angels. He had a beloved white milk cow, Blodwen (meaning White Flower); white cattle have Druidic associations (see pp. 65-67). In addition, Brynach tamed wild animals, including a wolf, and he was master of two magical stags. He is said to have died around 570 CE. Read more at http://www.goddess-pages.co.uk/index.php?option=com_content&task=view&id=699#ixzz1fPsA8cER.

The church is open daily. See map on p. 109.

More to Experience

There is much more to discover in Cwm Gwaun, including Dyffryn Fernant and Penlan Uchaf Gardens (http://www.penlan-uchaf.co.uk/); artisan ale at the Gwaun Valley Brewery (http://www.gwaunvalley-brewery.co.uk/); the intriguing incised standing stones in the garden of Llanychilwydog Church, now a private dwelling, located on the north side of the Gwaun River west of Pontfaen; and the old-fashioned Dyffryn Arms at Pontfaen, also known as Bessie's Pub (actually, her front room), where you can buy ale—and not much more; and Tregynon, which may be the site of an Iron Age fortification.

Instead of retracing your route to Fishguard, you can drive toward Pembrokeshire Candle Center

> Driving through Cwm Gwaun is a slow, leisurely, and sometimes challenging process. Although the valley seems quite remote, it is worth remembering that Pontfaen and Tregynon are located on what was the old turnpike road from Haverfordwest to Newport.

at Cilgwyn, run by Inger John, wife of Brian John, author of the popular Angel Mountain Saga, an eight-volume series set in the Preseli Hills. The fictional series recounts the life of Mistress Martha Morgan of Plas Ingli.

The Candle Center is a mile from the entrance to the Gwaun Valley and close to Ty Canol Woods and Pentre Ifan, and only a few miles from Newport (see map).

The best way to explore the Cwm Gwaun is to get in your car and drive, stopping at whatever church or standing stone attracts your interest. Or drive into the valley, park your car, and go for one of a number of walks. See http://www.experiencepembrokeshire.com/living-landscapes/walking-in-the-living-landscape-1 and http://www.walkingpembrokeshire.co.uk/.

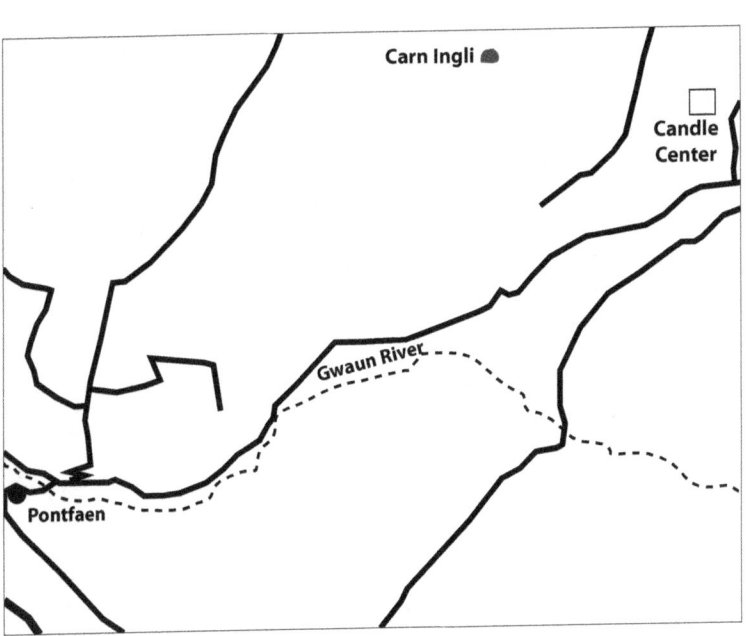

Eastern Gwaun Valley

Mynydd Preseli – The Preseli Hills I, Pembrokeshire

We met an amazing "indigenous" Welshwoman, deeply rooted in the Preselis. She approached us like a force of nature, her words tumbling out as fast as a waterfall. It was too much to grasp it all or all at once, but what I understood was: the south side of the Preselis has to do with the moon; the north with the sun. Seven underground energy streams run through the mountains. Gors Fawr Stone Circle is a complex astronomical machine. The entire Preselis are a huge observatory for calculating equinoxes, solstices, and eclipses. After millennia, ancient people's math skills improved and they were able to condense what previously had taken a mountain to measure. They compressed their observations into one monument: Stonehenge. They brought the bluestones from the Preselis to Stonehenge because they represented their ancestors. The Welshwoman told us, "If you write about my land you've got to get it right!" I promised we would do our best. (Elyn)

The Mynydd Preseli are part of the Pembrokeshire Coast National Park, although they are inland. Whether you call them hills or mountains is a personal choice. They stretch from Foel Eryr eastward to Y Frenni Fawr. The hills are dotted with evidence of long-standing human occupation, including Iron Age hill forts, Bronze Age burial cairns, standing stones, and ancient earthworks.

Some sites are found along the Golden Road, a 5000-year-old trackway across the central Preseli ridge. During the Iron Age, this was a popular route for travelers and traders journeying between Wessex in England and Ireland, perhaps returning with Wicklow gold. The Golden Road

> "... the prehistoric sun and moon watchers in Preseli had become aware of geometric order in the skies, ... the orientation and choice of location for many of their most impressive sites providing affirmation of this."
> Robin Heath, 2010, p. 154.

led across the ridge and on to Whitesands Bay, near what is now St Davids, where boats awaited. Today, one can drive across the Preselis but not along the Golden Road. To experience the Golden Road and its many megaliths, you have to go on foot.

The Preselis have been a place of spiritual significance for thousands of years and continue to be so today. You feel a difference in the atmosphere, as if it were subtly charged—and it is. Carn Ingli (Mountain of Angels) and Carn Enoch are igneous, capable of causing compasses to go haywire. In addition, Robin Heath is convinced that many of the sites have significant astronomical importance and were part of a megalithic calendar (See Robin Heath, 2010, for extensive archaeo-astronomy interpretations of the area.)

Carn Meini (Caermeini; Carn Menyn) is the origin of a number of the spotted dolerite bluestones used in the construction of Stonehenge. Recently, geologists have pinpointed the origin of another group of the Stonehenge bluestones, composed chiefly of rhyolites (another type of igneous rock) and sandstone. These stones came from the 76-yd-long area called Craig Rhos-y-Felin, which is northwest of Carn Meini, near the village of Pont Saeson, a little west and a little south of Crosswell/Ffynnongroes. This site is close to Pentre Ifan, which is located to the northwest. Future investigation may be able to determine the quarry site—if quarried they were, instead of transported by

> The bluestones are a kind of spotted dolerite, a dark igneous rock. When wet, the stone appears to be blue. Whether the bluestones at Stonehenge reached there by human means, superhuman means (Merlin is said to have magically transported them from Ireland—but there were Irish tribes in the Preseli area, so "Ireland" could have referred to the Preselis), or natural means (glacial movement) is open to debate. See Brian John's *The Bluestone Enigma* for a geologist's review of the data, but note that recent findings may change some of his conclusions.

glacier. See http://www.megalithic.co.uk/article.php?sid=28658 for map or http://www.dailymail.co.uk/sciencetech/article-2076050/Stonehenge-Has-mystery-stones-origin-solved.html.

The Preselis are also connected with King Arthur, his knights, and the magical Irish boar, Twrch Trwyth. "Culhwch and Olwen" is the earliest Arthurian tale in Welsh, dating to the tenth century but first written around 1100 CE. It is one of the additional stories in the *Mabinogi*. In it, King Arthur is called upon to help his cousin Culhwch in an Irish quest. During this adventure, they kill one of Twrch Trwyth's seven piglets (NB: the number "7" is often used symbolically). Enraged, the magical boar crosses from Ireland to the Preselis, pursuing Arthur and his knights to Foel Cwm Cerwyn (1760 ft), the highest peak in the range.

In most versions, Arthur and his knights drive the great boar into the sea at Cornwall. But in one version, Arthur and many of his knights are slain in the Preseli Hills. The knights turn immediately into stone, still visible as the standing stones at Cerrig Marchogion (the Stones of the Knights of Arthur). Arthur, it is claimed, was buried elsewhere, at Bedd Arthur, located along the ridge near Carn Meini. This oval (or eye-shaped) stone enclosure, 59 ft by 23 ft, is currently composed of 14 to 16 stones with an average height of 2.5 ft and backed by a low bank. It is located just southeast of the Golden Road, its axis is oriented toward the midsummer sunrise (Heath, 2010, p. 22).

Becky Thomas draws a connection between the Welsh Mother Goddess Ceridwen, whose animal association is the white sow, and the boar described above. Thomas suggests that in "Culhwch and Olwen," the white sow

> The name Ceridwen (Cerridwen, Kerridwen) comes from the Celtic *cerru*, meaning cauldron, a symbol of transformation. Ceridwen is the Welsh Mother Goddess, a sorceress who brews potions in her cauldron, and a wise woman who is a source of knowledge.

has been changed into a boar, and the story metaphorically describes the displacement of the goddess by Christianity (http://www.goddess-pages.co.uk/index.php?option=com_content&task=view&id=699#ixzz1fOrQsNwM, retrieved 2 Dec. 2011). Perhaps providing additional support for this interpretation are some of the Welsh traditions associated with Nos Galan Gaeaf (Halloween/Samhain). There are stories that link this night with the appearance of ghosts and other spectres. In the south, the ghost was most often "The White Lady"; in the north, however, it was usually the more frightening *Hwch ddu gwta* (tail-less black sow) that appeared. Possibly this tradition provides evidence for a similar transformation of white sow into black.

The Preselis are a hill-walker and megalith-seeker's delight. One trail, about 7.5 mi long, runs across the main Preseli ridge and moorland, passing by numerous megalithic sites on the Golden Trail. In the west, this hiking trail begins near Foel Eryr, which has a burial cairn on its summit. It skirts the Pantmaenog forest and climbs to Foel Feddau, with its cairn; it continues on to Bedd Arthur stone circle, near Carn Bica; and it ends near the tumulus at Crymych. Numerous other megalithic sites can be visited en route.

> "Perhaps the tale of Arthur's pursuit of the Twrch Trwyth tells of the downfall of the Goddess in her sacred places throughout Wales as Christianity took hold of the country, and maybe the tale marks the birth of the great Welsh male hero figures arguably dominated by Arthurian legend but reflected throughout medieval Welsh culture and tradition. The demise of the Goddess Ceridwen was ensured as the monks of the new religion recreated the great Welsh oral traditions. She, along with other great Welsh and Celtic goddesses such as Dôn, Rhiannon, Arianrhod and Blodeuwedd, were reduced to secondary characters in the stories of their male counterparts." Becky Thomas, http://www.goddess-pages.co.uk/index.php?option=com_content&task=view&id=699#ixzz1fOrQsNwM, retrieved 2 Dec. 2011.

Another popular route, called the Mynydd Preseli Walk, is 5.6 mi long. This half-day, circular walk starts at Mynachlog-ddu and includes Bedd Arthur stone oval and Carn Menyn (Meini). Other hikes begin at Rosebush, constructed as a Victorian resort and now famous for its atmospheric, sawdust-strewn restaurant/pub, Tafarn Sinc (Zinc Tavern). Or you may prefer to spend 7 days walking the 67-mi-long Preseli Circle Walking Trail.

The Preseli Green Dragon bus drops hikers at the eastern end of the Golden Road and picks them up at the other end. Check with the local tourist office in Fishguard or Newport for details. See http://www.greendragonbus.co.uk/, http://www.experiencepembrokeshire.com, and http://www.bbc.co.uk/wales/nature/sites/walking/pages/sw_maenclochog.shtml.

Carn Ingli (Carningli), Pembrokeshire
N51 59 54 W4 49 28

To the northwest of the main Preseli range is another important hill: Carn Ingli (Carningli; means "the Hill of Angels"). Separated from the Preselis by the Gwaun Valley, Carningli is one of the most sacred mountains in west Wales. It is probably the core of what was once an enormous volcano. The mountain is understood by some to be

> According to Brian John, geomorphologist and author, "the rocks on Carningli and Carn Enoch are igneous intrusives (dolerite, rhyolite and other complex rock types).... Strictly, volcanics are extruded rocks laid down at the surface—like lava and ash—but because these rocks at Carningli etc. belong to the 'Fishguard Volcanic Series' the term 'volcanic' is being used in a broader sense to mean any rock associated with volcanic activity." Personal communication, 21 March 2012.

the physical manifestation of the Goddess.

Although only 1300 ft high, Carn Ingli dominates its surroundings. Paul Devereux (p. 135) describes it as "the 'central symbolic focal point' for the Neolithic monuments in this area" (Devereux, p. 135), but not all researchers agree. Several hiking trails lead up its sides, and on a clear day you can see Ireland. See http://www.newportpembs.co.uk/articles/carningli-mountain-newport-pembs.php and http://americymru.net/video/sibelian-stones-carn-ingli for an evocative musical setting by Sibelian of Bob Reeve's poem on Carningli.

St Brynach (see pp. 111-112) spent a great deal of time on Carningli, escaping from the frantic life in his monastery at Nevern, which was on the pilgrimage route to St Davids. They say he used to retreat to the mountaintop and commune with angels. Still today, people camp at the summit, hoping to have inspired visions or dreams. Legend says that if you spend the night on Carningli, you'll either become a poet or go mad.

A similar story is told about Tinkinswood Burial Chamber and Cadair Idris

> "I have often seen bunches of flowers, ribbons and other keepsakes or personal mementos on the summit—and I can only assume that people use the mountain for prayers, for those who are ill or troubled, in exactly the same way as the people of Ireland use their roadside shrines." John, *Carningli*, p. 7. Carningli nowadays attracts many new visitors, fans of Brian John's eight-volume Angel Mountain saga.

(see pp. 56-59, 171-175). Perhaps these altered states are not surprising since research has shown that the magnetic qualities of iron-bearing stone can influence brain patterns, and Carningli is igneous.

> "...there is now abundant experimental and clinical evidence to indicate that changes in weak ambient magnetic fields can affect parts of the brain, causing sensations of dissociation ('ecstasy,' 'out-of-body experiences') and hallucinations or visions of various kinds." Devereux, p. 134.

Long before St Brynach sought isolation on its slopes, Carningli was inhabited. Ruins of an Iron Age hillfort and nearby Bronze Age hut circles are proof of its long attraction. The extensive hillfort dates from 1000 BCE, and at one time a defensive rampart surrounded the scree-strewn summit.

> "If we all have compasses in our heads, this is the place to be disorientated and whirled into other dimensions. It is a gateway to Annwn, the Celtic Otherworld, especially at certain times." Main, pp. 85-86.

Lawrence Main thinks that the summit of the mountain is on an ancient "spirit path." The Sleeping Goddess has her

Carningli

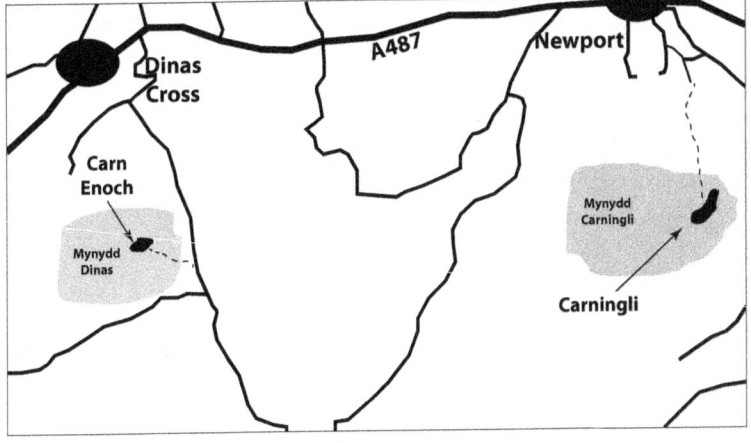

Area map

head to the south, feet to the north, and is about three to four months pregnant. Although Main sees the goddess figure as oriented south to north, others see her from a different angle. Viewed from the south, her head is to the west; to the right (east) are her upraised knees. There are other simulacra as well.

Getting There

Carningli can be reached on a steep path directly from Newport (see map).

"Recognising faces in nature, or 'Simulacrum,' is something that can be traced back through prehistory. It is likely that these images, when viewed through prehistoric eyes, would have been perceived as an expression of the living-spirit of the earth. The discovery of simulacrum at several of the megaliths supports the idea that such stones were considered to be endowed with special qualities, and possibly explains the specific selection and transport of certain stones over large distances in prehistory." http://www.ancient-wisdom.co.uk/stonefaces.htm, retrieved 5 Dec. 2011.

Gary on top of Carn Enoch

Carn Enoch, Pembrokeshire

N51 59 45 W4 53 50

To the west of Carningli and north of the Gwaun is another powerful place: Carn Enoch. It is one of two igneous projections (the other is Garn Fawr) that rise out of the surrounding moorland of Mynydd Dinas. Country lanes crisscross Mynydd Dinas, so you can drive, park, and then walk a short distance across the field to reach Carn

"Mynydd Preseli—The Preseli Hills—loomed over us during the weeks we stayed in Newport, disturbing my sleep, entering my dreams. Ancient trackways, a bluestone quarry, megalithic sites, a pregnant goddess reclining in the peaks, a holy mountain visited by angels and a saint, a craggy outcrop where my digital compass turned into an infinity sign—no wonder my cell phone didn't work and I couldn't sleep!" Elyn.

> Mara Freeman says about Carn Enoch: "There are just so many energies swirling around there . . . it seems to focalize patterns of many different beings: faery and ancestral from the surrounding moors and mountains, and also that higher angelic quality of light that streams up from St Davids Peninsula when it's clear." Personal communication, 14 Nov. 2011.

Enoch. The views are impressive: horses romping in the fields, the sea below, the Llŷn Peninsula in northern Wales and the Wicklow Mountains in Ireland visible on a clear day.

The main reason to go to Carn Enoch is to experience the energies. Wander around the tumbled grey boulders and see what you sense. In one location, your compass needle will swing from magnetic north to south. This mysterious phenomenon may have two causes. First, the high iron content of the rock may be interacting with the compass. Second, the molten rock that became Carn Enoch solidified at a time when the Earth's magnetic field was reversed; the magnetic material in the rock was "frozen" or "locked" into that alignment at the time of formation. This is an impressive phenomenon to witness and a clear indication of invisible energy (in this case, magnetism) at work.

Elyn felt rooted to the spot, both buzzed and peaceful, which was an unusual combination. Gary felt elemental energy in the stones, powerful earth energies that influence the nature of the people of Wales, long rooted in their land.

Toward the base of the outcrop, near the path from the parking lot, is a large boulder with dozens of curious diago-

> "In the Shadow of the Preselis," a chapter in *The Saints and Stones Pilgrimages*, provides detailed routes. The chapter is available as a brochure at some tourist offices, including Fishguard's Town Hall bookshop. For more information, go to http://www.saintsandstones.co.uk/.

nal grooves. They may be tallying marks or possibly Ogham script, dating to 400 CE when the Irish were settling in the region. An Ogham stone is on display at nearby Nevern Church, and there are two in Maenclochog Church.

Getting There

Drive west on A487 from Newport and turn left near Dinas Cross. The country road leads up to a parking area at the base of Mynydd Dinas and a short trail leads to Carn Enoch (see map on p. 121).

Mynydd Preseli – The Preseli Hills II, Pembrokeshire

A number of the Preselis' churches, holy wells, villages, and some important megalithic sites are accessible by car. We'll focus on three: Maenclochog Church, St Teilo's Well, and Gors Fawr Stone Circle.

Maenclochog Church, Pembrokeshire
N51 54 43 W4 47 18

Deep in the foothills of the Preselis, St Mary's Church in Maenclochog is located on a circular mound, indicative of its long history as a sacred site. The name may come from the Irish Gaelic *clochog*, which means "craggy ground." Or it might come from something else: *maen* is Welsh for boulders; *cloch* is Welsh for "bell"; so "Maenclochog" could

> The "indigenous Welshwoman" told us that some bluestones were shaped with a hollowed-out striking area. We were also told there is a ringing stone in the wall behind Pentre Ifan, but it no longer produces a very good-quality sound.

Maenclochog Church

mean "ringing stones." This derivation of Maenclochog seems probable since two large ringing stones used to stand next to St Mary's Well (Ffynnon Fair), half a mile to the southwest.

Maenclochog Church may have originally been built in the tenth century. It has been renovated several times, most recently in the nineteenth century, and was undergoing repairs when we were there in 2011. Inside are two Ogham stones, including one with a foliate cross: the ends of the cross-arms and the upright are splayed into three "fingers," perhaps representing the Trinity—or perhaps referencing the importance of three in Celtic tradition.

Area map

Cornel Bach Standing Stones are in a field to the right of a track on the north side of Maenclochog (http://www.megalithic.co.uk/article.php?sid=5903).

It seems counterintuitive for a stone to ring, but perhaps not: the universe is in constant vibration—so why shouldn't we be able to hear it sing? Although it has been said that "water plays the oldest music" (Tony Curtis, in his poem, "At Gumfreston Church"), perhaps stone sings as well as the babbling stream, if you know how to listen.

Getting There

Maenclochog is on B4313 south of Rosebush. The church is across from the general store.

St Teilo's Well, Pembrokeshire
N51 54 37 W4 45 45

A mile or so east of Maenclochog is St Teilo's Well, famous for millennia as a healing well. The well is near the ruins of Llandeilo/ Llwydarth Church, which was named after St Teilo.

Medieval visitors to the well would fill a skull, supposedly St Teilo's, with the holy water and drink from it. It was said to be an effective cure for chest illnesses. This is supposed to be the same skull now kept at Llandaff Cathedral, Cardiff. In 1927, however, an anthropologist determined that skull was the skull of a medieval Welshman who died sometime in the fourteenth or fifteenth century—not in the sixth century, when St Teilo lived. The legendary healing qualities of "Penglog Teilo" (St Teilo's Skull) recall the Celtic cult of the head. For an interesting discussion of the well and its history, go to http://people.bath.ac.uk/liskmj/

St Teilo's Well

 living-spring/sourcearchive/fs9/fs9ld1.htm; and http://people.bath.ac.uk/liskmj/living-spring/sourcearchive/ns2/ns2kb1.htm; and Davies and Eastham, pp. 55-56.

Getting There

Finding St Teilo's Well can be a journey into a strange, enchanted land, where things are not quite what they seem. In Maenclochog, drive to the church and turn left between the gas station and small convenience store; go over the bridge; turn sharp right down the hill; keep driving on the narrow country lane, past Temple Druid on left. Notice the shift in energy. At the T-junction (sign says, "Llanycefn 3 mi") turn left; drive up the lane and past the yellow house named "Maenteilo" on the left; pull over on the left and park. There is a tall, ivy-covered signpost and gate on the other side of the road; the signpost is difficult to see, but it points toward the well. St Teilo's Well can also be approached from the

St Teilo was probably born near Tenby, Pembrokeshire, around 500 CE, a native-born Welsh aristocrat and friend (possibly cousin) of St David. He became a bishop. After the yellow plague spread through Wales, around 549 CE, he took what was left of his community to Dol in Brittany, where they stayed for seven years and seven months (probably not to be taken literally, since seven is a sacred number). There, he and St Samson, Bishop of Dol, planted fruit trees. He also saved the country from a winged dragon by tying it to a rock in the sea. Later he returned to Wales and became one of its holiest men. He died, perhaps in 560, at Llandeilo Fawr. Legend says that after his death his body multiplied into three—one for each church that claimed him. He is often represented in Breton churches as riding on a stag, as is St Brynach. For more information, see http://www.stteilosbishopston.co.uk/stteilo/stteilo.htm and http://www.llandeilo.org/st_teilos.php.

village of Llangolman, following a hiking trail (see map on p. 125).

Open the gate, walk through it, and look for the wooden post for walkers located across the field, just before the trees. There is a big white stone to the left of the post. Cross the field, perhaps sensing meandering underground water lines. Beyond the post, walk down a set of grass-covered steps and enter a tree-filled faeryland of twisted, moss-covered trees.

Today, St Teilo's Well includes a large pond into which three springs drain. The pond, the size of a large swimming pool, is silting up and nearly dry, but it used to be 10 to 15 ft deep. Next to it are three circular springs, perhaps each originally with a separate healing focus. Our local guide, Russell, told us that the pond used to be filled with fresh, sparkling water, and it was surrounded by white quartz that shone in the moonlight. Little quartz remains, however, since much of it has been hauled off to

The sign pointing to St Teilo's Well

Roman road at St Teilo's Well

decorate people's gardens. When we visited the site, someone had apparently been shifting the energy of the place by disrupting the flow of water to and from the wells. Nonetheless, the place has a powerful, strong, solemn, "masculine" feel.

St Teilo supposedly lived there in the sixth century—perhaps in a shelter beside the bank, where we could see a crumbling stone retaining wall; or perhaps the ruins are what remain of an early chapel. A Roman road once went by the well, linking Llanglydwen (to the east) to Maenclochog, so the site would not have been as isolated as it is today.

> Our guide, Russell, said, "There's a chink in heaven's floor where the light shines through to churches—and to this well."

Take time to walk around the large well and to meditate while sitting on the large quartz boulder by the side of the farthest circular well. See what you experience. The faery energy and the pagan past are strong in this powerful place.

Gors Fawr Stone Circle, Pembrokeshire

N51 55 53 W4 42 47

Leaving the well and driving northeast toward Llangolman and Mynachlog-ddu (a good base for hiking up to Bedd Arthur and the Golden Road), you reach Gors Fawr Stone Circle, about 1 mi southwest of Mynachlog-ddu (see map on p. 132). The circle is located below the bluestone outcrop of Carn Menyn to the north.

The location is somewhat like a moonscape: the stone circle is in the midst of a treeless, marshy upland moor. Gors Fawr ("Big Bog") may not look like much—the stones are neither big nor impressive—but it has mysteries to reveal to those who take the time.

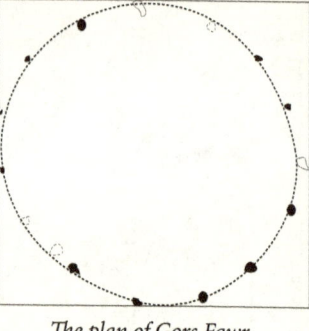

The plan of Gors Fawr

Called Cylch y Trallwyn ("Circle of Troubles") by locals, the stones barely poke out from the scattered gorse bushes that thrive on the boggy ground. Gors Fawr is approximately 74 ft in diameter and composed of 16 standing stones, at least 8 of which are local dolerite bluestones. The stones are arranged by height, ranging from 1.5 ft to 3 ft high. The tallest are in the SE.

Gors Fawr Stone Circle

> "And the Elders sat on rough hewn stones,/ Within a sacred circle,/And held in their hands the sceptral rods/ Of the loud proclaiming Heralds,/ On receiving which they then rose from the seats,/ And in alternate order gave good judgment." Homer, *The Iliad*, Book 18.1.585.

NE of the circle are two large standing stones, about 6 ft high. They appear to be aligned NE-SW and could have been used to mark midsummer sunrise or midwinter sunset, but there is no way to be sure that they are standing today where they were originally erected. For one thing, the ground is boggy and stones shift. Early antiquarian reports describe an avenue from the circle to these stones; if so, the stones would have acted as a portal (energetically and visually) for processions to and from the circle.

The more northern of the two outliers, which appears to have a natural seat, is called the "Dreaming Stone" and is associated with visionary experiences and activation of "the third eye." Part of this megalith has measurable magnetic qualities which have been proven to affect the brain. If a person sits on it, his or her head rests against the magnetic areas of the stone.

Local shepherds used to use Gors Fawr for astronomical observations. They would determine when to shear the sheep by observing when Deneb (a star in the constellation Cygnus) would rise in a cleft in the hills.

Spend time at the stones, counting them. Do you find 16?

Hilary on the "Dreaming Stone"

> The vibrational-medicine healer Jack Temple had an important encounter with Gors Fawr. "... it was that circle in Wales that showed me that the life force in the earth was even more powerful than I had believed before. Already certain of the powers of plants and crystals, I began to learn that a very different, stronger and older healing force was contained in certain stones that contained sun rays and moon rays, concentrated over thousands of years. They release their own vibrational rays and also send that energy into the earth around them." Temple, p. 82.

Hilary Wylde was told by Roger Worsley and Gordon Strachan that the stones are a complex calendar. Much remains to be revealed about these seemingly unimpressive stones. Sit on the "Dreaming Stone," described by the writer Liz Whittaker as "the fizzing stone." What do you experience?

Mynydd Preseli – The Preseli Hills III, Pembrokeshire

Looking to the north and west from Pentre Ifan dolmen, my eyes were drawn to a thick mass of trees, Pentre Ifan Wood. To the southwest, this becomes the ancient Tycanol Wood. Eagerly I made my way into the verdant wonderland of twisted, moss-drenched oaks and grey, lichen-dappled boulders. Light filtered through the open lacework of branches, turning everything green. Bronze Age standing stones, an Iron Age fort, and The Druid's Cave lie hidden in the lumi-

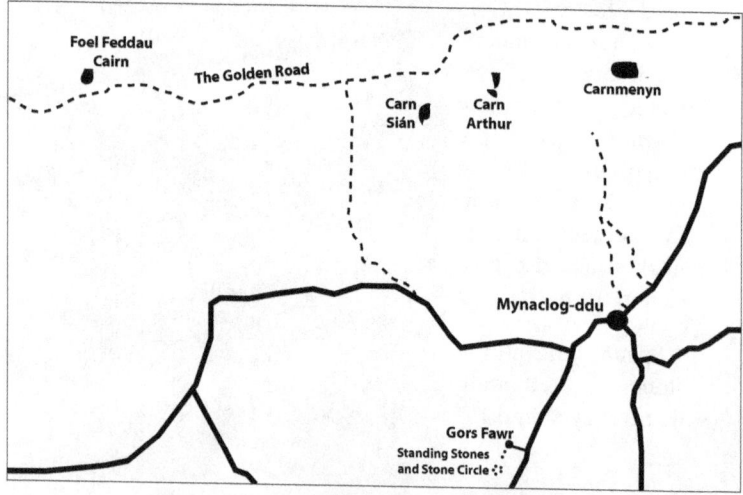

Area map

nescent, bright-green woods. The trail seemed to wind its way up and around the roots and branches, the toppled stones. I had entered another reality. (Elyn)

Pentre Ifan, Pembrokeshire
N51 59 56 W4 46 12

Pentre Ifan is one of the iconic images of Wales: tall, striking, assertive, its graceful capstone tilts back at a jaunty angle, supported at its wider end by two bluestone monoliths and at the narrower end by one. The chamber measures 10 ft long, 6.5 ft wide, and 10 ft tall. Its 16.5-ft-long capstone weighs some 16 tons. Erected around 3500 BCE, it is only 4 mi from Carn Menyn, location of the bluestone quarry, and 4 mi from Newport. The views are superb.

According to Robin Heath, Pentre Ifan was oriented to observe the midwinter sunset (Heath, pp. 88-90), as well as to participate in other important long-distance alignments. It is, for example, intervisible with Carreg Coetan and Llech-y-Tribedd (see pp. 140-141, 143-144).

Geomancer Laurence Main focuses on a different kind of alignment. He believes that one of the spirit paths linked to Pentre Ifan leads to the summit of Carn Ingli; this path ends in the north at the Witches Cauldron, an enlarged blowhole on the Pembrokeshire Coast Path (Main p. 90).

> Elizabeth Brown (p. 192) states "There is a general consensus…in the dowsing community that ley lines are lines of energy that link significant spiritual sites in geographical alignment and are in existence as a result of positive human intent."

Pentre Ifan

Pentre Ifan looked quite different when it was built. At that time, the stone chamber may have been covered with an earth-and-stone mound. It had a crescent-shaped façade at the entrance on the south, where there would have been a forecourt. The mound, which sloped down to the north, could have measured 120 ft by 56 ft and stood 15 ft high, making it very impressive indeed. The fence that currently surrounds the megalith roughly indicates the size of the original cairn. Recent archeological rethinking however, suggests that the cairn may have been only 3 ft high, a "low platform around the foot of the uprights" (Scarre, p. 71). This would have allowed repeated access to the interior (Burrow, p. 113)—but for what purpose remains unknown.

> "It was around Pentre Ifan burial chamber that W Y Evans Wentz recorded sightings of fairies in *The Fairy Faith in Celtic Countries*. Guarded by the giant in the rocks of Carnedd Meibion-Owen and at the eastern edge of the magical woodland where ghosts of chanting Druids and visions of Pan or Cernunnos have been seen, Pentre Ifan is one of the most important megalithic monuments in Wales" Main, p. 91. Even today, folklore asserts that Pentre Ifan remains the haunt of the Tylwyth Teg or Welsh faery folk.

> "The recent discovery of ritual cups used to hold narcotic beverages at Stonehenge and Callanish suggests this concept may not be too far-fetched and possibly was a practice inherited by the Druids from the aboriginal inhabitants of these islands." http://www.the-cauldron.org.uk/thewombofceridwen.htm

The archaeological assumption has been that Pentre Ifan was a burial chamber. However, no evidence of human bones or burials has ever been discovered. The entrance was blocked by a large stone, which would have made successive interments problematic. One suggestion has been that body parts or cremains (cremated remains) were pushed into the chamber through a side niche.

There is, however, another possibility. In local folklore, Pentre Ifan is called "the womb of Ceridwen." Julia Murphy (Dept. of Archeology, University of Wales) believes that Pentre Ifan was in fact not a burial place—it was a place of initiation. She bases her theory on folkloric analysis and literary descriptions recorded from the early seventeenth century. Local legend states that nearby Tycanol Woods was the location of a Druid college, and they used Pentre Ifan for initiations. "Allegedly, the neophyte had to spend a nocturnal vigil inside the burial chamber. They were given a special potion, probably made from narcotic plants, and left to experience contact with the Otherworld and its inhabitants" (http://www.the-cauldron.org.uk/thewombofceridwen.htm).

> "Pentre Ifan exists within an enchanted and magical landscape. Indeed it is located in an area of West Wales which is a 'hot spot' of psychic activity, legend and myth, both ancient and modern. … In this unique part of West Wales the veil between the worlds seems almost permanently thin. Pentre Ifan certainly changes its atmosphere after dark and this can be felt quite tangibly." Michael Howard, http://www.the-cauldron.org.uk/thewombofceridwen.htm.

We have no direct evidence that the megalith builders worshipped a goddess called Ceridwen, but perhaps they did. Or perhaps they used Pentre Ifan as an ini-

Another view of Pentre Ifan

tiatory womb of a goddess who was later known as Ceridwen. Or perhaps the megalith builders used Pentre Ifan

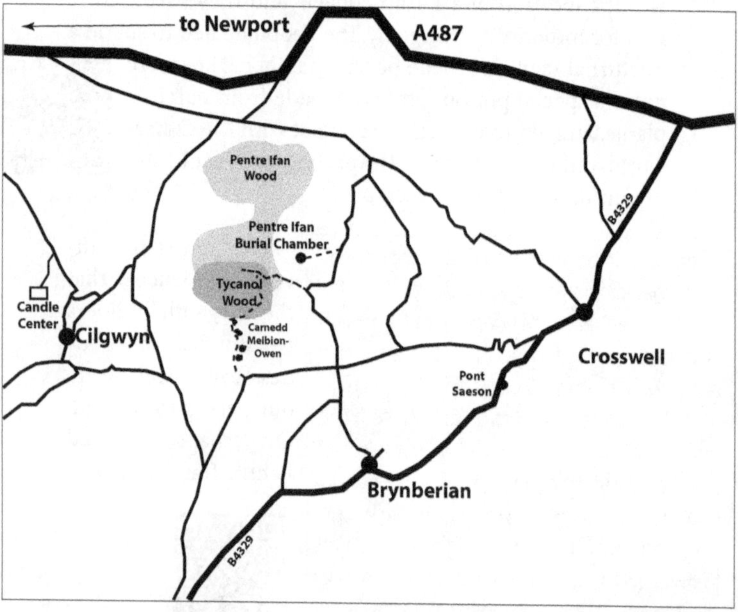

Area map

in one way and the subsequent Celtic settlers, who worshipped Ceridwen, used it in another.

Within view of Pentre Ifan is Carningli, with its simulacrum of a reclining giantess or Earth Goddess. The landscape is alive with images of the feminine, including Pentre Ifan as the "womb of Ceridwen."

Hilary Wylde suggests that although there is no direct evidence that the megalith builders in Wales worshipped a goddess called Keridwen, there may be sufficient indirect evidence from several sources—folklore, etymology, and even archaeology—to support quite strongly such a theory (see John Rhys and Kathy Jones). The following is a highly condensed and partial summary of her argument.

Hilary understands that *Ker*, in one of many derivatives, is one of the earliest names for the Great Goddess and the Grain Goddess. The bringing of agriculture is closely associated with the coming of the megaliths to the British Isles—thus suggesting a very early link to that name and the megalith builders. There seem to be Korreds, Kerions, Corics, Corriquets and hosts of other legendary beings, all with names that bear some relationship both to the erectors of standing stones or megalithic structures and to Ker. In folklore, the Korrigans were small, extremely strong, dark people who built the megaliths, carrying the stones on their backs. In Wales, in some places where there are concentrations of megalithic structures, the remains of ancient field systems have been uncovered.

Following the inception of this seemingly worldwide Goddess, way back in the mists of time, the preparation and fermentation of grain-based "inspirational" brews in many different vessels wouldn't have been far behind—another indirect connection with Keridwen and her cauldron. (Personal communication, 21 Aug. 2012)

Getting There

Pentre Ifan is located southeast of Newport on a series of minor roads off A487 (see map). The way is well signposted.

Tycanol (Tŷ Canol) Wood, Pembrokeshire
N51 59 42 W4 47 2

South and west of Pentre Ifan is Tycanol (Tŷ Canol) Wood, a mysterious and powerful place. It is one of the few remaining ancient woodlands in Wales, and some of the surviving gnarled oak trees are over 800 years old. The woods are home to nearly 400 species of lichens, many of them rare. Hidden among the crags near the top edge of the woodland is The Druid's Cave. Although there is no proof that Druids frequented Tycanol Woods, local legend states that they did. Buried in the rocks and ferns is an Iron Age fortification, proof that the woods were inhabited long before the Christian era. Tylwyth Teg (the "Fair Folk"—the Welsh faeries) are said to be there still. Perhaps they move between Pentre Ifan and the woods.

Tycanol Wood

> According to Robin Heath (2010, p. 149), Tycanol Wood is "an 'interesting' place where you need to be clear and know your own motives."

There are several approaches to the woods. One takes you past four large igneous outcroppings known as Carnedd Meibion Owen. They are said to mark the graves of the sons of Owen Glendower, waiting for the signal to rise up and fight for the land of their father. Or they might be the graves of three giant sons who killed each other quarreling over who would inherit their father's kingdom. Or—and this is historic—this is the site where three sons of Owen ap Robert fought each other over the family inheritance (John, *Carningli*, p. 47). These "legends of place" show how life mirrors myth—or perhaps the other way around.

Spend time in the woods, experiencing the energy in different places. Be still, center yourself, and see what you encounter.

Getting There

From Pentre Ifan continue south on the minor road until you come to a trailhead that leads into the woods. See map on p. 136. Contact David Wheeler, Reserve Manager, telephone: (0)1545 590 434, for further information and more detailed maps.

More to Experience
Newport, Pembrokeshire

Newport (Trefdraeth) is a fine base for exploring the region. It has a range of accommodations, several excellent restaurants, including Llys Meddyg, and several cafés with gluten-free options. A number of walks start from Newport, including a relatively easy, two-hour ascent to Carningli and the riverside "Pilgrims' Way," which follows the Afon Nyfer east to Nevern. Stroll down to the Parrog, Newport's nearest beach, or to the Traethmawr, on the other side of the estuary.

Getting There

Newport is on A487 between Fishguard and Cardigan.

Carreg Coetan Arthur, Pembrokeshire

Carreg Coetan Arthur (AKA Arthur's Quoit)—not be confused with Coetan Arthur near St Davids—is a dolmen situated in the middle of a Newport housing development, within view of the sea. On A487 to the east, turn left on Feidr Pen-Y-Bont in the direction of the Newport Golf Course. After a few hundred feet, turn left at Carreg Coetan and park near the monument (see map on p. 141). Surprisingly, the surrounding fence manages to provide an effective boundary between this 5000-year-old megalith and the neighborhood.

Carreg Coetan Arthur

Arthur's Quoit looks a bit like a large, ungainly, four-legged mushroom. Two uprights (two others no longer touch the capstone) delicately support the massive, sloping capstone. Burnt remains of bones have been discovered in the chamber, along with pottery sherds from a later period, suggesting that the dolmen continued in use for a long time. Legend relates that Carreg Coetan was formed from stones thrown from the summit of Carn-ingli, perhaps by King Arthur.

It is puzzling that so many sites in Pembrokeshire and elsewhere in Wales are linked to Arthur. According to Steve Blake and Scott Lloyd, this is because Arthur was a Welsh king and fought his battles in Wales, not in England. See their book (2003) for an intriguing revision of Arthurian history. Of course, why Arthur is associated with megalithic sites is a different question. Folk memory attaching to a mysterious, large solid object?

Robin Heath (2010, p. 85) says Carreg Coetan Arthur is aligned to the midsummer sunset in or around 2800 BCE and is also a lunar observatory, "detecting the southern transit of the moon when it is at the major standstill position in the summer" (2010, p. 105). Children and Nash (2008, pp. 36-37) think that Carreg Coetan's capstone appears to replicate the rocky summit of Mynydd Carningli to the south, thus "drawing the landscape within the architecture of the tomb." If the megalith was originally covered with a mound, this replication would have been unseen. Regardless of the details, it is clear that Coetan Arthur and many other megalithic sites were built in relationship to the landscape around them and oriented with a sophisticated awareness of the movement of the moon, sun, and stars.

Brithdir Stone Circle, Pembrokeshire

Brithdir Stone Circle is both an ancient and modern stone circle, located SE of Newport, below Cilgwyn Road, near a cottage called New England. Before 2000 CE, there was little trace of the original circle.

Ros Briagha writes, "I went to visit some friends with a farm in Pembrokeshire, at the foot of the Preseli Mountains, and they asked me to look at a strange ring of stones in one of their fields. The stones were buried, with a few inches of height and about a square foot of stone showing, and I offered to help expose them and create a true circle. The local ancient stone circle, Gors Fawr, has stones of approximately 2-3 tons and I assumed these would be the same. However when we dug down, it became clear that they were much bigger than that, about 6-8 tons each, and our little project suddenly got bigger too!" http://www.rosbriagha.org/stone_circles.html.

Ros Briagha and a local geomancy group dug up fourteen of the stones and placed them in an egg-shaped ring, carefully calculating contemporary astronomical alignments (http://www.geomancygroup.org/stone_circles/brithdir_page1.html).

> Lawrence Main did a many-year-long dream project on Carn Ingli, which overlooks Brithdir. In one dream, "he saw the hands of the Goddess coming up out of the ground, Her fingertips being the stones of the circle... which was not above ground or visible at that time." Ros Briagha, personal communication, 20 Dec. 2011.

Ros described the construction process: "... most of the stones we simply raised out of the ground so they were pretty much in the same place as when they were buried. My first map of the stones, when they were all still completely buried, was close enough to a circle to make it obvious that it was a circle. However, we certainly moved several quite some distances, so it is NOT the same circle as I first mapped. However, if an original purpose of the stones was to act as a calendar, amongst other uses no doubt, then it is probably close to what the original builders were aiming for. Our aim was to put a stone to mark the major rising and setting points of the Sun and Moon, and we put in some fillers as well so there were no obvious gaps. We did not know it would become an egg

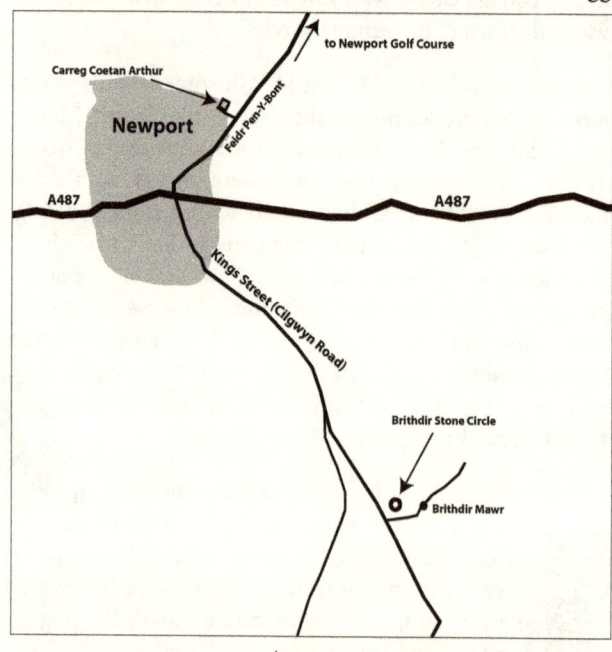

Area map

shape.... this was because the 3 biggest stones were at the "point" of the egg and would NOT allow themselves to be in any other position. We broke 2 poles trying.... So my feeling is the ring is the way the stones want to be! And it may well be a new dance for them. Of course, we do not have any confirmation that this was ever a stone circle before; the archaeologists who came along were no help at all." (Personal communication, Ros Briagha, 20 Dec. 2011.)

Ros told us (7 March 2012), "The stones are not inanimate objects. They are animate, conscious—they just move much more slowly than humans." Her group chanted to the stones and sensed where each stone "wanted" to be placed. If the stones were put in their proper place, in the proper way, they almost "leapt" into the spot. But if they tried to put the stones where they didn't want to go, they wouldn't budge. Ros compared this to the experience of a dancer trying to lift another dancer: if the "liftee" is willing, it is easy; if not, it is impossible. It's the difference between "animate" and "dead" weight.

Today, the Brithdir Stone Circle is once again used for rituals. The reconstructed circle is not the same as the original. Do you think that matters? If you visit the stones, see what you feel and experience.

Getting There

According to Ros, Brithdir circle is accessible to the public. It is accessed along a public footpath coming down from the Cilgwyn road (see map on p. 142).

Llech y Drybedd, Pembrokeshire

Llech y Drybedd dolmen (also known as Lleich-y-Drybedd or Llech-y-Tribedd, meaning "Tripod Stone," or Samson's Quoit) is in the middle of a field, with a clear view in all directions, taking in the north Mynydd Preseli range. It has three squat uprights, which form a tripod, two of which support the capstone, which is oriented toward

Carningli. Robin Heath (pp. 75, 102-103) considers it an important example of a precision lunar observatory, as well as being on an alignment from Bardsey Island and Pentre Ifan. Access permission is required from Penlan Farm.

St Brynach's Church, Nevern (Eglwys St Brynach, Nanhyfer), Pembrokeshire
N52 01 30 W4 47 42

A high stone wall surrounds Nevern Church, the arched entrance partly hidden under the spreading branches of an immense, dark-green yew. The energy shifted immediately when we crossed the threshold into the churchyard: the air felt static-filled and charged. We walked between two rows of ancient, brooding yews. These "tree beings" stood watch, evaluating us as we passed by. (Elyn)

Only about 2 mi as the crow flies from Newport, Pentre Ifan, and Castell Henllys (a reconstructed Iron Age hillfort), Nevern is a tiny hamlet in the Nevern (Nyfer) Valley. It was once an important ecclesiastical center located on one of the main Pilgrims' Ways leading from Holywell and Strata Florida in the northeast to St Davids in the southwest. The tiny hamlet is situated on the banks of the Nevern

Entrance to St Brynach's churchyard

> "Nevern's heartland is magical, resonant of being a *nemeton*, a sacred Druid grove at the almost edge of the land...." Hughes, 2006, p. 221."

(Nyfer) River and its tributary the Gamman (Caman). It is famous for its church with the bleeding yew and its ruined castle. The Caman stream borders the churchyard and joins the Afon Nyfer below the church.

Legend says that Irish St Brynach (see p. 111-112) founded the church at Nevern in the sixth century and established a monastery on the site. The current church dates from the fifteenth century, except for its older Norman tower, and was renovated in the nineteenth century.

The church is approached through a gate in a high stone wall, overshadowed by looming trees. You enter an avenue of ancient yews, four on each side of the path. The second tree on the right is the famous "bleeding yew," whose reddish sap oozes like blood from a gash on its trunk where a branch was sawed off during Victorian times. This is a botanical mystery yet to be solved. Legend states that a man was hanged from this tree and it has been bleeding ever since—and that the tree will continue to bleed until a Welshman sits on the throne in (ruined) Nevern Castle.

Apparently the bleeding is most obvious in spring, at which time other trees also appear to bleed. When we were there in 2011, the trees weren't bleeding, but that might have been because of an extended drought. The southern boundary of the churchyard is marked with 26 Irish yews, planted in 1928 to commemorate the local soldiers who died in WW I.

The bleeding yew tree

The 13-ft-tall Celtic high cross to the south of the church dates from the tenth or eleventh century. It is rare in Wales to find such a high cross, with such fine decoration, and in such an

> "[St Brynach] introduced agriculture to the people and taught them how to yoke wild stags to the plough and to milk the hinds. He also chopped wood from the trees and had these deer draw it to the place where he built a church on the site of the present one." See http://www.earlybritishkingdoms.com/bios/brynach.html for more legends.

excellent state of preservation. It is carved out of the local dolerite bluestone, identifiable by its spotty covering of orange-colored lichen, which favors that particular stone. Legend says the cross was a gift from St David to St Brynach, although they lived at least 400 years before the cross was sculpted. This anomaly is easily explained by those faithful to the legend. They say the current high cross is a replacement for the original—but subsequently lost—gift.

The first cuckoo to return to Wales each year is expected to land on the high cross on St Brynach's Day (7 April). Traditionally, Mass in the church could not begin until the bird's song was heard. One story recounts that one year the congregation waited impatiently, then worriedly, for the bird to arrive. At last it fluttered through the air, staggered onto the cross, let out an exhausted tweet, and dropped down dead.

> The yew is an important tree in Celtic tradition. It has powers of regeneration: the center of the trunk may be spongy but it puts out new growth and gets broader in circumference. Some yews are over 1000 years old—or even 3000 or (some claim) 5000 years old. For Druids, the yew was a symbol of eternity, death, rebirth, and regeneration. They planted it in sacred groves called *nemetons* in pre-Christian times. In recent years, researchers have developed the anti-cancer drug Tamoxifen, also known as taxol, from Pacific yews.

Near the high cross is the Vitalianus Stone, a worn standing stone inscribed in Latin and Ogham script, dating from around 500 CE. The churchyard contains a number of interesting graves.

The Celtic high cross in the churchyard

Inside the church are several important engraved stones, including the sixth-century Maglocunus Stone, with Latin and Ogham inscriptions, set into a windowsill. The intricate, interlaced Cross Stone, 48 in x 12 in, is set in another windowsill. The unusual design resembles graceful, intertwining branches or ribbons. Inside the expanded triangular head of the cross is a triskel. According to Robin Heath, the Cross Stone design was constructed using the sacred geometry of the vesica piscis (2010, p. 173). Perhaps you can see the shape of a goddess in it.

Becky Thomas has explored the legends of Brynach in depth and links his legend with the goddess Ceridwen (see pp. 135-137, 188-190). She writes that, according to some accounts, the angels instructed Brynach to leave Carningli

The Maglocunus Stone

The Cross Stone

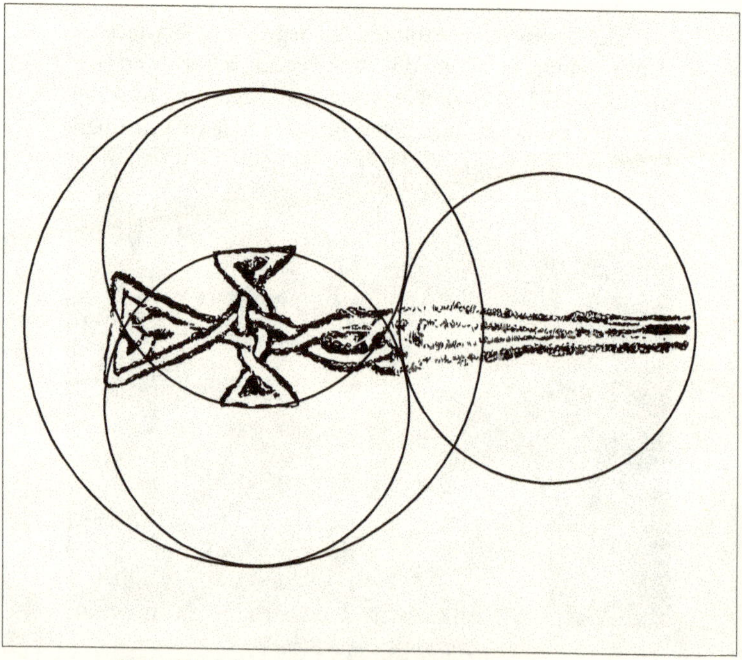

Vesica Piscis in the Cross Stone (after Heath, 2010, p. 173)

after 40 years of retreat and build a church. They told him "that he would know the place when he came to it for he would find there a Great White Sow. The white sow is long known to be a symbol of the Welsh goddess Ceridwen. As white sow, she is guardian of the underworld, keeper of souls. So Brynach left the hill of angels and walked until he came to a beautiful river valley. Here, as promised by the angels, Brynach came upon Ceridwen the Great White Sow and built his church where she guided." (http://www.goddess-pages.co.uk/index.php?option=com_content&task=view&id=699#ixzz1fPt9DUVO, retrieved 2 Dec. 2011.)

Some claim that Nevern is the valley through which King Arthur and his knights pursued the magic boar Twrch Trwyth. Once again, we have a white sow, Ceridwen, a boar—and instead of Arthur, a saint with Druidic associations. Is there a message hidden beneath the imagery, describing the shift from Celtic beliefs to Christianity?

The avenue of yews in St Brynach's churchyard

Some also say that "Caman llan" ("the Sacred Enclosure at the Gamman") is Camlan, where Arthur's last battle took place, and that the river that flows nearby is the one St Brynach turned to wine. Clearly, this is a location filled with mythic resonances.

> Remember BLESSING and ECOLOGY (see pp. 9-10). Center yourself, ask permission, and enter with respect.

According to Robin Heath, Nevern is on a number of important alignments. For example, he has discovered that Nevern Castle (just north of the church), Carningli, and Pentre Ifan form an equilateral triangle (Robin Heath, 2010, p. 155). Laurence Main has found a spirit path that leads from Carn Ingli to the High Cross in the churchyard.

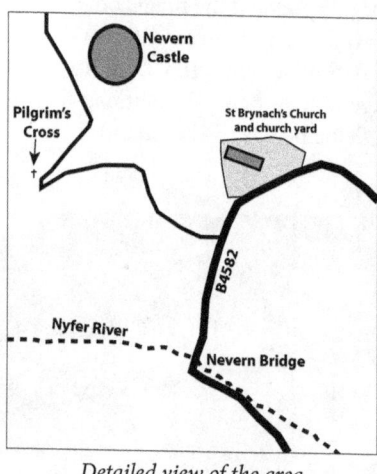

Detailed view of the area

Myth, geomancy, and archaeo-astronomy, all assert that Nevern is a powerful place. Notice how the energy shifts as you walk between and beneath the yews. Stroll slowly around the churchyard and see what you experience. One of our companions described the churchyard as a complex network of intersecting energy lines. Sense, see, feel, and listen. What do you discover?

On the hill 160 yd to the NW of the church are the ruins of a massive motte-and-bailey twelfth-century Norman castle built over a previous Welsh fortress. It may not look like much, but it is also a powerful place, hidden among the beech trees. Some have described the large mound as a faery mound (see http://www.neverncastle.com/).

The "Pilgrim's Cross"

The Pilgrim's Cross is found carved in relief into the exposed stone hillside a short distance to the west of the church, above the village, on a narrow, wooded lane that was once the old Pilgrims' Way. At its base in the slate steps are impressions worn down by the knees of the pious, or by their numerous footsteps— or perhaps it was a ledge for offerings. It is probable that this was a wayside shrine where pilgrims would pray for safe travel.

Follow the worn and rocky path past the cross into the forest, then turn around and walk back down. Imagine yourself a medieval pilgrim, following a wild and sometimes dangerous route to a holy shrine. Imagine your feelings when you come across this cross, etched into the living rock. Imagine falling to yours knees and praying, perhaps in gratitude, perhaps in need.

Getting There

Nevern is on B4582 north of A487 near Temple Bar. The way is well signposted.

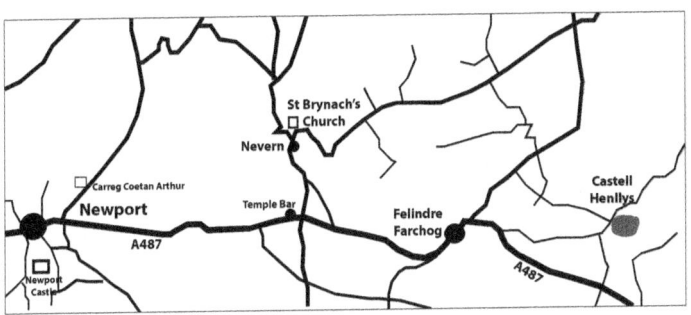

Area map

More to Experience

Castell Henllys, Pembrokeshire

Castell Henllys ("Castle of the Old Fort") is located a few miles to the east of Nevern. It is an Iron Age and Romano-British fort that has been reconstructed as a living history museum. Ongoing archeological excavations continue to give new insights into Iron Age life. Entry fee; free guided tours may include storytelling (http://www.castellhenllys.com).

> A *castell* is a stone fortification; a *dinas* is an earthen fortification.

Getting There

Take a minor road off A487 near Felindre Farchog. The way to Castell Henllys is well signposted (see map on p.151).

Ffynone Waterfall (Ffynone Cwm Cych), near Abercych, Pembrokeshire
N52, 55 W4 33 40

We strolled down the path to a waterfall at Ffynone, located on the river Dulas, which flows into Cwm Cych (Cych Valley). There was a steep, forested slope on one side, the rushing Afon Dulas on the other. Legend says the clearing is the entrance to the "other realm," the place where Pwyll, Prince of Dyfed, encountered Arawn, a king of Annwyn, the Celtic Underworld. Walking slowly, I fell behind the others. I felt something watching me from the hillside and turned to look. A face appeared on the trunk of a tree, and then another came

and went in the shifting fronds and branches. As I continued down the path, I passed through an invisible gateway and then another. Stepping through the energy was like brushing against cobwebs. I was in a "thin place" but the air felt thicker, not thinner, on the other side. Had I entered the Underworld? The waterfall tumbled fast and clear down the rocky cleft, forming a deep pool. Full immersion baptism seemed called for, an initiatic dip into this other world. (Elyn)

"There is a feeling about a place that we call 'thin places' that is thicker and stronger. A sense of something peaceful and yet gloriously alive; of Joy lurking somewhere in the landscape." Molly Wolf, quoted in http://thedailyofthedivineoffice.blogspot.com/, 22 Jan. 2011.

It is a pleasant walk from the parking lot alongside the Dulas River to Ffynone Waterfall, on its descent to Cwm Cych. The clearing may be one of the locations described in the *Mabinogi* as an entrance into the underworld of Annwyn. If you weren't familiar with the story of Pwyll and his encounter with Arawn, a king of Annwyn, perhaps you wouldn't find anything unusual at this site. Or maybe you

Ffynone Waterfall

would, for it is a powerful place, a "thin" place where this world and the Otherworld seem to reach out to each other and embrace.

According to the First Branch of the *Mabinogi*, Prince Pwyll was out hunting one day in Glyn Cuch (Cwm Cych), when his dogs came across a stag that had been brought down by another pack of hounds—the huge Cwn Annwn—shining, gleaming white, with red ears. He drove away the pack and fed his own hounds on the stag. Soon another hunter appeared, the owner of the faery hounds, outraged at this violation of courtesy. He was not to be messed with, for he was Arawn, a king of Annwn, the Celtic Underworld.

Pwyll sculpture in Rhos-y-gilwen concert hall (see p. 156). Phil Forder, sculptor. Courtesy of Glen Peters.

But all was not lost. Pwyll apologized and agreed to rule Arawn's kingdom for a year and then kill Hagfan, Arawn's main enemy, another king of Annwn. Arawn and Pwyll magically exchanged appearances and spent the year ruling each other's kingdoms. Their subjects were none the wiser. At the end of that time, as a reward for the honorable way in which Pwyll had conducted himself (including not having sex with Arawn's beguiling wife), Arawn gave Pwyll the title King of Annwn.

As you follow the sylvan path to the falls, if you pay close attention, you may notice that you pass through "energy gateways." They may feel a bit like brushing against cobwebs. They vary in intensity, depending on many factors. One of these gateways is near the beginning of the walk, near the dam on the stream, where the water cascades down.

When we visited the falls, the "thinness" of the place was palpable. Elyn "got" that this was a place of initiation, which would make sense, for what else is a journey into the Underworld than an initiation? Later she read about a modern Druid who had, indeed, used the pool for a "full-immersion" baptism (http://www.druidkirk.org/druid/articles/baptism.html).

On the way back from the waterfall, we encountered a young couple. He looked very unhappy, and he told us he had grown up in the area, fishing in the river and playing

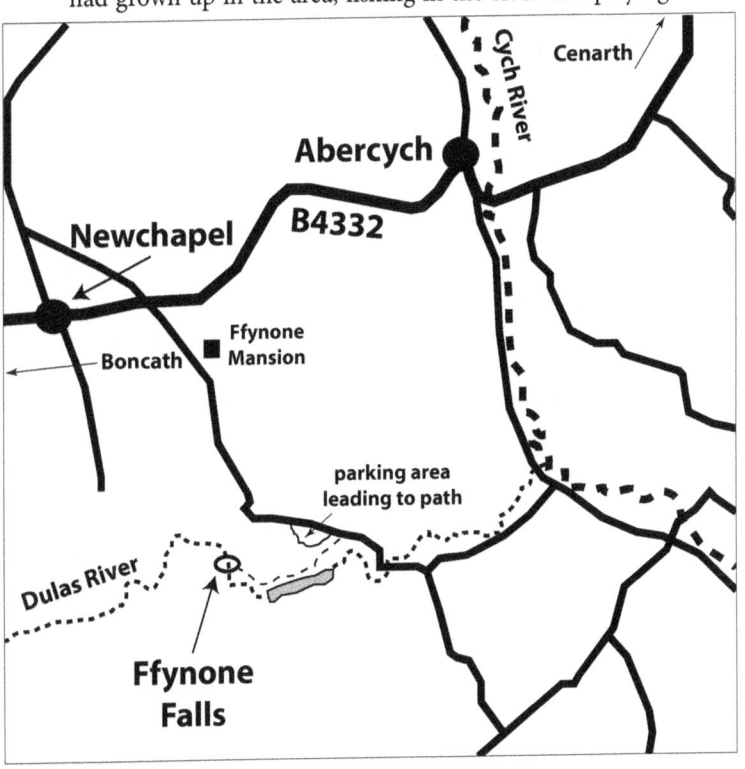

Area map

in the woods. He said, "It's really weird, but the world is dying. Now there are only small fish on the river, and the lake is silted-up because it hasn't been properly taken care of." Although for us, just passing through, the place was still powerful, the young man was mourning the loss of what he had known when he was younger.

Getting There

From Cenarth, take B4332 in the direction of Boncath. After passing Abercych/Penrhiw, take a left at the next crossroads, before reaching Newchapel. Pass Ffynone Mansion. When the lane has dropped most of the way into the valley, park in the parking area on the right. A track leads from the upper end of the parking area to the waterfall. The river will be on your left. Keep walking. A track turns left in front of a cottage; keep straight on. When the path forks again, take the left-hand track, passing some old dog kennels on your right. Keep walking to the falls—perhaps 15 minutes total. See maps on pp. 155 and 158.

More to Experience
Rhos-y-gilwen, Pembrokeshire

If you plan to spend time in the area, check out Rhos-y-gilwen (see map on p. 157), a delightful music and theater venue buried deep in the countryside. The owners have constructed a purpose-built concert hall on the grounds, which is well worth visiting. If you can, attend one of the many first-class programs, some with optional dinner arrangements (http://www.rhosygilwen.co.uk). Billed as a "Pembrokeshire Country Retreat," the lovingly restored Rhos-y-gilwen Mansion now offers short-term accommodations and can be used as a retreat center (http://www.retreat.co.uk/).

Rhos-y-gilwen mansion

Cilgerran Castle, Pembrokeshire

Cilgerran Castle is a moody place, located on a wooded promontory 4 mi by road to the east of Cardigan. It stands at the juncture of the Teifi River and the Plysgos stream. The castle has a dramatic history. Shortly after it was first constructed, Prince Owain of Powys may have raped and abducted Nest (the "Welsh Helen of Troy") from the castle on Christmas Day 1109. At her urging, her Norman husband, Gerald of Pembroke, escaped from the invaders in a most unusual fashion: he slid down a toilet waste chute. The result of the abduction was a broken truce and war between the Welsh and Normans. It is likely that the story is much more complicated: see http://en.wikipedia.org/wiki/Nest_verch_Rhys.

Existing masonry is from the thirteenth-century rebuild. If you are interested in ruined, scenic castles, it is worth a visit. Managed by Cadw; entry fee; opening hours.

Annual coracle races take place on the river; coracles are ancient hide and wicker boats. The Teifi Marshes Nature Reserve is only a mile or so to the north.

Getting There

Drive on A478 south from Cardigan to Pen-y-bryn. Turn east (left) to Cilgerran (see map below).

Cenarth, Carmarthenshire

Cenarth, 7 mi upstream from Cardigan, is a charming little town, famous for its "rapids"—actually, a series of low cataracts. The National Coracle Center is located here, and you can visit its museum to learn more about these pre-Christian boats, still used by traditional fishermen on the Teifi (http://www.coraclemuseum.co.uk/).

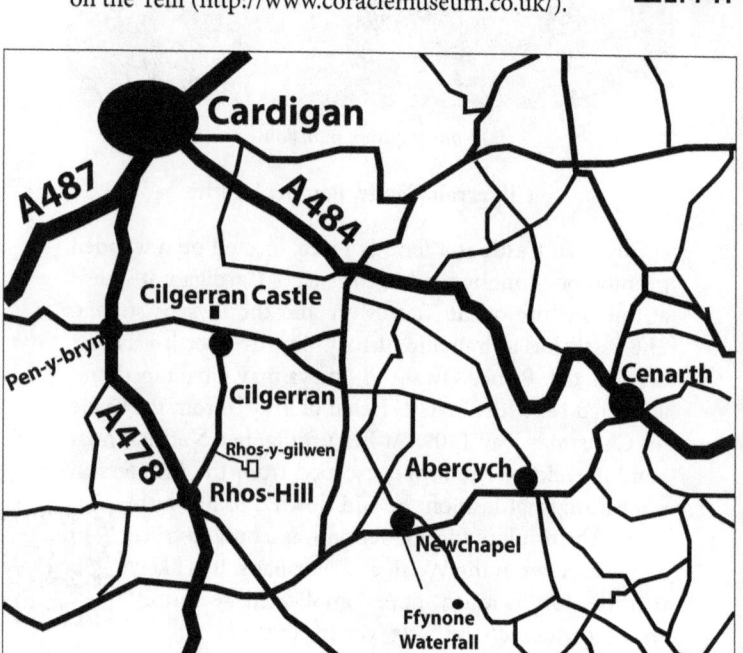

Area map

Getting There

Drive on A484 southeast of Cardigan (see map on p. 158).

The "rapids" at Cenarth

Mid Wales (Ceredigion, Cambrian Coast, Powys, part of Gwynedd, and the Brecon Beacons)

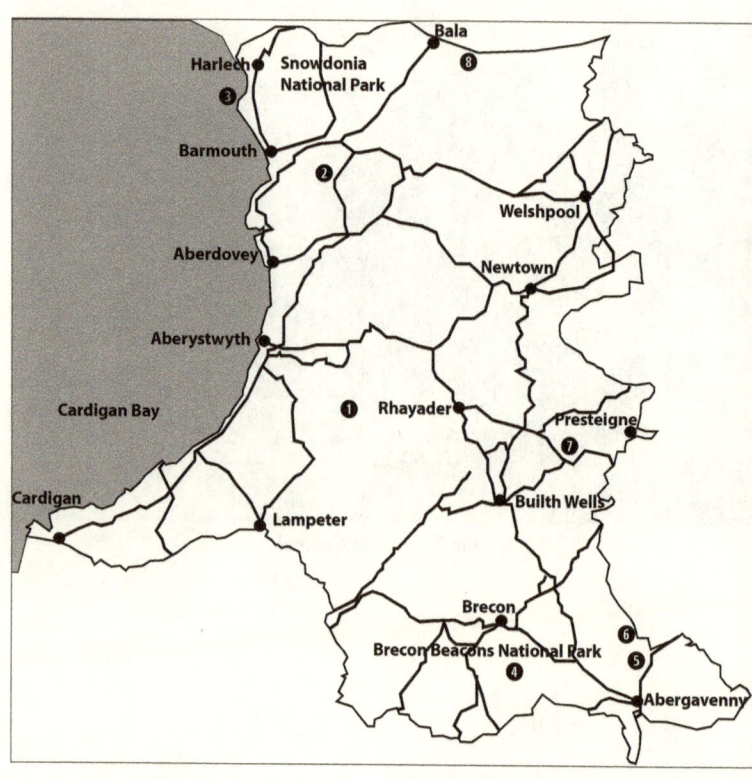

1. Strata Florida Abbey, Ceredigion
2. Cadair Idris, Snowdonia National Park, Gwynedd
3. The Cambrian Coast
4. Brecon Beacons National Park
5. Patrisio (Partrishow) Church and Holy Well, Powys
6. Llanthony Priory, Monmouthshire
7. Radnor Forest, Cascob Church, and St Michael's Church in Discoed, Powys
8. St Melangell Church, Pennant Melangell, Powys

Ceredigion is a county in midwest Wales noted for its charming fishing villages, inviting beaches, nature reserves, scenic railroads, walking trails, Cambrian Mountains, and its deeply Welsh rural communities hidden in the hills. Its coastline sweeps around Cardigan Bay and includes the new Ceredigion Coast Path. Modern Ceredigion includes much of the same territory as historic Cardiganshire, a county founded in 1282 by the English king Edward I. The area hosts many rare species of plants, animals, and birds, in particular the rare, beautiful red kite.

The Cambrian coast runs from Cardigan in the south to Harlech in the north; it includes the southern part of Snowdonia National Park. The historic county Merionnydd in the north of the Cambrian coast is now administratively part of Gwynedd.

Powys and the Brecon Beacons are located in the center and west of this region of country roads, quaint villages, market towns, high waterfalls, Roman ruins, medieval churches, spa towns, megalithic sites—and more red kites. Excellent hill-walking and hiking opportunities abound in the Brecon Beacons National Park, with its snow-capped mountains, moors, and forests.

Powys and "the Brecons" are characterized by organic agriculture, sustainable energy—and sustainable lifestyles. This is rural Wales, sparsely populated, with sheep grazing on the green, rolling hillsides. Southern Powys is Wales' foodie heaven: the annual Abergavenny Food Festival draws gourmets from around the world.

The myths and legends of this middle region of Wales revolve around the goddess Ceridwen and the bard Taliesin. They appear in "The Tale of Gwion Bach" and "The Tale of Taliesin," two of the addition stories in the *Mabinogi*. Another legendary figure is (H)elen, who appears in "The Dream of Macsen Wledig," another *Mabinogi* story. The Grail—or "a" grail—also makes an appearance.

> "In all things of nature there is something of the marvelous."
> Aristotle.

Strata Florida Abbey (Abaty Ystrad Fflur), Ceredigion
N52 16 31 W3 50 22

We were told that Strata Florida Abbey is a powerful, "heart-chakra" kind of place, sweet and peaceful. But we arrived there just before a funeral in the parish chapel next to the ruined abbey and in the middle of an international motocross race. The rrhuumm rrhuumm rrhuumm of mud-spattered motorcycles speeding by did nothing to enhance our experience of the subtle energies of the abbey. At one time the Grail—or "a" grail, the Nanteos Cup—was held within the now-ruined walls. Surely, I thought, this was, or had been, and should be, a very powerful place. I tried to meditate and caught a faint whiff of stale incense, of unhappy monks muttering prayers in the side chapels. Perhaps on a different day.... (Elyn)

Strata Florida Abbey is located in a lush valley beside the River Teifi. The original church was founded in 1164 by Cistercian monks from Whitland Abbey at a site 2 mi away in Ystrad Fflur, a Latinized version of the Welsh Uh Strad Fleer, meaning wide valley or vale of flowers. Or perhaps the name is Latin for "layers of flowers."

Looking down the nave at Strata Florida

Soon the monks moved their community to the current location of Strata Florida. In 1184 the abbey came under the patronage of Rhys ap Gruffydd (d. 1197). Rhys the Great, Prince of Deheubarth (one of the ancient Welsh kingdoms), combined military ascendancy with enthusiastic support of the new religious orders. Under his patronage, Strata Florida expanded in size and possessions. It is probable that the abbey included a school and hospital devoted to herbal medicine.

Lord Rhys's and his son Rhys Gryg's physicians were Rhiwallon of Myddfai and his three sons were (see pp. 197-200) the most able medical practitioners in the area. They probably practiced at Strata Florida.

The Cistercians (AKA the White Monks because of their white hooded habits) were a reform order of the Benedictines, founded at Çîteaux in Burgundy in 1098. Bernard of Clairvaux (d. 1154) was their most important and powerful abbot. They were austere, known for seeking out remote and isolated sites for their abbeys and working industriously to make the land highly productive. Cistercian architecture tended to be simple and utilitarian, avoiding elaborate ornamentation.

Strata Florida Abbey became an important keeper of Welsh traditions and history. It housed an important scriptorium. Monks at Strata Florida wrote the manuscript that was the source of *Brut y Tywysogyon (Chronicle of the Princes)*. They also copied other works of Welsh literature—as well as collecting and writing down, often for the first time, oral lore and stories. It is because of their efforts that native Welsh traditions were not lost.

Detail of the Norman-style west door

During the thirteenth century, Strata Florida remained an ardent supporter of the Welsh cause against the English, and many members of the Deheubarth dynasty were buried there. In 1238 Llywelyn the Great, who had unified the Welsh under his rule, called other Welsh princes to Strata Florida to pay homage to his son Dafydd. Over time, the abbey gained 6000 acres of land. The close connection between church and state was both an advantage and a detriment, depending on who the ruling powers were.

The abbey was damaged during the wars between King Edward I and Llywelyn ap Gruffydd, prince of Wales (1276-77 and 1282-83). It was remodeled in the early

Decorative tiles in one of the side chapels

fourteenth century. The abbey was forced to close in 1539 because of King Henry VIII's dissolution of the monasteries, and it was soon left in ruins.

Even the ruins are impressive, including the huge Norman-style west door, the remains of fourteenth-century, decorated red-brown tile pavements, and chapels in the north and south transepts. The bucolic setting is outstanding, with lush green hills visible through the ruined stone walls.

The massive west doorway opens onto grass and broken stone walls, the remains of the once-great abbey. The doorway is adorned with five (originally six) nesting "ropes" of stone, with a seventh roll-molding across the tops of the arch. The doorway is banded with thirteen bands of stone, each ending in a spiral, as does the roll molding across the top. Surely there is significance in these numbers: coded reference to the apostles and Jesus, perhaps? Or to the lunar year?

Near the center of what had been the choir, slightly off-center at the crossing between the nave and the transept, is a stone-lined basin situated about 3 ft beneath ground level. Four steps at the east end and four at the west end lead down to this puzzling feature, which was discovered between 1935-1949 during site excavations.

No one knows its purpose. It might have been used in the mandatum, a rite on the Thursday of Holy Week during which the abbot washed the feet of various monks and lay brothers. However,

The stone-lined basin

this ritual as a rule took place in the cloister, not in the middle of the church. Another possibility is that the basin had something to do with a drain under the site, but again, this is not very likely.

According to the assistant in the Cadw visitor's center, they have discovered that the pit is actually a spring—and it is connected with another one in the hill to the east. TJ Hughes (p. 195) asserts that the "stepped stone hollow" was a holy well associated with healing. This would make sense, given the tradition of healing at Strata Florida, except that there is no record of its use as such. Clearly, this "pit" is a very significant feature, but how was it used? It remains a fascinating puzzle.

> The Welsh visionary writer Megan Wingfield (pp. 67-79) thinks the pit was a Celtic initiation site. Later it became a place where monks passed into a "new life"; walking through the water-filled pit raised their vibrational level. Wingfield writes that she and her companions experienced angelic presences at the abbey. She also "got" that Joseph of Arimathea and Mary, mother of Jesus, had visited what is now Strata Florida, a location that was sacred to the Druids and to those who had been there long before they arrived.

Using dowsing rods, Gary located a fire line running down the nave. Not surprisingly, it crossed a water line at the stone-lined pit. In our experience, such crossings are usually quite powerful. We frequently find the crossing of a fire line with a water line in churches, often where the nave crosses the transept, and also under the altar. We also find this pattern in certain dolmens. You can think of such crossings as places where the "heat" of the fire line meets water and creates "esoteric" steam and hence "power."

The Nanteos Cup, named after the "stream or valley of nightingales," is associated with Strata Florida. It may or may not be the Cup of the Last Supper—i.e., the Grail. Robert de Boron's Joseph d'Arimathie and subsequent

> Peter Redgrove (pp. 93-110) describes "total body dowsing" as the human response to a "webwork of forces" that include electric, magnetic, electromagnetic, acoustic, and olfactory stimulations.

medieval legends claim that Joseph of Arimathea arrived in Britain in 36 CE with the cup and perhaps with Mary, mother of Jesus. The cup remained at Glastonbury until the dissolution of the monasteries in the 1530s. According to one legend, the custodians carried it westward, hoping to take it to the Irish Mellifont Abbey to keep it safe, but they were forced to return to Wales. They took refuge with the Stedman family, owners of much land, including Strata Florida, and the Stedmans became the guardians of the Nanteos Cup.

Laurence Main (pp. 62-63) thinks that the Nanteos Cup is the cup brought to Glastonbury by Joseph of Arimathea. Main asserts that it was taken to Strata Florida in the sixth century, not the sixteenth, after King Arthur was mortally wounded at the Battle of Camlan. Three warrior saints, who later became known as Sir Galahad, Sir Percival, and Sir Bors, carried the Grail to Strata Florida for safekeeping.

> Other legends assert that the Grail resided in various Spanish locations, including Our Lady of Montserrat Basilica, the isolated monastery of San Juan de la Peña, and Valencia Cathedral, where a "Santo Cáliz" (Sacred Chalice) has been venerated since 1437. Some claim it is buried under Rosslyn Chapel in Scotland or somewhere in Glastonbury, England. A different approach asserts that the Grail was never a cup: rather, the image stood for Mary Magdalene, pregnant with Jesus' child. Graham Phillips (2000) suggests the Grail was the Virgin Mary, brought to Anglesey by Joseph of Arimathea. Perhaps the Grail represents the interior search for spiritual enlightenment.

The Stedmans later married into the Powell family, and they built Nanteos House in Aberystwyth in 1739. As keepers of the Nanteos Cup/Grail, the Powells would pour water in the cup, then give the water to people to drink for healing. Some people broke or chewed off pieces of the cup to take home as relics, thus markedly diminishing its size. The Powells remain the guardians of the Nanteos Cup, although they no longer live at Nanteos. Today they keep it in a bank vault. Recent investigations of the cup have concluded that it is probably a medieval mazer or food bowl made from wych elm (holm)—not a 2000-year-old drinking cup made of olive wood.

After experiencing the energies at Strata Florida, be sure to visit St Mary's parish church, just to the north of the abbey. An early pre-Norman slab of stone, now located behind the east end of the church, was found in the churchyard, so it is possible that the church predates the abbey. A huge tree shades the simple church.

> An often-repeated story says that Richard Wagner was a guest of George Powell and that during his stay at Nanteos House, he was inspired to write the opera *Parsifal*. But although Powell and Wagner knew each other, there is no evidence that Wagner visited Nanteos.

In 1539, 39 yews were recorded in the churchyard but now only two remain, a male and a grand, storm-battered female. The Cistercians are said to have planted the female yew to indicate the spot where Dafydd ap Gwilym (b. 1315/1320; d. 1350/70) lies buried. Dafydd ap Gwilym was one of the most important medieval European poets. He wrote about nature and love—and sometimes wrote quite erotic and humorous poems. See http://en.wikipedia.org/wiki/Dafydd_ap_Gwilym.

A stone retaining wall and a rough memorial below the massive yew mark Dafydd's supposed grave. However, it has

Ancient female yew tree in the churchyard

been convincingly argued that the famous Welsh poet lies beneath the much smaller male yew growing by the wall to the northwest (Morton, pp. 112-113).

Time has taken a toll on both yews, but it is impressive to witness the way they re-generate themselves, sending out new sprouts and branches despite time's devastation. Whether it is "the poet's tree" or not, take time to commune with the ancient female yew. Approach respectfully, request permission to draw near, and see what unfolds.

Strata Florida is managed by Cadw; entry fee; unrestricted entry.

Getting There

Drive northeast of Tregaron on B4343 to Pontrhydfendigaid. There take a minor road east to Strata Florida (see map). There are adequate signs showing the way.

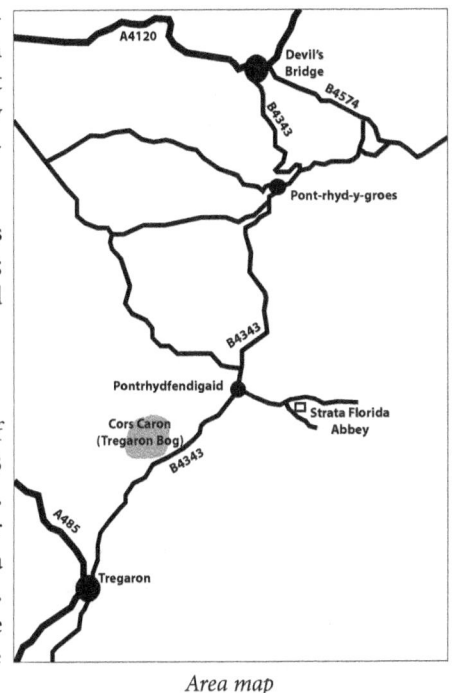

Area map

More to Experience
More Holy Wells, Ceredigion

In addition to the spring in Strata Florida Abbey and the holy well on the hill, three other holy wells are found in the vicinity. One of these has just been made accessible. To reach it, follow the road past Strata Florida for about a mile until it ends. There you'll find a new forest road; follow it approximately 1.5 mi and you'll reach the holy well. The forest well is thought to be a leg well (for healing leg issues) and has stone steps going into it somewhat like the steps in the church. Another well in the area is thought to be an eye well. Mara Freeman provides a moving account of her visit there: http://marafreeman.blogspot.com/2011/07/freeing-waters-two-rediscovered-holy.html. There is also a Neolithic site nearby, perhaps a burial chamber—additional evidence that this area was sacred for millennia before Strata Florida was established.

The Devil's Bridge (Pontarfynach), Ceredigion

The Devil's Bridge, 12 mi east of Aberystwyth, is reachable by car and by the Vale of Rheidol Railway (see map on p. 169). It is actually three bridges, one on top of the other: they span the River Mynach where it joins with the Rheidol River. Waterfalls drop 300 ft through the stunning gorge. At the top is the iron road bridge, built in 1901; below is the stone bridge from 1753; and below that is the original bridge, dating from the eleventh century and perhaps constructed by monks from Strata Florida. This lower bridge is the Pont-y-gwr-drwg (Bridge of the Devil), so-named because a legend says the devil built it and waited to claim the soul of the first being to cross. A wily old woman sent her dog across first.

The scenery is spectacular. Two nature trails provide different experiences: the longer walks include a "Jacob's Ladder" of 100 slippery stone steps leading down to the torrent's edge. Because it is so popular—and has been for centuries—avoid peak times and seasons. Charges for access to the paths (http://www.devilsbridgefalls.co.uk/).

Tregaron, Ceredigion

Tregaron is a traditional Welsh market town, a center for Welsh language and culture, with an excellent jewelry shop and café, Rhiannon Welsh Gold Center. Tregaron Red Kite Center and Museum provides information about these birds of prey and lets visitors watch the kites feeding during winter months (see map on p. 169). To the north is Cors Caron, the Tregaron Bog, a national nature reserve and "prodigious wildlife area." This ancient bog was created when a glacier retreated at the end of the last Ice Age and created a natural lake. Sediment and vegetation filled the waters, and the peat surface grew. There is a short walkway and a 3-mi circuit along the railway and the river. See http://www.ccw.gov.uk/landscape--wildlife/protecting-our-landscape/special-landscapes--sites/protected-landscapes/national-nature-reserves/cors-caron.aspx?lang=en.

Getting There

Tregaron is on A485 (see map on p. 168). The Tregaron Bog is just to the north on B 4343. The main access to the reserve is from the new car park on B4343.

Cadair (anglicized as Cader) Idris, Snowdonia National Park, Gwynedd

So much to experience, so little time. We drove on narrow twisting roads through the southern Snowdonia region. Everywhere we turned, multi-peaked Cadair Idris loomed overhead. We could not escape its ominous, domineering presence. The story goes that anyone who spends the night on the Chair of Idris will either become a poet or go mad—a story we have heard before. I felt no urge find out which would be my fate. (Elyn)

Cadair Idris (the Chair of Idris), with its massive 7-mi-long ridge, dominates the southern reaches of Snowdonia National Park. On a clear day you can see the Isle of Man and as far as the Irish coast from the top of the hulking, glacier-scraped summit, Penygadair (Top of the Chair). Standing there, you are 2927 ft above sea level. After Mt Snowdon, Cadair Idris is the second most popular Welsh mountain to climb.

> "It is said that Hounds of the Underworld fly around [Cadair Idris'] peaks, and strange light effects are often sighted in the area." Atkinson and Wilson, p. 244.

The largest glacier-created amphitheater on the mountain is called Cwm Gadair, and some think that is the place to spend the daredevil night. Others think that Idris' Chair is a seat-like rock formation on the summit ridge, and that's where you should try to sleep, though what dreams might come might give you pause. Tradition says that Druid bards slept on the mountain, seeking inspiration. Perhaps the modern "superstition" is a distorted memory of that ancient practice.

Much of the area around Cadair Idris is a national nature reserve, but it was a different kind of nature that drew us there: the "nature" of Idris, the "nature" of a rock ridge that could drive one mad or transform one into a poet.

Myths and legends swirl around Cadair Idris like the thick fog that often cloaks its summit. Gwyn ap Nudd, the Celtic Lord of the Underworld, is said to have lived on Cadair Idris, and some say that his malevolent Hounds of Hell (Cwn Annwn), fearsome white dogs with red ears, still inhabit the Cadair, eager to spirit people away to their eternal doom. The fog and mist that naturally occur on the mountaintop add veritas to the myth. Day-hikers report that Cadair Idris has a special feel, a mysterious atmosphere, which draws them back repeatedly.

Some say the mountain was named after Idris Gawr, the fabled Welsh giant, poet, astronomer, and philosopher, who

> "Snowdonia National Park was established in 1951 and is the third largest of the 15 National Parks in the UK [and the largest in Wales]. The Park covers 2,132 square km (823 square miles) and stretches from Cardigan Bay's High Water Mark in the west, to the Conwy Valley in the east and from the River Dyfi and its estuary in the south to the coast of Conwy Bay as far as Conwy in the north." http://www.eryri-npa.gov.uk/visiting/snowdonia-national-park, retrieved 17 March 2012.

made the summit and bottomless Llyn Cau Lake his chair (*cadair*). One of the "Welsh Triads" asserts that Idris the Great (the Giant), Gwydion, son of Dôn, and Gwynn, son of Nudd, were the three great priestly astronomers of the Island of Britain, able to foretell the future with their knowledge of the stars. How appropriate that Idris would sit high on a mountain: where better to observe the stars!

Others think that the name comes from the seventh-century Welsh prince, Idris ap Gwyddno, who won a battle against the Irish on the mountain. Cadr is Welsh for stronghold and similar to cadair. According to this theory, over time the "Stronghold of Prince Idris" became the "Chair of Idris" (http://en.wikipedia.org/wiki/Cadair_Idris, retrieved 12 Dec. 2011). This Idris is a symbol of Welsh pride and evokes memories of King Arthur, a native Briton though not Welsh, who bested, for a short time, the invading Anglo-Saxons.

Still others think the mountaintop was the stronghold of King Arthur. This idea appears to be due to a mistranslation of the hill as "Arthur's Seat" and hence is a modern invention. However, legends of Arthur do abound elsewhere in the Snowdonia hills (see pp. 251-253).

Idris is an antediluvian name, dating back to before the biblical Flood. Idris is the same person as Enoch, the great-grandfather of

> "Listen. This is the noise of myth. It makes/ the same sound as shadow. Can you hear it?" From Eavan Boland's poem, "Listen. This is the noise of myth."

Noah. In Judaism, Enoch was "a pious man" and, like Elijah, he was "taken up by God" and thus did not experience death (Gen. 5:21-24). In Muslim tradition, as in Welsh tradition, Idris/Enoch is associated with the study of astronomy, the origin of writing, and other technical arts.

> Two novels in Susan Cooper's young-adult fantasy series, *The Dark is Rising*, take place in this area of Wales. The "Grey King" is the evil Lord of the Dark who opposes the Powers of the Light. He lives on Cadair Idris, and the "mist that men called the breath of the Grey King" (p. 549) is dreaded, for it disguises the edge of the mountains precipices, and unwary hikers may fall to their death.

Cadair Idris is like a palimpsest, a parchment that has been scraped clean and written over—and over and over. Idris/Enoch is an ancient name linked with writing and astronomy. Idris is also the Welsh name of a "giant" among men and a poet, perhaps a faded remembrance of Druid bards who went to the mountaintop in search of inspiration. And Idris is the name of a native warrior who bested the invading Irish. These overlapping associations resonate from the top of an impressive, dangerous massif, its trails

Cadair Idris above Tal-y-llyn lake

Gwyn ap Nudd

often shrouded in mist, a mountain that has its own powerful energies—perhaps personified as the Celtic Lord of the Otherworld and his hounds.

Several routes lead up to Cadair Idris, some easier than others (see http://www.trekkingbritain.com/cadairidristheminfforddpath.htm and http://www.docbrown.info/docspics/wales/walespage02.htm). Route information and current weather reports are available from the Dolgellau Tourist Office and National Park Information Center; tel. (0)1341 422888; email tic.dolgellau@eyri-npa.gov.uk. We recommend OS Explorer map OL23, "Cadair Idris and Llyn Tegid."

Cadair Idris towers over the tiny settlement of Tal-y-Llyn and the beautiful glacier fingerlike, TalyLlyn Lake (Llyn Mwyngil; "Lake in the Pleasant Retreat"). The shallow lake is popular with trout fishermen, and the setting is idyllic.

Next to the lake is the onetime parish church of St Mary, dating from before the ninth century, which would make it one of the oldest churches in Wales, or from the twelfth century, depending on the source. Although the church is currently closed to visitors, it is worth walking through the tangled, unkempt churchyard.

Church of St Mary in Tal-y-Llyn

More to Experience

TalyLlyn Railway, Gwynedd

Wales is home to a number of scenic railways, many of which were originally designed to connect mines and quarries to shipping points on the coasts. When the mines and quarries ceased operation, some of these railways were converted to tourist attractions. The narrow-gauge TalyLlyn Railway is one of Wales' most charming steam-powered railways. It puffs its way up from Fathew Valley to Abergynolwyn, with scenic stops en route (http://www.talyLlyn.co.uk). It stops short of Cadair Idris.

Getting There

Drive north to Tywyn from Aberdovey on A493 (see map on p. 177). The TallyLlyn Railway begins at Tywn Wharf.

Llyn Barfog (The Bearded Lake), Gwynedd

Llyn Barfog is an intriguing lake, often covered with water lilies. One medieval story claims that King Arthur came to Llyn Barfog to slay the *afanc* or *addanc*, a beastly cross between a dragon and a crocodile. Arthur lassoed it with a chain and then his powerful horse, Llamrai, dragged it from the waters. A rock near the lake is known as Carn March Arthur, "the Stone of Arthur's Horse," because of the hoof-like impression it bears. One ending of the story claims that Arthur killed the beast, but another ending claims that he dragged it to Llyn Cau on Cadair Idris and released it there, far from people. See http://www.glyn-yr-aur.com/Llyn%20Cau.htm.

The lake is located in the hills above Aberdyfi (Aberdovey; pro. "aber-DUV-ee"), 2.5 mi from Cwrt, near Pennal. SN 65398 98858. Driving directions: from Glyn-yr-aur, take A470 from Dolgellau and then travel on A487 toward Machynlleth. Just before reaching this town, turn right

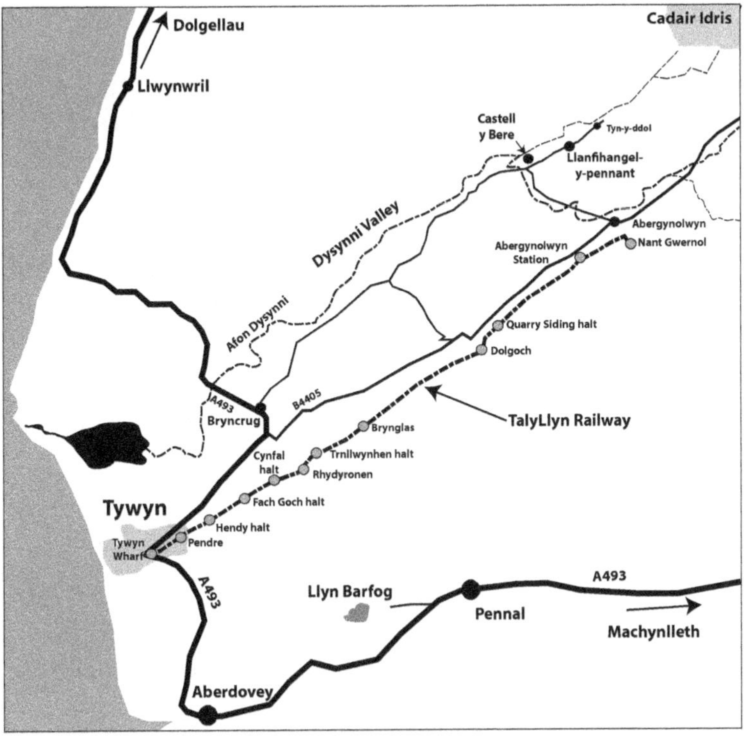

Area map

onto A493. Take a right turn into Cwm Maethlon (Happy Valley) soon after reaching the village of Pennal. Once on this country lane, travel for 10 minutes or so to a car park that is signposted for Llyn Barfog or the Bearded Lake (see map above). See http://www.glyn-yr-aur.com/Barfog.htm.

Walking directions: you can walk from Aberdyfi/Aberdovey. The walk is approximately 10 mi and should take around 4 1/2 hours (http://visitaberdovey.co.uk/bearded-lake/).

Dysynni Valley, Gwynedd

The isolated Dysynni Valley offers much to experience, including green hillsides dotted with heather and grazing sheep. The thirteenth-century Welsh hilltop fortress Castell-y-Bere is now in ruins, but it remains evocative in setting and memory (see map on p. 177).

Llywelyn ap Iorwerth (Llywelyn the Great) built the fortress in 1221 to control the mountain passes. It was one of the most massive of Welsh castles but was only used for 60 years before being captured by the English. When the Welsh regained control in 1285, they destroyed it.

The path may be a bit mucky at first, but persevere and continue walking through the woods to the castle, which seems to grow out of the rocky crag on which it stands. Managed by Cadw; unlimited access.

Nearby Llanfihangel-y-Pennant church (Church of St Michael) is in a powerful setting, deep in the Dysynni Valley. The church contains exhibits describing sixteen-year-old Mary Jones' famous barefoot 25-mi walk to Bala in 1800 to purchase a copy of the Welsh translation of the Bible from Thomas Charles. Daughter of a poor weaver,

Castell-y-Bere

Mary Jones

she had saved money for six years. Charles had no more copies available, so he gave Mary his own copy. The incident inspired him to establish the British and Foreign Bible Society.

In the vestry of the church, replete with memorabilia of the Bible-seeking local, is a Plexiglas-encased, 14-ft-long 3D patchwork scale map of the area. Unfortunately, when we were there the case was covered with rodent droppings and the displays were thick with dust.

The churchyard is round and planted with yews, indicative of its long history. A spring bubbles forth outside the yard, to the left of the lychgate. The setting is powerful but when we were there, the church had a very unpleasant energy, palpable as soon as we crossed through the lychgate. Elyn got an instant headache that didn't stop until she left the churchyard. Maybe you will have a more pleasant experience.

Further up the lane at the ruined Tyn-y-ddol is the beginning of a 10-mi-long path up Cadair Idris. It includes a 2900 ft ascent and

Entrance to Llanfihangel-y-Pennant Church

takes approximately seven hours. This is a longer route than some of the others.

In the other direction, toward the sea, is Craig yr Aderyn/Craig y Deryn (Birds' Rock). This 760-ft-high rocky hill is the only place in Wales (and perhaps Britain) where cormorants breed inland. Over the years, the sea has receded from the base of the rock so that now it is 4.3 mi inland. It has a brooding, powerful feel. For directions for a walking excursion, go to http://www.walesdirectory.co.uk/Walks/Abergynolwyn_Castell_y_Bere_Walk.htm.

The Cambrian Coast

The Cambrian Coast, connecting mid to north Wales, is full of powerful places and megalithic sites.

Harlech (Harddlech), Gwynedd

Harlech is a good town to use as a base for exploring the area and its numerous hiking trails. Harlech means "Bold (or Beautiful) Rock," and it is indeed a stunning setting, with its castle perched on a rocky outcrop 200 ft above the shore. Edward I of England began building the imposing castle in 1283 (Cadw; opening hours; fee). The sea originally came up to the foot of the bluff but the coastline has now changed.

Harlech Castle was constructed on the site where, according to the Second Branch of the *Mabinogi*, Brân the Blessed and his sister Branwen entertained Matholwch, the Irish king who came to ask permission to marry her.

Harlech Castle

Senior members of The Golden Dawn (an esoteric order) used to meet at what is now the Plas Tearoom and Café on High Street. Apparently they, like Edward I and Bran, were drawn to the energies of Harlech town. The Beach Road below the town and castle offers access to an excellent beach and sand dunes (http://www.walesdirectory.co.uk/Towns_in_Wales/Harlech_Town.htm).

Ardudwy Megaliths, Gwynedd

Numerous stone circles and megaliths dot the heather-covered Rhinog Mountains to the east and around the Harlech area. The Neolithic Dyffryn Ardudwy Burial Chambers, also known as Coetan Arthur, is signposted off A496 in Ardudwy. Cadw; unrestricted entry.

"Ardudwy has a remarkable and well-preserved group of chambered tombs of the early Neolithic period, all within an area of some eight miles in extent, suggesting a single population group, made up of several related local communities." http://www.heneb.co.uk/ardudwycharacter/ardudwyintro/ardudwythemeseng.html, retrieved 13 Dec. 2011.

Dyffryn Ardudwy/Coetan Arthur is composed of two chambers, some 25 ft apart, surrounded by a rough pavement of stones, the vestiges of the cairn that once covered them. The larger, eastern chamber now has brick supports to keep its capstone from falling in. The smaller, western chamber was built earlier and was later incorporated with the other chamber into a single cairn. The cairn would originally have measured some 130 ft by 55 ft. Despite the location and reconstruction, the burial chambers are surprisingly powerful and sweet. Elyn felt that they were waiting patiently over the millennia for something—perhaps for appreciative visitors. In their presence, you become aware of an immense time span (http://www.isleofalbion.co.uk/sites/136/dyffryn_ardudwy.php).

Taith Ardudwy Way is a well-signposted upland hiking trail that traverses Ardudwy, an ancient commote (a medieval administrative area). It is 24 miles long and stretches from Barmouth in the south to Llandecwyn in the north. The route is divided into three sections, each with a descriptive leaflet. It visits each of the parishes bordering Cardigan Bay and crosses the geological formation of the Cambrian Rocks, amongst the oldest in Wales, known as the Harlech Dome. The modern Way, based on the prehistoric trackway, was developed to take in some of the best coastal and mountain views in Wales, visiting ancient sites and offering the chance to see varied vegetation and rare birds of the area. http://www.taithardudwyway.com/northern.html, retrieved 13 Dec. 2011.

Getting There

Follow A496 into Dyffryn Ardudwy and turn into the cul-de-sac called Bro Arthur, which is near a school. Park and return to the main road, turn left, and you'll easily find the footpath leading beside the school to the dolmens.

Bryn Cader Faner ("Outlook Post on the Hill") is a stone circle lying above Harlech on a spur of land that rises above the prehistoric Ardudwy Trackway (http://www.megalithic.co.uk/article.php?sid=526). Its outward-tilting stones resemble a crown of thorns. Another stone circle located near the trackway is Moel Goedog ("Goedog Hill") West.

Two Waterfall Walks, Gwynedd

Dolgellau makes a convenient base for exploring the parks and waterfalls in the area.

Surrounded by Coed y Brenin Forest Park, the Waterfall Walk begins 5 mi north of Dolgellau at Ganllwyd. A path in the National Trust's Dolmelynllyn estate leads through heath and oak woodlands along the fast-flowing Afon

Gamlan to Rhaeadr Ddu. The "Black Waterfall" is one of the most spectacular in Wales. It's a short stiff climb into the woods (ten minutes at most) but well worth the effort. The mossy green woods are enchanting, and the sight and sound of the white rushing water and the waterfall dropping 60 ft over glistening black rocks are impressive—depending, of course, on the amount of recent rainfall.

Rhaeadr Ddu

Rhaeadr Ddu is accessible from Ganllwyd. Heading north on A470 from Dolgellau, pass Tyn y Groes hotel on the left. Enter town; pass the speed limit sign; note the parking sign on the left point-

Elyn on the footbridge on the Rhaeadr Ddu waterfall walk

ing right. Pass a black-painted town hall with white arched windows on the left. Just beyond on the right is the parking lot and public toilets. Walk down past the black building and enter the path through the gate beside the stream. Climb up the hill on the asphalt lane along the stream; when the road curves to the right, you'll see a waymarker ahead in the woods. Walk to it, turn left, and follow the rocky, slippery trail to the footbridge. The waterfall is on the right. Cross the footbridge, turn right, and walk a little way up the trail for a great view of the falls. Bring a walking stick in case the trail is slippery.

Another walk easily accessible from Dolgellau is the popular 2-mi-long, lowland Brithdir Torrent Walk. It follows the course of the Clywedog River. You stroll downstream past cascades, through gnarled old woodland. From Dolgellau drive 2.5 mi east along A470; then take B4416 (signposted to Brithdir) to a sign on the left-hand side marking

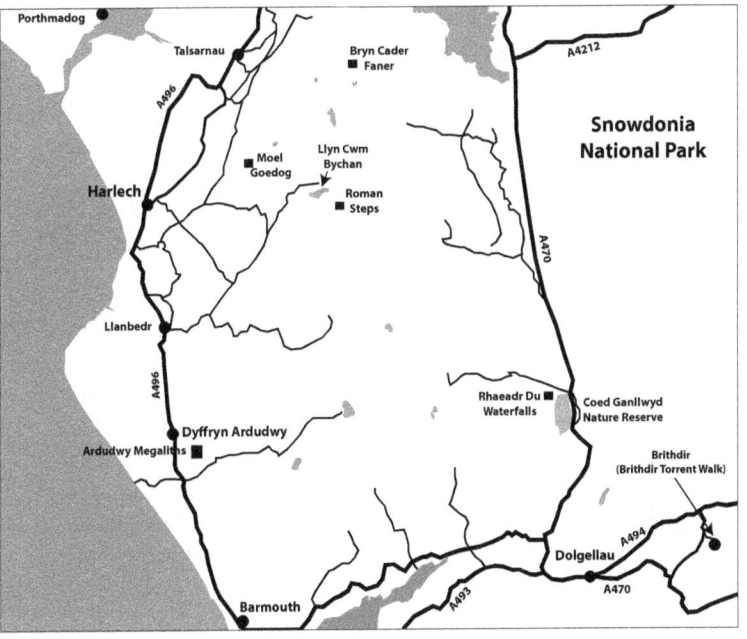

Cambrian Coast area map

the beginning of the walk (http://www.snowdoniaguide.com/torrent_walk.html).

A few miles south of Harlech is the village of Llanbedr. From there, follow the road signs for Cwm Bychan. Llyn Cwm Bychan is a naturally formed lake (*llyn*) that holds brown trout and a fish known locally as the red-bellied char. The char is related to the trout but has been isolated in the lakes high in the mountains for so long it has lost its desire to migrate. It is a beautiful location and views of the tumbling River Artro on the 7-mi ascent are lovely. The canyon road becomes very narrow and you have to respect other drivers; it is often difficult to pass and a fair amount of reversing may be required. There is a car park (fee payable) at the far end of the lake. From there is a path leading to the Roman Steps (http://www.walesdirectory.co.uk/Towns_in_Wales/Harlech_Town.htm).

The Roman Steps are a series of hundreds of steps that climb through the rocks and heather of the Rhinog Mountains. The Roman Steps are probably not Roman; instead, they formed part of a late-medieval trade route for travel between the coast and England, or for transport by packhorse of wool from the Bala area to Pensarn harbor, 2 mi south of Harlech. In the valley, look for wild goats on the rugged hills. Four waymarked trails take in the once-productive gold mines, waterfalls, nature trails, and an old copper works (http://www.visitmidwales.co.uk/Dolgellau-Coed-Ganllwyd-Nature-Reserve/details/?dms=13&venue=1012033).

We recommend purchasing a guidebook for walks in the area. Kittiwake publishes a series that includes *Walking to Mid Wales' Waterfalls* and *Walks Around Coed y Brenin*. The inexpensive booklets include detailed information for walks of various degrees of difficulty and are available from http://www.kittiwake-books.com and at the Dolgellau Tourist Information Office.

Aberdovey (Aberdyfi) and Tre Taliesin, Gwynedd

Aberdovey (Aberdyfi) is a resort at the mouth of the River Dovey (Dyfi). It is highly civilized, with a yacht club, rowing club, golf course, and numerous upscale holiday rentals. A Victorian ballad called "The Bells of Aberdovey" recounts the legend that a great kingdom lies drowned in the nearby sea, and that on quiet evenings one can hear the bells ringing out from beneath the waves (http://en.wikipedia.org/wiki/Aberdyfi). It is possible that such legends of sunken cities are an ancient folk memory of a time 10,000 years ago when the sea level, which had been much lower, began to rise (see p. 27).

On the south side of the Dyfi Estuary is a small village called Tre Taliesin. The name links it with Taliesin, the mythical and medieval bard. Although the village was given this name in the nineteenth century, probably as part of the romantic Welsh Revival, it has an older association with Taliesin. A mile or so to the east of Tre Taliesin is the Bronze Age tumulus known as Bedd Taliesin, which is traditionally regarded as the site of the grave of the Welsh bard.

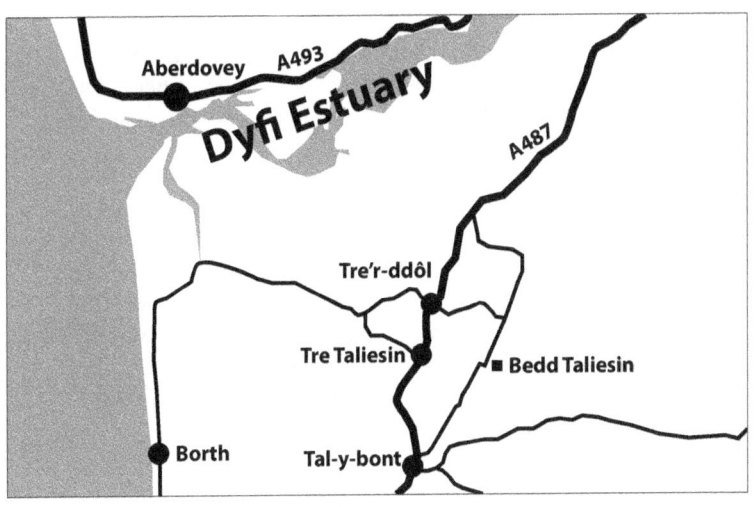

Area map

Taliesin's birth is described in "Hanes Taliesin" (the "Tale of Taliesin"), a story included in Lady Charlotte Guest's 1849 translation of the *Mabinogion*. Subsequent scholarship suggests it was not a part of the original collection written down between 1350-1400, but was written down in the 1600s.

Gwion Bach and the cauldron

"The Tale of Taliesin" is a story in some ways reminiscent of the Irish tales of Fionn Mac Cumhaill. In the Irish story, Fionn is responsible for grilling the salmon of wisdom for someone else. He accidently licks his thumb when the grilling fish splatters it and thus gains the wisdom intended for another.

In the *Mabinogi* tale, the goddess/noblewoman/sorceress Ceridwen (whom we may have encountered at Pentre Ifan) lives on the shores of beautiful Bala Lake in mid Wales. She has a beautiful daughter, Crearwy, and an ugly, stupid son named either Afagddu or Morfan. She wishes him to have respect, so she studies the books of the mystical alchemists known as the Fferyllt and concocts a mixture of herbs. In some versions of the story, she already knows the magical mixture and doesn't need any help.

She sets the concoction to boil for a year and a day in a cauldron. When the potion is ready, the first three drops will confer wisdom and knowledge on whoever imbibes it, but the rest of the liquid will be poison. A blind man stirs the cauldron and a young man named Gwion Bach is hired to keep the fires going. Somehow (details differ), when the potion is ready, three drops bubble forth from the vessel—and into the waiting mouth of Gwion Bach.

> "The Welsh legend of Ceridwen, her cauldron and the potion that changed Gwion Bach into a bard, has been seen as a mythical representation of initiation into the Mysteries" (http://www.the-cauldron.org.uk/thewombofceridwen.htm). In other words, Taliesin has undergone three initiatic "births": the first as Gwion Bach, the second through Ceridwen's womb, and the third when he is named "Shining Brow."

Knowing that Ceridwen will be enraged that he has "stolen" the potion, Gwion Bach flees, and as she chases him and as he flees, they transform into various creatures: he changes into a hare, she into a greyhound; he into a fish, she into an otter; he into a bird, she into a hawk. Finally, he becomes a kernel of corn—which Ceridwen, transformed into a black hen, finds and eats. The transformation continues, however, because she becomes pregnant with Gwion Bach. She gives birth to him but is determined to get rid of him. So she puts him into a wicker, leather-lined basket (or a leather bag) and sends it down river or casts it into the sea.

But the basket is caught at the river's mouth in fishing traps (weirs)—perhaps near Tre Taliesin?—where Prince Elphin of Ceredigion, fishing for salmon, discovers the child. Surprised by the brightness of the child's forehead, he names him Taliesin, which means "Shining Brow." Immediately the child composes beautiful verses, for the wisdom and knowledge he gained from Ceridwen's potion has survived all his transformations. Taliesin becomes a Welsh bard of great renown, perhaps even attending the court of King Arthur.

The Book of Taliesin (Llyfr Taliesin) is a fourteenth-century collection of early manuscripts, some dating from the tenth century, purported to be the poems of

Taliesin rescued from the basket

the sixth-century bard Taliesin (http://en.wikipedia.org/wiki/Taliesin). Scholars believe that some of the poems are the authentic works of this sixth-century poet and that he was not merely a fictional creation. The Welsh monk Nennius, a ninth-century historian, describes Taliesin as an historic figure and a great bard. Myth and history mingle in peculiar ways in Wales, and it is not sufficient to dismiss a legendary character as false.

More to Experience

Aberystwyth, Ceredigion

For a complete change of pace, visit bustling Aberystwyth, AKA "Aber," with its attractive seafront. It is the site of the prestigious Aberystwyth University and the National Library of Wales, with its permanent and changing exhibits (http://www.llgc.org.uk). Library holdings include the oldest extant Welsh text, the twelfth-century *Black Book of Carmarthen,* and the earliest manuscript of the *Mabinogi.* Aberystwyth is an emphatically Welsh town—and proud of it.

Cardigan, Ceredigion

The market town of Cardigan (Aberteifi), Ceredigion, was one of the greatest seaports in Britain until the river Teifi silted up in the nineteenth century. But don't expect to find much of its former glory. It is a town that has seen better times, although its arts and theater scene is growing in importance. The Ceredigion Coast Path starts (or ends) at the Teifi estuary, opposite the Cardigan Heritage Center, and the Pembrokeshire Coast Path ends at St Dogmael's, a mile west of Cardigan town center.

Cardigan is home to the Roman Catholic shrine of Our Lady of Cardigan (AKA Our Lady of the Taper), who holds a flame that is never extinguished (http://en.wikipedia.

org/wiki/Our_Lady_of_Cardigan). According to the story, the shrine was originally founded in the twelfth century, after the discovery of a buried statue of the Virgin Mary holding a burning candle. For centuries it was a place of pilgrimage, but in 1538, after the dissolution of the monasteries, the original image was taken away and burned. In the mid-1950s a new statue was carved, and fourteen years later a new shrine was consecrated.

"Come see the cardigan in Cardigan": In 2010, over 200 knitters from as far away as New Brunswick, Canada, knit pieces of a giant cardigan to mark Cardigan's 900th anniversary. The sweater is 16.4 ft wide by 8 ft long. Its multiple designs, including knitted mermaids, coracles, portraits of people, and castles, provide a 3D fiber-art view of the culture, history, and architecture of the town. The peripatetic cardigan has been displayed in different galleries in Cardigan.

The cardigan of Cardigan

Mwnt Church, Ceredigion

About 3.5 mi to the north of Cardigan is Mwnt's Church of the Holy Cross. It is beautifully situated, sheltered behind a headland hill from the fierce Atlantic storms and prospective sea raiders. It gets its name Mwnt (pro. "moont," means "mound") from the steep, 250-ft-high conical hill beside it.

> Lord Cardigan led the Charge of the Light Brigade in 1854; the button-front woolen sweater is named after him. The name of the town of Cardigan is anglicized from the Welsh Ceredigion, meaning "Ceredig's land."

Mwnt Church

The oldest church in Ceredigion, Mwnt was on the Pilgrims' Way to Bardsey Island, as well as on the Pilgrims' Way to St Davids. The church stands above an attractive, sandy cove, site of a Flemish invasion in 1155 that was repelled. Over the centuries, many pilgrims (alive or dead) traveled by sea from Mwnt to Bardsey.

The stolid, primitive, whitewashed little church with a slate roof dates from the thirteenth or fourteenth century, but its foundations date back to the sixth. Its raised oval churchyard, surrounded by stone walls like an Iron Age fort, is evidence of its great age. The remains of an Iron Age fort have been found between it and the sheltering hill. A 5-ft-high stone wall surrounds the churchyard. The path to the church and church itself appear to have been dug into the churchyard, which rises 3-5 ft above the level of the path. The church is surrounded by a drainage ditch. Whether the churchyard grew up over time or the church was dug into it, we could not determine.

The churchyard seen from the entry to Mwnt Church

Take time to center yourself in the church and open yourself to see, sense, and feel your surroundings. Experience the energy both within and without the cave-like shelter. You might even hike up the cone-shaped hill, where there used to be a stone preaching cross and a mortuary chapel, but be careful of the powerful wind on the seaward side. For more information, http://www.welsh-cottages.co.uk/ceredigion/mwntchurch.php.

> "A short path leads like a gully from the gate to a door so low it must be entered stooping, until surrounded by solid walls of leaning stone. It is like entering the chamber of a dolmen." Hughes, p. 176.

Brecon Beacons National Park (extending through several counties)

The Brecon Beacons has it all. It's a hill-hiker's delight, complete with megaliths, Roman roads, challenging summits, and easier moorlands. Within the park boundaries are excellent restaurants and accommodations. History and legend morph in this romantic wilderness, in this expanse of nature where fork-tailed red kites soar and wheel in the air, and where a faery who lived in a lake taught her half-human sons how to be healers. (Elyn)

Walking in the Brecon Beacons National Park is like walking across the skin of Mother Wales. One of three Welsh National Parks (the others are Pembrokeshire Coast and Snowdonia), it is the least crowded. It covers 520 sq mi and is wider than it is high. It encompasses the Black Mountain range in the west, porous limestone caves and waterfalls in the southwest, the Brecon Beacons range in the center, and the Black Mountains in the east (http://www.breconbeacons.org/).

Ferran Blasco reminds us that "Nature is the true temple," and in the Brecons we enter into an expanse of place uncluttered and only minimally developed for human purposes. Visiting the Brecons is an opportunity to remember that places can be sacred in and of themselves, not because humans have claimed them and named them holy.

The western Beacons include the uplands of Black Mountain (Mynydd Ddu). Although the name is singular, Black Mountain is actually a range of unpopulated barren peaks and high moorland that tower over streams and glacial lakes. Between the Black Mountain and central Beacons is Fforest Fawr (Great Forest), a range of mostly unforested sandstone hills, administered by UNESCO as a geopark. The name "forest" comes from an old use of the word to indicate a hunting ground. Fforest Fawr is known for its

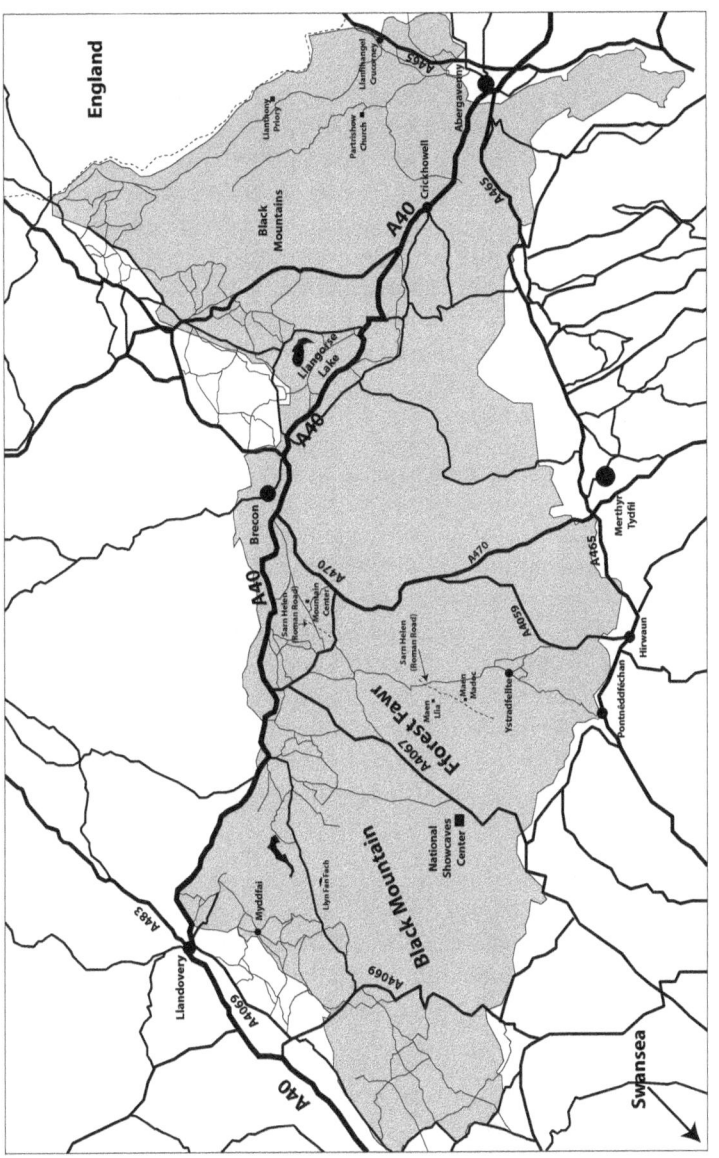

Brecon Beacons National Park

rushing streams and spectacular waterfalls, many of them near the village of Ystradfellte. To the south is the National Showcaves Center (admission charge; http://www.showcaves.co.uk/).

The central Brecon Beacons (Bannau Brycheiniog) are high, flat-topped hills that include Pen y Fan (2907 ft) and Corn Du (2863 ft), the two highest peaks in south Wales. The most popular walk in the park is to climb these two. To the southeast is the Usk Valley, a wide, fertile land that is heavily populated and filled with castles, churches, ruins, and excellent restaurants and accommodations—and more hiking trails. In the northeast of the park are the Black Mountains (Y Mynyddoedd Duon), a wild region of tiny villages buried in crevices in the rolling green hills and heath-covered ridges.

There is much to experience in this varied landscape. Some places can only be visited on foot, either during a short stroll or a long hike. Three long-distance trails include The Beacons Way, a 100-mi-long hiking trail from Abergavenny to Llangadog (http://www.breconbeaconsparksociety.org); the Taff Trail, a walking and cycling route from Cardiff in the south to Brecon in the north (http://www.tafftrail.org.uk/); and Offa's Dyke Path, based on the original 178-mi-long fortification (see p. 215), which runs along the eastern fringe and passes by Llanthony Priory (see pp. 212-216).

 Car, bus, or train can reach other sites. A detailed guidebook to the Brecon Beacons will provide the information you need for a few days or a week of exploration, including various kinds of transportation (http://www.breconbeacons.org).

We'll focus on two places you can reach by car: a legendary powerful place—a faery lake—and a Roman road, built because of a dream.

Myddfai and Llyn y Fan Fach, Carmarthenshire
N51 57 21 W3 47 20

The legend of the Physicians of Myddfai (Meddygon Myddfai) takes place in the Black Mountain area, in the western part of the park. The story goes that a faery lady lived in Llyn y Fan Fach with her faery cattle. A young farmer saw her and fell hopelessly in love. He courted her with gifts of bread. The first was too hard; the second too soft; the third, half-cooked, was just right. At last he was permitted to marry her, but with the condition that if he struck her three times, she and her faery cattle would return to the lake.

They married and lived happily, and she gave birth to three sons. Unfortunately, her husband lightly struck her three times, each time for behaving inappropriately by human standards. Sadly, she took her livestock and returned to her watery abode. However, she returned in secret to teach her eldest son, Rhiwallon (or Riwallon), herbal remedies.

> Ros Briagha Foskett (http://www.rosbriagha.org) suggests that this is really a story about farmers meeting up with hunter-gatherers or herders. The latter were smaller, indigenous people, the former larger because of their better nutritional status. The offering of bread thus represents the offer of agriculture. Perhaps the cattle are a faint memory of reindeer herding. There may also be echoes of a shifting balance between masculine and feminine, since the faery lady is quite strong willed and in charge of her own destiny—and does not accept physical abuse.

History and legend morph in this story, for the healers of Myddfai, said to descend from this faery mother, did exist and Myddfai was an important healing center. Rhiwallon was a famous doctor, physician to Lord Rhys and/or his son Rhys Gryg, benefactor of Strata Florida and lord of Dinefwr (see pp. 162-169) in the late twelfth century. Rhiwallon and his three sons (and maybe their sons) wrote down their remedies and guidelines for healthy living. Their treatise is included in *The Red Book of Hergest*, a manuscript completed in the years following 1382. These early documents show that the Myddfai physicians were quite advanced for the period; in fact, some of their herbal remedies are still in use.

A Myddfai herbalist

Although Myddfai might seem isolated, over the centuries the physicians of Myddfai exchanged medical knowledge and personnel with the important medical school in Salerno, Italy, and they were familiar with the work of Hippocrates, Galen, and Avicenna. The last direct descendant (through the male line) of the Physicians of Myddfai was Dr. John Jones, who died in 1739 or 1743 and whose gravestone can be seen in the porch of St Michael's Church—more than 500 years after the first physician plied his trade.

Another source, however, says the last direct descendent died in 1842. Robin Gwyndaf writes (p. 198) that in the twentieth century, direct descendents of the family (through the female line) continued to practice medicine

> Robin Gwyndaf calls this story "one of the best known and best loved of all Welsh folk narratives since the *Mabinogion*." He also points out (p. 196) that "From the fourteenth century onwards the fame of the Myddfai Physicians is well attested in Welsh literature. Yet there is no recorded tradition connecting them with fairy descent prior to the printed version published in 1821 and that of Williams in 1861."

Packer (p. 17) says that some researchers think "that the famous [Myddfai] physicians, consulted by St Louis of France in the second half of the thirteenth century and claimed to have been among the most renowned medical practitioners of the middle ages, had derived their medicines from Druid lore." However, he thinks it " more likely that their remedies were the product of contact with Moorish medicine along the pilgrim route [to Santiago de Compostela]."

in Wales. We have also been told that descendents of the physicians are practicing medicine in other countries, including the USA (http://www.myddfai.com/salerno-myddfai.aspx).

At the center of the village is St Michael's Church, which is probably 1000 years old. Ty Talcen, the new community center/café, offers Myddfai-brand organic herbs, herbal teas, and specialty bath products for sale, part of a community development initiative started in 2010 (http://www.myddfai.com/). For guided herb walks, contact medical herbalist LaraBernays@hotmail.com. There is also a 5-mi-long walk (about 2.5 hours) called "The Physi-

Entrance to the town of Myddfai

cians Trail." You can pick up a brochure for the trail at Ty Talcen, where the trail begins. The faery lake, Llyn y Fan Fach, is not part of the Physicians Trail, though it can be reached on foot via a different route. Located beneath the scree-buttressed summits of the Carmarthen Fans, it is an evocative sight, especially when viewed from the summits.

Getting There

Drive A40 to Llandovery. In the town turn on Bridge Street and cross the river. The way to Myddfai (3 mi south) is well signposted from there.

Sarn (H)elen, Brecon Beacons
N51 55 35 W3 29 57

Traces of Sarn Helen, the name given to Welsh Roman roads, can be found in the Brecon Beacons. The name "Elen" refers to one of the additional tales in the *Mabinogi*, "The Dream of Macsen Wledig." Magnus Maximus (Macsen Wledig in Welsh) dreams of a beautiful maiden sitting on a red-gold throne, dressed in gold. He falls in love with her and cannot rest until he finds her. He sets off for Caernarfon (a town in northwestern Wales), where he meets Elen Lluyddog ("Elen of the Hosts") and courts her successfully. At her request, he gives Elen the three islands of Britain and stays in Britain—thus, according to Welsh legend, transferring sovereignty of Wales back to the original Britons.

Elen proceeds to build roads from one Roman fortress to another to protect her domain. These roads are called Elen's Roads or Sarn Helen. After spending seven years in

Sarn (H)elen

Wales, Macsen Wledig loses his throne. But, according to legend, he enlists a Welsh army, marches on Rome, and regains his power. The two rule happily ever after.

Myth and history intertwine in (H)elen's legend. There was a Roman emperor named Magnus Maximus. Born in Spain, he became a Legionary commander in Britain, assembled a Celtic army, and was Emperor of the Western Roman Empire from 383-388 CE. He married Elen Luyddog, "Elen of the Hosts," daughter of a Welsh chieftain. He was defeated in battle in 388 and beheaded at the direction of the Eastern Roman Emperor. Whether (H)elen had

"Sarn" refers to an ancient paved road or causeway; "Helen" is a confusion generated from mistaking Elen Lluyddog for the Roman St Helene, mother of Constantine the Great (see Prevett, pp. 55-57).

(H)elen of the Roads, Elen of the Ways, and Elen of the Hosts are associated by the Welsh with Beltane, with fire and light, and with the land. "She is certainly a pre-Roman goddess, and possibly much older than the Celts. The first trackways across Britain are said to have been reindeer tracks; Elain is Welsh for deer, and it is possible that Elen is one of the horned goddesses portrayed in Celtic art, such as the two figures found at Lackford and Icklingham. Female reindeer are the only female deer that grow antlers; they died out in Britain at the end of the last Ice Age, so race memories of her must be very ancient indeed. Some of the Sarn Elen tracks are associated with the Wild Hunt, led in some places by the Horned God, and in others by the Death Goddess. Some say that the tracks we call ley lines are spirit paths that the souls of the dead travel to the afterlife." http://www.merciangathering.com/elen.htm, retrieved 12 Dec. 2011.

anything to do with building roads is unknown.

Bits and pieces of Sarn Helen (Elen's Road) can still be seen, stretching some 160 mi from Aberconwy in the north to Carmarthen in the south and connecting various Roman sites. Another Sarn Helen passes through the Brecon Beacons, across the bleak moorlands of Fforest Fawr. Possibly Sarn Helen was based on old "straight tracks" long predating the Romans.

Emperor Magnus Maximus and Elen of the Roads

The modern Sarn Helen Trail is a challenging long-distance mountain bike route (http://mbruk.co.uk/mbruk_SarnHelenTrail_details.htm). It runs 270 mi from Conwy to Gower, loosely following the old Roman route and passing through Snowdonia and the Brecon Beacons. One can also walk a trail called Sarn Helen Way, but it is not well marked. Long stretches of it are now buried beneath modern highways, while other sections have been lost (http://www.ldwa.org.uk).

Several megaliths in the Fforest Fawr area of the Brecons seem to be associated with Sarn Helen (http://www.breconbeacons.org/visit-us/about-the-brecon-beacons/standing-stones). The impressive diamond-shaped standing stone known as Maen Llia is located between Ystradfellte and Sennybridge, a short distance from the minor road leading from Ystradfellte to Heol Senni. The 13-ft-tall megalith is visible for miles at the junction of two valleys. It may have marked an ancient trackway; at any rate, it is located quite near what became Sarn Helen. It is a short walk from the road to the megalith. Maen Madoc is an 11-ft-tall standing stone, located alongside Sarn Helen and perfectly aligned with Maen Llia, 2 mi away.

One short stretch of Sarn Helen is located near the Brecon Beacons Visitor Center near Libanus, southwest of Brecon. This short stretch of Roman road is easy to reach on a short walk but very difficult to see. Inquire at the information desk and see if they can help.

Getting There

To reach the Brecon Beacons National Park Mountain Center turn south from A40 to A470 for about 7 mi. There is good signage for where to turn on the minor road into the center. To visit Sarn Helen inquire at the information desk in the center. For instructions about reaching the Maen Llia and Maen Madoc standing stones visit http://www.brecon-beacons.com/archaelogy-Sarn-Helen-Maen-Madoc-Maen-Llia.htm.

More to Experience
Brecon (Aberhonddu), Powys

Brecon (Aberhonddu) is a lively town located at the northern edge of the Brecon Beacons. It has numerous services, several outdoor equipment stores, bookstores, coffee shops, a large cathedral, a promenade along the River Usk, and touristy canal-boat cruises on the Monmouth and Brecon canal (http://www.brecontown.co.uk/). It's a nice place

River Usk in Brecon

to use as a base for exploring the region. Inside St Mary's Church is a somewhat quirky luncheon café and coffee shop, offering fresh fare; the proceeds help support the costs of maintaining the church.

The Brecon Beacons Mountain Center (the National Park Visitor Center) is 6 mi to the southwest off the A470 (turn off at Libanus and drive 1.5 mi). On summer bank holidays and Sundays, it is possible to explore the Beacons on the Beacons Bus from Brecon (http://www.travelbreconbeacons.info).

Getting There

Brecon is just off A40 in the north-central area of Brecon Beacons National Park (see map on p. 195).

Abergavenny (Y Fenni), Brecon Beacons

Abergavenny (Y Fenni), on the eastern edge of the Brecon Beacons National Park, is a foodie haven. It has excellent restaurants and is the site of the annual Food

Abergavenny Castle

Festival in September, one of the most prestigious in Britain (http://www.abergavennyfoodfestival.co.uk). The ruined medieval castle, site of a treacherous massacre of Welsh leaders by the English, is atmospheric and has an interesting museum. The parish church of St Mary contains numerous medieval tombs and effigies, including a twice-life-size recumbent statue of King David. Abergavenny is a good location for exploring the Black Mountains and nearby villages.

Getting There

Abergavenny is on A40 in the southeast part of Brecon Beacons National Park (see map on p. 195).

Llangorse Lake (Llyn Syfaddan), Brecon Beacons

Llangors Lake (Llyn Syfaddan) is the largest natural lake in south Wales, with the only intact *crannog* (artificial island) in England or Wales. It is a short drive from Brecon.

The crannog *in Llangorse Lake*

The well-done interpretive center includes a thatched building and information plaques; it extends out from the shore and describes the ninth-century crannog and the local ecology. The twelfth-century chronicler Gerald of Wales reported a local legend about a submerged city under the waters.

Llangorse Lake is popular for water-sports enthusiasts, but when we were there in September (off season), it was a lovely, peaceful area, with white swans and ducks floating on the water, birds chirping, reeds and rushes rustling with the breeze. See http://www.breconbeacons.com/llangorse-lake.htm.

Getting There

Llangorse Lake is located 8 mi from Brecon on a minor road off A40.

Patrisio (Partrishow) Church and Holy Well, Powys

N51 53 45 W3 3 5

It was an adventure to get to Patrisio Church, the twisting roller-coaster country lane hemmed in by hedgerows, but we found our way and parked outside the imposing lychgate. The church perches precariously on the side of a hill; tombstones line the path leading to its doors. The main sanctuary was a spooky place, however, and we were eager to leave. We walked outside and entered the low doorway into the original chapel, perhaps St Issui's hermit cell. I took a deep breath and slowly exhaled. This place felt peaceful and sweet, simple and comforting. Perhaps the saint's spirit abides there still. (Elyn)

Sign to Patrisio Church

The narrow country lane winds its way deeper and deeper into the valley of the Grwyne Fawre, at the eastern edge of the Black Mountains but still within the Brecon Beacons National Park. Expectations rise as you journey deep into this isolated, hidden landscape. A sharp turn over a tributary of the Grwyne Fawr, a steep rise up the hill—and there is Partrishow Church of Merthyr Issui (Martyred Issui), dark grey stone silhouetted against the deep green hillside. The churchyard's edge is a near vertical drop. The setting is exceptional.

Legend says that Issui, a sixth-century Celtic missionary, built a hut beside the stream in the hollow below the church. There, beside a spring, he devoted himself to healing the

Entrance to Patrisio Church

sick and preaching until an ungrateful traveler killed him. One account explains that, in the public mind, his healing powers were transferred to the well, which acquired a great reputation. A more likely story is that the holy well was famous long before the Christian saint arrived, and Issui's healing powers came in part from the well.

Because of St Issui's sanctity and the healing waters, the site became a place of pilgrimage. In the eleventh century the waters cured a wealthy leper. In gratitude he left money to build a church higher up on the hill. Later the building was expanded.

Along the south wall of the current, somewhat reconstructed church are two doors. The western door, which you encounter first, leads into an older chapel (the Shrine Chapel), probably the original eleventh-century church. The eastern door, with its fourteenth-century covered porch, opens into a slightly more modern chapel.

Patrisio Holy Well

The Shrine Chapel

This latter church is famous for its ornately carved wooden rood screen and the frescoes on its walls. Winged dragons writhe at the ends of the elaborate fifteenth-century rood screen, intertwining with oak leaves and grapes. Faded frescoes decorate the thick, whitewashed walls, their scriptural texts and sober admonitions painted over earlier apocalyptic images. The Grim Reaper (or Time, or Death), with its sweeping scythe, spade, and hourglass, has gradually emerged from its coat of whitewash, demonstrating the impossibility of denying the inevitable.

Below the great figure of Death are the eleventh-century font and the parish chest, said to be the oldest in the country. At the back of the church, on the same west wall as the Grim Reaper, is a deep-set "squint" that resembles a barred window. It provides a view into (and from) the older chapel.

We (Gary and Elyn) found the newer church unsettling and eerie. We felt chilled by more than the rain and wind that blew around the windows and battered at the door. We quickly exited the main sanctuary and entered the Shrine Chapel. The atmosphere changed immediately. Here was peace and calm, tranquility, a gentle sweetness. Later, a local Welshman told us he, too, had felt an unpleasant shiver go up

> Patrisio's is "the definitive Welsh mountain church. Each of the eras of the church—the Celtic reverence for spirit of place; the Catholic screened rituals and relics; the Protestant plastering with the Word—are encapsulated here in a way which tells the spiritual history of Wales with especial clarity." Hughes, p. 181.

his spine when he entered the church, and he, too, had left in a hurry.

The roof in the Shrine Chapel dates from the fourteenth century. For many years the small chapel was used as storeroom, but in 1991 it was refurbished and rededicated to the purpose for which it was clearly intended. An attractive modern statue of Celtic St Issui is placed in a niche on the east wall.

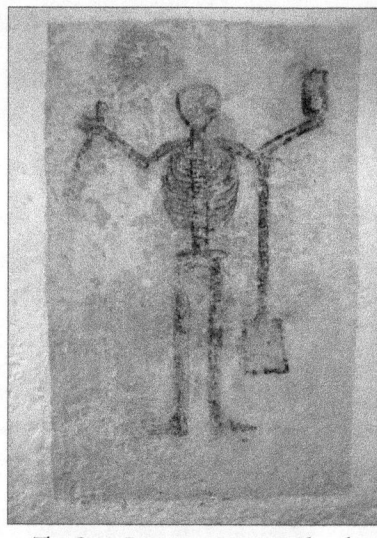

The Grim Reaper in Patrisio Church

A slightly damaged medieval preaching cross still stands in the churchyard. It is probable that in 1188 Archbishop Baldwin preached the Third Crusade from this cross, in the presence of Giraldus Cambrensis (Gerald of Wales) and a group of local Christians. Although today the church and its yard seem isolated, that was not always the case. According to Canon Arthur Reed, former rector of Patrisio, "Until fairly recent times, the main road from Abergavenny to Talgarth, and so into mid-Wales, came this way."

The unsignposted spring is located in the wooded hollow downhill from the church, where the road makes a sharp turn near the parking turnout. Stand in the parking area, face back uphill to the church. Notice Nant Mair (St Mary's stream) flowing from left to right. Embedded in the ground to the right of the road is a flat pilgrim stone incised with the Maltese cross. Notice

---

An excellent exercise in sensing subtle energies is to spend time in both sections of the church, the Shrine Chapel and the newer chapel, and notice the differences. They are both sanctified spaces, connected—and separated—by a wall. Center yourself, breathe, and sit in silence for a few minutes. Pay attention to how you feel, what you sense and smell. What do you notice? Then do the same in the other sacred space. What do you notice? Why might that be?

Detail of the rood screen in Patrisio Church

the stone wall on the right; the well is around the corner of the wall that faces the pilgrim stone. Flat paving stones lead the way. Homemade crosses of bark and twigs decorate the stone ledge beside the spring, along with an unusual assortment of broken pencils, shells, stones with inscribed prayers, pinecones, water-drenched candles, and plastic toys. People continue to come to this holy well and leave offerings.

Getting There

Drive on A465 north from Abergavenny, turning left into the Honddu Valley. Continue on minor roads to the site, which is well marked. The plaque on the lychgate says the church is open every day. The rectory is in Llangenni (tel.: (0)1873 812 593), and it might be worth calling first. There is space for two cars to park beside the lychgate near the church. If there is no room, drive back down the hill and park at the turnout near the stream and holy well. Or, better yet, park below and approach the church on foot: you will have a sense of "getting there," not just arriving.

Llanthony Priory, Monmouthshire
N51 56 39 W3 2 9

We wandered through the immense grey stone ruins, trying to visualize what the priory had once looked like. Long ago, black-robed Augustinian canons strolled through the stone halls, prayed in the spacious sanctuary. But now, an interior colonnade of rhythmically repeating arches opens onto green grass and the tree-covered hills beyond. Perhaps instead of wondering why so little remains, I should be surprised that so much still stands. (Elyn)

In the Black Mountains, halfway up (or down) the Vale of Ewyas, are the ruins of Llanthony Priory, a thirteenth-century Augustinian priory and once one of the great medieval buildings in Wales. Llanthony may be a corruption of the Welsh "Llan-ddewi-nant-honddu," which means the

Ruins of Llanthony Priory

> Gerald of Wales wrote that here "is a site most suited to the practice of religion and better chosen for canonical discipline than that of any of the other monasteries in the whole Island of Britain." Quoted by Main, p. 111.

"ancient parish/sacred enclosure of St David on the River Honddu." The setting is wild and beautiful, with rushing river and windswept mountains. The location is a favorite for hikers on Offa's Dyke Path, which runs along the Hatterall Ridge behind the ruins.

Legend says that in the sixth century, St David came to this isolated place and built a cell on what is now the site of St David's Parish Church. In the eleventh century the Norman knight William de Lacy was lost in the woods and came across the remains of St David's cell. He was so captivated by the place that he renounced his sinful, worldly life and founded a hermitage on the site, rebuilding the ruined shelter. Soon after, in 1103, Ernisius, chaplain to Queen Matilda, wife of Henry I, came to visit de Lacy. He, too, found himself drawn to this powerful place. Together they built a church, and soon others with a religious vocation joined them. The first Augustinian priory in Wales grew out of this, established no later than 1120, with Ernisius as prior.

The current ruins are the remains of what were once a magnificent church and extensive buildings, erected be-

Llanthony Priory in 1734

tween 1175-1230. This was an isolated area, however, with many brigands roaming the hills, and occasionally the canons were killed or forced to flee. Trouble hit Llanthony again in 1399 during the revolt of Welsh nationalist Owain Glendower.

> The Augustinians are known as the Black Canons because of the color of their habits. They are canons, not monks. Each canon is an ordained priest, hence responsible for preaching and leading local services. This is not as introspective an order as the Benedictines or Cistercians.

Revenues were hard to collect during times of upheaval, and the old priory gradually lost much of its importance. In 1538 it fell victim to the dissolution of the monasteries and was sold to the Chief Justice of Ireland. In 1790 it was sold to Colonel Wood of Brecon, who transformed the south tower of the west front into a shooting lodge. In 1807 the temperamental English poet Walter Savage Landor acquired the property, hoping to restore it. He planted numerous beech, larch, and chestnut trees, but he failed to get on with the locals, and eventually had to leave. Gradually, the priory fell further into ruin, but

Llanthony Priory Hotel

> For 1500 years people have been drawn to this place—long before it was the site of a major medieval priory. St David, de Lacy, and Ernisius are only a few of the religious seekers drawn to the spot. Is there something here, intrinsic in the location (its isolation, its beauty, perhaps its earth energies) that encourages a spiritual life? Spend time meditating in the ruins and see what you experience.

in the twentieth century it was taken under the care of Cadw, which has provided protection and information plaques.

The thirteenth-century Church of St David, across the driveway from the priory ruins, is a powerful place, constructed on the site where St David lived and where de Lacy and Ernisius built their church in 1108. The current church was originally the infirmary for the priory. It served the sick and needy, as well as being a place of worship. Today it is the parish church and services are held regularly. It has been a location of worship and retreat for 1500 years. Spend time in the church, seeing what you sense and feel.

Llanthony Priory Hotel (AKA The Abbey Hotel) is built in part out of the 1790s hunting lodge. It claims a twelfth-century bar and unusual tower rooms—without plumbing, as befits a twelfth-century priory. It's a good place for lunch and local brewed ales (http://www.Llanthonyprioryhotel.co.uk).

A section of Offa's Dyke Path runs along the ridge behind the priory. The Path is 177 mi long and follows what remains of the eighth-century earthwork divide, constructed to separate Wales and England. It is strenuous and best walked from south to north (http://www.offas-dyke.co.uk).

Getting There

Drive on A465 north from Abergavenny, turning left into the village of Llanfihangel Crucorney (see map on p. 195). Turn left after the Skirrid Mountain Inn and drive for about 5 mi to Llanthony Priory, on the right.

Radnor Forest, Cascob Church, and St Michael's Church in Discoed, Powys

I asked permission from the ancient yew to draw near, then pressed my back against its rough, expansive trunk. I felt something almost like static, as if something was gently stroking my energy field. The Discoed yew is said to be 5000 years old, but it may be only 2000 or maybe 3000 years of age. Only. Imagine! I had never been so close to a living being that is so old. I asked myself and I asked the tree: What is it like to live so long, and live it as a tree? (Elyn)

Radnor Forest, with its deep ravines and forested hillsides, conifer woods and broad, featureless plateaus, is a popular hiking and bird-watching area. It is a rock dome, a forest only in the medieval sense of "an unenclosed place to hunt."

It is surrounded by lush green hills and filled with an abundance of churches dedicated to St Michael, archangelic victor over dragons. "Mihangel" is Welsh for St Michael, and "Llanfihangel" means something like "sacred enclosure of St Michael." The ley-hunter Alfred Watkins devoted a great deal of study to Radnor Vale. He discovered that it is an area with numerous ley lines.

It is said that the last Welsh dragon is sleeping in Radnor Forest and that four churches dedicated to St Michael were built around the edges of the forest to

St Michael the Archangel is often represented in Western Christian iconography as an angelic warrior holding a lance with which he pins down a dragon, serpent, or devil. This has been variously interpreted as referring to his conquering the indigenous earth-centered religions, conquering the materialist ego, or controlling the telluric energies that flow under the location dedicated to the archangel. Many St Michael's churches are built on high places, and many are built over pre-Christian sacred sites and caves. In Carnac, Brittany, St Michael's Chapel is perched on top of a very large mound that covers an ancient passage grave. (See *Powerful Places in Brittany*, p. 44; http://www.ancient-wisdom.co.uk/stmichael.htm.)

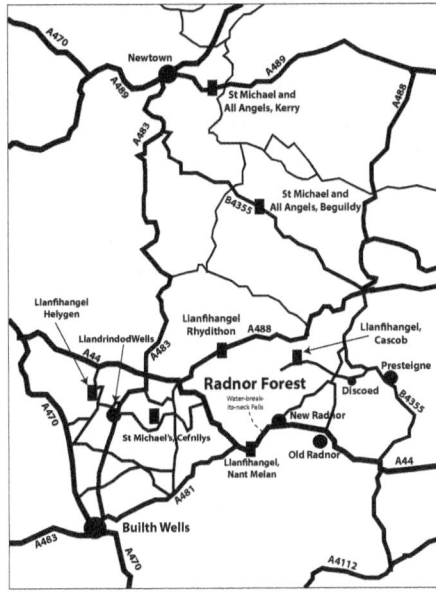

St Michael churches in the Radnor Forest area

imprison it. The four churches are Llanfihangel Cascob, Llanfihangel Nant Melan, Llanfihangel Cefnllys, and Llanfihangel Rhydithon. If any of these churches is destroyed, the legend asserts, the dragon will awake from its slumber and escape, wreaking havoc on the land.

Perhaps in Radnor Forest the dragon is a metaphor for unstable earth energy. According to Laurence Main (p. 77), St Michael "slays or tames the raw dragon energy of the spirit force in the leys and puts it to good use." Or perhaps the encircled, sleeping dragon refers to Druidic traditions and their conquest (or immobilization) by Christianity.

St Michael's Church, Cascob, Powys

N52 17 26 W3 06 59

Although Cascob is no longer on the road to anywhere, until 1767 it was part of the Great Road from London to Aberystwyth. Built on a mound, the tiny St Michael and All Angels Church is one of the four that guard the sleeping dragon. The name "Cascob" probably derives from Cascope, "a mound overlooking the Gas," Gas being the name of the stream running nearby.

It is possible that the thirteenth-century church was built over a prehistoric burial mound. It has a very large, irregular, D-shaped churchyard, filled with impressive, powerful trees—including a huge female yew at the far end, southwest of the imposing church tower. The yew's trunk is 25 ft in circumference. When we were there, the yew appeared to be the favorite resting place for the sheep that grazed freely in the churchyard.

The size and shape of the churchyard, and what might be the remains of an earthen rampart surrounding it, indicate this might have been a Bronze Age settlement, although no artifacts indicate who was here before (Gregory, pp. 115-116). The place has the feel of great age.

For most people, the fame of the church comes not from its role guarding a sleeping dragon but from the "Abraca-

St Michael's Church, Cascob

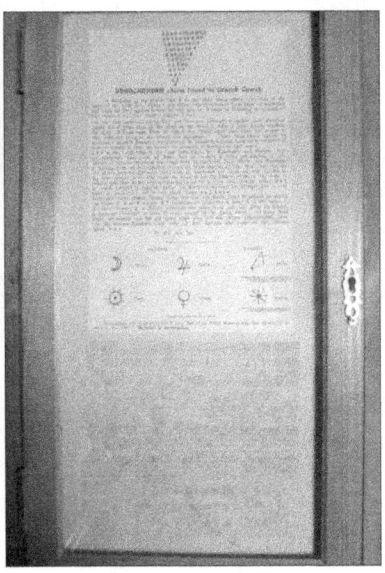

The Abracadabra charm

dabra charm," dating from 1700. The charm was discovered either buried in the churchyard or in the church archives, depending on who tells the story. Mysterious motifs, astrological symbols, a mixture of English and mock Latin, and the word "abracadabra," repeated in truncated form to create an inverted triangle, are handwritten in faded ink on an old piece of parchment.

Scholarly decipherment indicates that the charm was cast to drive out evil spirits besetting a parishioner, Elizabeth Lloyd. Some of the phrases were taken directly from writings by Dr John Dee, court astrologer, mathematician, and occultist to Queen Elizabeth I. Since the family home of John Dee is at Nant-y-groes, 2 mi away, one wonders whether perhaps he was directly connected with the amulet.

Cascob Church is a strange church, hunkering down, its west square tower rising from a mound that was probably put there for structural reasons. Its north side is virtually without windows; only two tiny slits in the stone wall let in light. According to TJ Hughes (p. 136), the north side of the church is the traditional shield against the devil, so perhaps this lack of doors or windows is an effort to provide an unbroken barrier against evil. Even the east wall, which usually has a large window to welcome the rising sun, symbol of resurrection, has only a small opening. Maybe the lack of windows has something to do with the prevailing winds rather than with fear of the devil.

The inside of the church has none of the closed-off, guarded feeling of the exterior. When we were there, several displays of fresh flowers brightened the sanctuary. The parchment charm was actually of little interest, an oddity for the curious locked behind a glass display cabinet attached to the wall on the north side of the nave. We had expected to find a church steeped in esotericism or occultism; instead, we found a homey church that smelled of fresh herbs. Maybe we missed something hidden and deep; maybe not.

The church was restored in 1895 and redecorated in 1965. A fine oak screen dates from the fourteenth century;

Tiles in the floor at the altar

Ancient yew tree in the churchyard

in the sanctuary are a triangular aumbry (wall cabinet for holding ritual items) and a square piscine (basin for holding holy water) from the thirteenth century. The octagonal font is from the fourteenth century.

William Jenkins Rees was rector of Cascob from 1806-1855. He played an important part in the revival of the Welsh National Eisteddfod and was editor of the Welsh Manuscripts Society. We wonder whether his interest in the past was encouraged by the time he spent at Cascob Church.

The churchyard has a number of impressive trees, including, but not limited to, the powerful yew in the southwest. Wander around; see if you are attracted to one tree or another. Ask permission to approach and, if granted, spend time experiencing the nature of that tree. If you have time and interest, do the same with another tree that draws your attention.

A group called Friends of Cascob Church is responsible for raising money to keep the church in repair. Norma Olds is the prime mover in this project. She lives in the cottage across

> When we first visited Cascob, the church was locked and no one was in the cottage across the road. So we spent time walking around the churchyard, visiting the trees. We felt that, even from outside, the church had a strong, powerful atmosphere. Was this because of the building itself, or did the "atmosphere" come from other things like the setting, the landscape, the trees—and especially the huge female yew?

the road and has the church key; her telephone number is (0)1547.560.331. It might be wise to call ahead.

Getting There

Drive on B4355 north from Presteigne, turning left on a minor road (see map on p. 217). The churchyard is entered through a gateway between a large stone building on the left (once a school, now a private home) and a red phone booth on the right. Beware of stinging nettles along the fence line; if stung, look for dockweed growing nearby (see photos, p. 37).

Entry gate to the churchyard

St Michael's Church, Discoed, Powys
N52 16 34 W3 03 42

St Michael's Church in Discoed (also spelled Disgoed and Discoyd) is 3 mi east of Casgob. In the front yard, to

the left of the main entrance, is a 5000-year-old (or maybe 3000- or 2000-year-old) male yew. There are two yews in the churchyard. The largest, which is split down the trunk, is the oldest. Like most churches dedicated to St Michael, it is on a slight rise above the surrounding countryside. It is medieval but with extensive Victorian modifications. The churchyard is raised, an indication of great age.

> The center of the yew tree's trunk is long gone, now cavernous and empty. Its grayish-red branches are twisted and gnarled, but new green sprouts and sprigs spring forth—verdant demonstration of why the yew is linked with regeneration and renewal.

When we visited, an art and craft exhibit was being installed in the church. Although the church is still sanctified for worship, the congregation has diminished and the minister is only present once a month. In order to help raise money for maintenance and repair, the church is often scheduled for other, secular events—including exhibitions and small-scale musical events.

Spend time with the ancient male yew tree. Ask permission to approach, and if you sense a "yes," enter the tree's aura slowly. Pamela Petro (2005) writes about the "slow breath of stone," but here is your opportunity to experience the slow breath of the yew tree—not as old as stone but more responsive. Contemplate its age. Imagine what might have been happening here when the yew was planted. Perhaps it

Interior of St Michael's Church, Discoed

> We initially found the multi-functionality of Discoed church (and the café in St Mary's Church, Brecon) unusual, but we later learned that Welsh churches have always been multifunctional, serving as community halls as well as places of worship. The north side of the churchyard was often used for ball games, markets, and patronal feasts, complete with dancing and drinking; only the south churchyard was consecrated for burials. During the Middle Ages, often only part of the interior of the church was sanctified, to lessen the amount of upkeep for which the Welsh Church was responsible. Secular activities—including cockfighting on occasion—took place in the unsanctified nave, whose upkeep was the responsibility of the community. (See Gregory, pp. 13-14).

The churchyard and the ancient yew tree

was first planted by the ancient megalith-builders, or perhaps it was planted several thousand years later by Druids who considered the site holy. Romans followed them, and then Christians.

Getting There

Discoed is on a minor road off B4356 just north of Presteigne. Drive slowly; there's a sign to the church and a sign pointing with an arrow straight up. Turn onto the narrow lane and go uphill; then you turn left at the T-junction. The church is very close (see map on p. 217).

> Imagine. How. The. Yew. Experienced. These. Events. How does the yew sense and feel and see and hear? Imagine. Being. That. Old. That. Old.

More to Experience:
Presteigne, Powys

Nearby Presteigne is a good place for lunch and shopping, complete with delis and arts and crafts galleries. Locals recommend the Hat Shop Café. The Judge's Lodging provides an interesting view into the lifestyle of circuit judges in 1870. Presteigne is a "touch of England" in Wales: in fact, it is on the Welsh bank of the river that separates the two countries.

Getting There

Presteigne is on B4355 north of Kington (see map on p. 217).

Main street, Presteigne

Old Radnor, Powys

Old Radnor, 6 mi southwest of Presteigne (see map on p. 217), was the home of King Harold. He was killed by William the Conqueror's troops at the Battle of Hastings in 1066. Its imposing Parish Church of St Stephen contains examples of fourteenth-century building design, as well as an eighth-century font made from a glacial boulder. New Radnor is 2 mi to the west, originally a Norman settlement; the remains of a castle overlook the village. This is the town where, in 1187, Archbishop Baldwin and Giraldus Cambrensis began their tour of Wales. During their journey, Baldwin preached the Third Crusade at Patrisio Church, among other places. He was the first archbishop to visit Wales. As Archbishop of Canterbury, he crowned Richard I.

Radnor Forest, Powys

North of New Radnor is the Radnor Forest (Fforest Faesyfed). Hiking trails abound. You can drive part way to Water Break-Its-Neck waterfall. A lane turns north off A44 a mile west of New Radnor and leads to a parking lot and picnic area (see map on p. 217). From there, a trail leads to the Water Break-Its-Neck waterfall (http://www.forestry.gov.uk/website/ourwoods.nsf/LUWebDocsByKey/WalesPowysRadnorWarrenWoodWarrenWoodWaterBreakItsNeck). One can follow trails from here to Cascob in the northeast. See also http://www.forestry.gov.uk/website/recreation.nsf/$$SearchPlacesToGo?Openform&n=Radnor&nt=&g=uaem&op=wc&x=y&ct=All%20Counties&cr=Wales and http://www.walkingbritain.co.uk/walks/walks/walk_b/3023/.

Nearby is Llanfihangel Nant Melan with its atmospheric St Michael's Church—another one of the four that encircle the sleeping dragon. The church was completely rebuilt in 1846 and modeled on a Norman church. In the twelfth century, it was the property of the Knights Hospitallers. The setting is evocative, including a somewhat circular, raised churchyard with five (originally twelve) very large, impressive yews—one with a stone imbedded. At one time, a stone circle enclosed the site, and church literature suggests there were probably prehistoric burials near the present church. The churchyard seems to glow green from the moss that covers the trees and gravestones.

St Melangell Church, Pennant Melangell, Powys

N52 49 38 W3 26 56

Pennant Melangell church is a long way from anywhere, nestled near the head of a deep, steep-walled valley. Getting there requires a pilgrimage of sorts—most fitting, since for centuries it has been a pilgrimage destination. The surrounding hillsides seem to embrace the holy site. We walked through the stone lychgate and crossed into a powerful sacred space, a churchyard encircled by five ancient yews and the remnants of a Bronze Age stone circle. The energy shift was palpable; everything looked just a little misty. (Elyn)

Located near the head of the Tanat Valley, Pennant Melangell is an ancient, powerful place, drenched in Celtic lore and the holy spirit of the Age of Saints. The site has been an important Christian pilgrimage shrine for over 1200 years and was undoubtedly a sacred site long before then.

Legend tells us that in 604 CE, St Melangell (Monacella) was praying in the Tanat Valley when a hare was chased in her direction by a pack of dogs belonging to Brochwel, Prince of Powys. The hare ran under her cloak for safety. Prince Brochwel urged on the hounds but they fled howling; the prince drew his horn to call them back but the horn stuck to his lips. Clearly, Melangell was able to perform miracles.

> "The more remote, ascetic, lost in nature a Celtic sacred site aspired to be, the holier it became and—the paradox is—the more it was sought out. The pilgrim trails to Pennant Melangell wound over the mountains through moorland, mist and bog, leaving traces of ruined shelters, seeking out the healing and sanctuary of Ffynnon Ewyn and Melangell's care and intercession to be wrapped in her llan's enfolding cloak like the throbbing, dew-bedabbled hare of her legend." Hughes, p. 185.

Prince Brochwel soon learned that Melangell was the daughter of an Irish king. She had fled to the valley fifteen years earlier to avoid a forced marriage and to live a life of contemplation. The prince found Melangell's gentleness and godliness so moving that he offered her the valley in which to build a religious community. And she accepted. Or so the story goes. The *Historia Divae Monacellae*, a "Life" of Melangell (Monacella), mentions "both a female community founded by Melangell and a male community of abbots living under Melangell's sanctuary" (Morton, p. 43).

We wondered if the real story wasn't somewhat different: rather than a generous prince giving the land to a saintly woman, perhaps the valley was already hers. Maybe it was, or had been, the location of a female Druid community, similar to that at Kildare in Ireland,

St Melangell

> "The Celts believed that the goddess Eostre's favorite animal and attendant spirit was the hare. It represented love, fertility, and growth and was associated with the Moon, dawn and Easter—death, redemption, and resurrection. Eostre changed into a hare at the full Moon. The hare was sacred to the White Goddess—the Earth Mother—and as such was considered a royal animal. Boudicca was said to have released a hare as a good omen before each battle and to divine the outcome of battle by the hare's movements. She took a hare into battle with her to ensure victory and it was said to have screamed like a woman from beneath her cloak." http://h2g2.com/dna/h2g2/A2465426, retrieved 17 Dec. 2011.

which was later converted into a Christian sanctuary. After all, the hare that hid under Melangell's skirts was an ancient goddess symbol long before a Christian prince hunted it.

The circle of yew trees that surround the ancient circular churchyard, along with the remains of a Bronze Age stone circle, lend support for this alternative interpretation. In addition, recent archeological evidence proves that Pennant Melangell church was built over a pagan burial ground, in use at least 1000 years before St Melangell settled in the valley.

The church dates to the eighth century, though most of it is from the twelfth century. Today, it is a well-loved church, nurturing, gentle, sweet, and feminine in its energy. As recently as thirty years ago, however, it was in such bad repair that its survival was in question. Fortunately, the apse was rebuilt, and major restoration efforts were completed in 1992.

Inside the church, a fifteenth-century carved oak screen shows the story of Melangell and Prince Brochwel. Melangell, the prince, dogs, and the hare are at

> "It may be that the earlier pagan site was used in later times either because it was already 'sanctified' in some way, or because the presence of an existing place of veneration gave the local community 'authorization' to continue its use as a place of burial." Morton, p. 44.

center stage. The greatest treasure of the church, however—aside from its atmosphere—is the twelfth-century shrine of St Melangell, the only surviving Romanesque shrine in Britain. The stone construction stands on six stubby columns with ornately carved capitals.

During the Reformation the shrine was dismantled and its stones repositioned in the walls of the church and lychgate. In 1894 the stones were recognized as belonging to the shrine, and in 1958 they were recovered and used to reconstruct it. The shrine was placed in the *cell-y-bedd* (the square extension on the east end of the church) until 1989, when the *cell-y-bedd* was destroyed and replaced by the current rounded apse. The shrine was rebuilt in 1991 in the chancel behind the altar.

Because this is a pilgrims' church, it is possible to walk behind the altar and around the impressive shrine, sculpted with a mix of Celtic and Romanesque motifs, with perhaps some Islamic design elements as well. Numerous prayer cards are piled up in the space beneath the raised shrine.

St Melangell Church

Interior of the church

They are a moving memorial to faith and hope—and to St Melangell.

Melangell's grave lies under the raised stone slab in the cobblestone-paved apse. This room had been built as a square addition (a *cell-y-bedd*) in the eighteenth century. Archaeological excavations during the reconstruction of the church disclosed the original twelfth-century semicircular foundations and Melangell's grave, so the apse was reconstructed in a more authentic manner.

There are a number of opportunities to participate in this powerful place, to interact with the sacredness of this sanctified space. One is to light a candle in honor of a friend or loved one, and to send them a card that says, "A candle has been lit for you at the shrine of St Melangell." Another is to pray or meditate. Another is to sense the shifting energies as you move from nave to chancel to the grave of St Melangell.

As you spend time in this pilgrim church, sinking into the ambience, you will find other ways in which you can become part of its ongoing traditions. One could be to take a contemplative walk around the perimeter of the churchyard to experience the trees.

> "In the long hours of the night, and throughout the day, in thousands of churches and temples all over the world, candles and votive lamps are burning: a symbol of our need to invoke a power beyond our limited selves. To light a candle in this way is an act of poetry as well as an act of piety. It speaks to us of a larger dimension and remind us that each of us carries a single lamp for humanity." James Roose-Evans, *The Tablet*, 8 March 1997.

The seven yew trees that surround the churchyard generate part of the atmosphere of Pennant Melangell. One of the yews is recently planted—in spring 1878—but four of the other six are of considerable age. Two of them, one male and one female, growing on the eastern perimeter bank, appear to be the oldest. The male tree east of the apse is more than 28 ft in circumference; the female yew next to the lychgate is over 23 ft in girth (Morton, pp. 44-45). At least one of these trees has been certified as over 2000 years old. This would indicate that the yews (or at least that yew) predated the Christian establishment—as do the ancient burials.

> "Circles of yews (which are unique to Wales) within the circular churchyards, like the small holy islands encircled by the sea, seem to echo the map of the Celtic cosmos, a concentricity of circles for the upper and lower worlds." Hughes, p. 14.

Pennant Melangell church has been a place of pilgrimage for more than 1500 years, and in recent years its focus has been as a healing shrine. In 1987 a retired priest, the Rev'd Paul Davies, arrived in the area with his wife, Evelyn. They spearheaded the effort to restore the church, which was falling into ruin. Mrs Davies had a particular mission, driven by her recovery from cancer. She found money to convert the cottage garage into a palliative-care center and turned Melangell into a place of healing pilgrimage and spiritual counseling, establishing the St Melangell Center charity. She left after twelve years, and the

The shrine of St Melangell

center has continued to choose an individual with expertise in healing ministry as priest guardian of the shrine and director of the Center.

The Shrine Church of St Melangell is open daily. Frequent services are held, including Sundays at 3 pm and a Holy Eucharist with laying-on of hands and anointing with oil. In 2011, the priest guardian was Rev'd Lynette Norman. There is no resident congregation. A gift shop with an "honor box" for payment is at the west end of the church beneath the tower, and purchases and donations help support the church.

Contact the Melangell Center at (0)1691 860 408 for more information and the current worship schedule (http://www.st-melangell.org.uk/index.htm). The center is open weekdays from 10 am to 4 pm. NOTE: The nearest public toilets are in the car park in Llangynog village.

Getting There

St Melangell Church is in Pennant Melangell, 2 mi outside of Llangynog on a minor road (see map). A trail leads from the church to Pistyll Blaen-y-Cwm, the waterfall at the head of the valley.

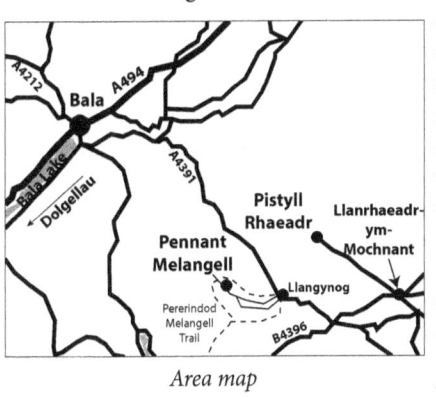
Area map

If you want to take a longer walk, consider following the Pererindod Melangell Trail. This is a challenging 15-mi linear walk between the Vyrnwy and Tanat Valley. The county council created the trail after the modern revival of the Melangell shrine. It is a reconstruction of the centuries-old, undulating route followed by pilgrims, quarrymen, and drovers. See http://tourism.powys.gov.uk/index.php?id=78 and http://www.ldwa.org.uk/ldp/members/show_path.php?path_name=Pererindod+Melangell. Peter Robin suggests a variant that follows more closely the ancient Pilgrims' Way (http://pilgrim.peterrobins.co.uk/wales/melangell.html.)

More to Experience

Bala Lake (Llyn Tegid), Gwynedd

N52 53 0 W3 38 0

Lake Bala (Llyn Tegid; "Lake of Beauty" or "Serenity") is associated with Ceridwen. It was here that the ancient goddess resided and stirred her magical cauldron (see pp. 135-137). Llyn Tegid is the largest body of water in Wales, 4 mi long by 1 mi wide, clear and very deep. Its waters are abundant with trout, pike, eel, and *gwyniad*, a white fish of the salmon family unique to Llyn Tegid, which apparently became trapped 10,000 years ago, at the end of the Ice Age. Llyn Tegid is also said to be the home of Teggie, an elusive, crocodile-like beast rumored to live in the lake. And there are legends that deep beneath its waters lies a drowned city.

Bala is a market town, founded by the Romans if not before. It is a "Walkers are Welcome" town and a stronghold of Welsh language. There are numerous hiking trails, opportunities for water sports, and a popular steam railway (http://www.bala-lake-railway.co.uk/).

Getting There

Bala is on A494 northeast of Dolgellau (see map on p. 233).

Pistyll Rhaeadr, Powys

N52 51 14 W3 22 24

Nearby in the Berwyn Mountains is Pistyll Rhaeadr (means "Spout Waterfall"), a dramatic down-rushing exuberance of white, sparkling water. It is considered one of the Seven Wonders of Wales. Pistyll Rhaeadr is one of the highest waterfalls in Wales. Propaganda says it is the highest single-drop waterfall in England and Wales, but this is inaccurate.

At Pistyll Rhaeadr, the Disgynfa river drops vertically for 100 ft before filling a natural cauldron called "the Druid's Bowl." It then passes through a natural rock arch, the Fairy Bridge, before completing its spectacular descent of 240 ft. Various trails lead up to the arch and to the top.

Legend says the waterfall was sacred to the Druids, and other legends (probably apocryphal) associate it with

Pistyll Rhaeadr Falls

King Arthur. Some say that the ancient Britons thought the Berwyn Mountains were the physical and geographical location of Annwn, the Celtic Otherworld, the place of the spirits of the dead (http://www.pistyllrhaeadr.co.uk/berwyns.html). The land around is filled with myth and mystery—and heather moorland, blanket bog, and megalithic sites.

> "What shall I liken it to? I scarcely know, unless it is to an immense skein of silk agitated and disturbed by tempestuous blasts, or to the long tail of a grey courser at furious speed. I never saw water falling so gracefully, so much like thin, beautiful threads as here." George Borrow, *Wild Wales*.

> In Welsh, pistyll means spout; rhaeadr means waterfall. Some waterfalls are called by one name, others by the other, depending on their appearance.

Standing at the bottom of the falls, we felt invigorated, probably because the falling water generates ozone. The area has a magical feeling, but that might be due to the oxygenated air. Or maybe not. Maybe it is due to something else: maybe it is another Welsh "thin place," where one is indeed in closer proximity to the Otherworld.

> "The gateway to Arthur's ancient lands and the kingdom of the Celtic Otherworld is represented by Pistyll Rhaeadr. Walking up the south face of the Berwyns and traversing east along the ridge as far as possible leads to a place called Bwrrd Arthur (Arthur's Table). Here, had you been Arthur, you could have stood with pride and viewed your lands stretching from the mountaintop to the sea." http://www.pistyllrhaeadr.co.uk/berwyns.html, retrieved 12 Dec. 2011.

Pistyll Rhaeadr is stunning and the surrounding scenery beautiful, but it can get very crowded. Somewhat destroying the ambiance is the riverside café, coffee shop, B&B, and campsite in the nearby field. The dead-end road is narrow, with frequent pull-offs, making it vulnerable to traffic jams, especially on weekends and holidays.

Getting There

Drive on B4396 to Llanrhaeadr-ym-Mochanant. In Llanrhaaeadr, drive through the main square past the Wynstay Arms. Turn on Waterfall Street near the Greatorex shop. The waterfall is signposted at that point. Pistyll Rhaeadr is about 4 mi from Llanrhaeadr (see map on p. 233).

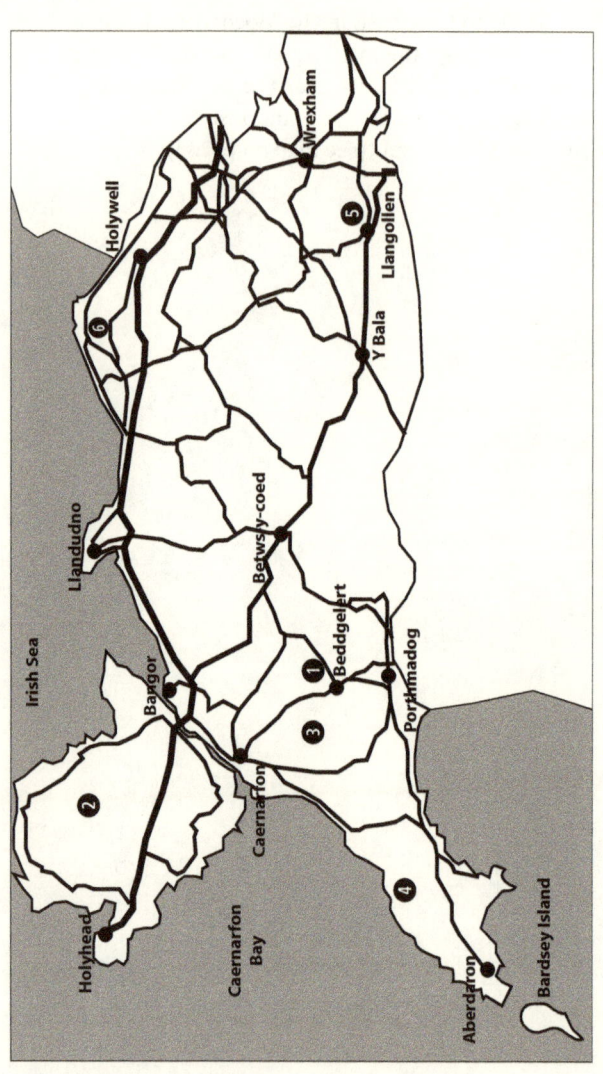

North Wales

1. Dinas Emrys
2. Anglesey
3. Driving toward the Llŷn Peninsula
4. The Llŷn Peninsula
5. Castell Dinas Brân
6. Gop

North Wales (Snowdonia, the Isle of Anglesey, the Llŷn Peninsula, the North Coast, Denbighshire, Flintshire)

North Wales is the ancient stronghold of the Druids. It is still intensely Welsh and Welsh speaking, especially as you move west from the English border toward Anglesey (Ynys Môn) and the Llŷn Peninsula. The region is a mixture of holiday resorts, industrialized farmland, rural agriculture, isolated mountain villages, defunct slate quarries, copper and gold mines, the rolling Clwydian Range, narrow-gauge railways, Snowdonia National Park, medieval castles, and the largest collection of megalithic and pre-Christian sites in Wales.

The northern coast is noted for its inexpensive British holiday resorts, especially toward the east. But you also find St Winifred's Well at Holywell, likened to the French Lourdes; Gop, an artificial hill that (according to Elyn) is one of the most powerful places in Wales; and Great Orme Copper Mine, in use for over 4000 years.

Snowdonia National Park is the largest of the three Welsh national parks. It extends from the north into mid Wales. It includes dramatic scenery, the highest mountain (Snowdon) in Wales, and a number of hill ranges and hiking trails through what remains of the vast forests that once covered Wales.

The Isle of Anglesey (Ynys Môn) is often called "The Mother of Wales," both because of its fertile fields and its history. It is a land set apart, steeped in pre-Christian and Welsh tradition. It was on this island, barely separated from the mainland, that the Welsh made their last stand against the Romans. Ynys Môn is a mix of rolling hills, fertile farmland, beautiful coasts—and an extensive assortment of megalithic sites.

The Llŷn Peninsula (also spelled Lleyn) is a secluded, traditional area of Wales. Some 100 mi of its shoreline have been designated Areas of Outstanding Natural Beauty. Bardsey Island lies 2 mi off the tip of the peninsula, and intrepid medieval pilgrims traveled across Wales to reach it. Megalithic monuments, hill forts, churches, holy wells, and ancient place-names that recall Modron, the Welsh Mother Goddess, are all within close reach.

North Wales is filled with myths and legends that are imprinted on the land. The Second Branch of the *Mabinogi* takes place in the north. It tells the story of the giant Brân "the Blessed" and his sister Branwen, both called "Children of Llŷr," a sea god, and Branwen's ill-fated marriage to the Irish King Matholwch. He asked for her hand at Harlech (p. 181). The story goes on to describe Bran's death in a disastrous battle in Ireland between his men and the Irish warriors, provoked by Matholwch's abuse of Branwen. Branwen and seven survivors returned with Bran's head to Wales. She died of a broken heart and was buried on Anglesey (see p. 286). The warriors, carrying Bran's head, spent seven years at Harlech Castle before eventually traveling to London to bury Bran's head.

Brân and Branwen oak sculpture in Rhos-y-gilwen concert hall (see p. 156). Phil Forder, sculptor. Courtesy of Glen Peters.

The Fourth Branch of the *Mabinogi* also takes place in the north. The complex episodes are filled with sorcery, shape-shifting, sexual violence, and with the struggle between feminine and masculine social dominance.

Gwydion and Arianrhod, children of Dôn, are sky deities. Gwydion is also a mighty astronomer. Caer means "stronghold" in Welsh, and the Milky Way is called Caer Gwydion, in honor of Gwydion. Arianrhod's name comes from Welsh *arian*, meaning "silver," and *rhod*, meaning "wheel." She is known as the Goddess of the Silver Wheel and is associated with the full moon and the weaving of human interactions. She has a ship, Oar Wheel, in which she carries dead warriors to Emania (Moon-land). "Hers also are the circumpolar stars known as Caer Arianrhod [the Corona Borealis], her spiral castle, where she houses and passes judgment on the souls of the dead. The stars are also her spinning wheel, and she spins the patterns of the universe, and the thread of life, death and rebirth, an eternal thread with no ending and no beginning, but marked by time." http://www.merciangathering.com/arianrhod.htm, retrieved 23 Dec. 2011.

Math, son of Mathonwy, is tricked into war with Pryderi (son of Pwyll and Rhiannon) by his nephew Gwydion, son of Dôn (mother goddess; similar to Danu, mother goddess of the Irish Tuath Dé Danann). Gwydion foments the battle because his brother, Gilvaethwy, is obsessed with the maiden Goewin, Math's "foot-holder." Gilvaethwy takes advantage of Math's contrived absence to rape Goewin. Math later marries her but punishes Gwydion and Gilvaethwy for several years by turning them into animals: first deer, then hogs, then wolves, alternating which of them is male and which female—and which will become pregnant and give birth.

Later, Gwydion counsels Math to choose Arianrhod, his sister (and Math's niece) for his next lap-maiden. Arianrhod lives in Caer Arianrhod, a revolving castle in the sea near Caernarfon. Cernarfon is located between Snowdonia and the Menai Strait.

Arianrhod is tricked by Gwydion to prove she is a virgin. She fails the test and gives birth to two infants, perhaps fathered by Gwydion. She flees in shame, leaving the babies behind. One of the infants is named Dylan of the Waves. As soon as he is baptized, he leaps into the sea near Caernarfon and swims like a magnificent fish. Gwydion secretly raises the other infant near Dinas Dinlle, 3 mi south of Caernarfon (see pp. 294-297). Arianrhod has cursed the child to have no name, never bear weapons, and never have a wife of any race that is on the earth. Gwydion tricks her again, and she gives him weapons and the name Lleu Llaw Gyffes,

> Hilary Wylde suggests this story is a veiled description of the social shift from women-centered matrifocal clans to patriarchy, mirrored in the shift of power from the Goddess to the Gods. Although Arianrhod's castle is located in the sea, Gwydion and Arianrhod's attributes demonstrate the patriarchal culture's greater emphasis on the celestial realms.

which means "the fair-haired one with the skillful hand."

Determined that Lleu shall have a wife, Gwydion and Math conjure one out of flowers. She is called Blodeuwedd—"Flower Face." She and Lleu marry and live together in the province of Ardudwy. But she falls in love with Gronw Pebr and is unfaithful. Worse, they plot Lleu's death. They almost succeed, but, seriously wounded, Lleu transforms himself into an eagle. In revenge, Gwydion chases Blodeuwedd and her ladies to Llyn Morynion (the Lake of the Maidens), located in the hills near Ffestiniog. The ladies drown and Blodeuwedd is transformed into an owl.

Lleu and Boldeuwedd oak sculpture in Rhos-y-gilwen concert hall (see p. 156). Phil Forder, sculptor. Courtesy of Glen Peters.

Other medieval Welsh tales tell of King Arthur and Merlin, supposed to have lived in the north, as well as the south, of Wales. "Proof" is found in the numer-

> It is probable that Arianrhod, Blodeuwedd, and Ceridwen are the Welsh representation of the Triple Goddess: mother, maiden, and crone. "[Arianrhod] is also said to be one of the five Goddesses that originate from the isle of Avalon; the other four being Blodeuwedd, Ceridwen, Branwen and Rhiannon." http://sacredmistsblog.com/goddess-of-the-week-arianrhod

ous locations bearing their names. Still other stories hint at the presence of St Joseph of Arimathea and the burial place of Mary, mother of Jesus, in Ynys Môn.

A well-versed and "attuned" guide, such as Hilary Wylde or Eric Maddern, can make the hills and lakes come alive with the stories that still reside within the land.

Dinas Emrys, Snowdonia National Park

N53 01 12 W4 05 21

As we walked up the trail to Dinas Emrys, our guide, Eric Maddern, regaled us with the legend of Vortigern, the young Merlin, and the prophecy of the twin dragons. We could almost hear the clash of swords, the snorting horses, the clang of armor. Dinas Emrys was where it all happened, or so the story goes. The trees seemed to wave their branches in agreement. Thus primed, we hiked up the hill to the ruined hillfort and a reed-filled pool surrounded by gnarly, lichen-covered trees. Meditating, I felt a presence and turned to stare—young Merlin, riding on a stag, passed by. (Elyn)

Dinas Emrys is an ancient hillfort near Beddgelert, in the heart of Snowdonia National Park (Parc Cenedlaethol Eryri). *Dinas* means "fortress" in Welsh. It is the legendary site of the encounter between the child Merlin, the warlord Vortigern, and two dragons.

> Eric Maddern writes, "For me the most potent place in Snowdonia is Dinas Emrys, a modest hill at the heart of the mountains in the valley below the summit of Yr Wyddfa. Inside the pregnant belly-shaped hill is a womb-like little valley with a small reedy pool whose outlet trickles over the edge and disappears underground." http://www.caemabon.co.uk/#/historic-setting/4560175251, retrieved 3 Feb. 2012.

Vortigern (AKA Vortigen, Vortiger, and, in Welsh, Gwrtheryn) was probably a historical figure, a fifth-century Briton warlord, first mentioned in the sixth-century *On the Ruin and Conquest of Britain,* written by the historian cleric Gildas. With the agreement of his counselors, Vortigern invited Saxon mercenaries to England to help fight the Picts and Scots. Unfortunately, the mercenaries soon revolted and Vortigern fled to northwestern Wales.

> Over time, the early, relatively non-judgmental account of Vortigern's life changed, and he was described as a character of insatiable lust, overweening pride, and avarice—in other words, a brutal tyrant. Other additions to the original story include Merlin and the dragons buried at Dinas Emrys.

Legend says that as Vortigern fled to the west, his advisors told him to build a fort on the near-impregnable hilltop near Beddgelert. The masons worked each day to raise the tower, but each night it fell down. Vortigern's wizards/wise men/Druids told him that the only way to keep the fortification upright was to sacrifice a "fatherless" child (born of a virgin, in one account) and sprinkle his blood on the walls. Troops were sent in search, and soon they found the child, named Ambrosius (Emrys, in Welsh), whose mother was a nun and

> Eric Maddern suggests that the real meaning of "a fatherless child born to a nun" is that the mother was a priestess, chosen because of her wisdom and purity, to take part in the Great Rite with a masked man. Because he wore a mask, she could always say she didn't know the father. This ritual was undertaken in order to "bring through" a being—Merlin, in this case—to help humanity. Personal communication, June 2011.

whose father was unknown or unnamed. They brought him to the hilltop.

To save his life, young Ambrosius/Emrys prophesized, stating that a white dragon and a red dragon were buried in a pool beneath the site, and when they awoke (which they did periodically), they fought, destabilizing the tower. He also said that although the white dragon (the Saxons) would appear to win, in the future the red dragon (the indigenous Britons/Welsh) would be victorious. He told Vortigern he should flee the area; local legend says he fled to Nant Gwrtheyrn (see pp. 302-306).

The builders dug and found the fighting dragons, just as prophesized. Ambrosius/Emrys' life was saved, and he went on to become Merlin, the prophet/magician/advisor to King Arthur. Or so the story goes.

Dinas Emrys probably takes its name not from Ambrosius/Emrys but from the warrior Aurelius Ambrosius, known as Emrys Wledig or the Emperor. He claimed the fort after Vortigern had fled.

The tale of two dragons originated long before the story of Vortigern and Merlin. According to the "Welsh Triad 37," there are "Three Concealments and

The young Merlin prophesying to King Vortigern

Three Disclosures of the Island of Britain: The Head of Brân the Blessed, son of Llŷr, which was buried in the White Hill in London. And as long as the Head was there in that position, no Oppression would ever come to this Island. The second: the Bones of Gwerthefyr the Blessed, which were buried in the Chief Ports of this Island. The third: the Dragons which Lludd, son of Beli, buried in Dinas Emrys in Eryri [Snowdonia]." (http://www.vortigernstudies.org.uk/artcit/dinas.htm, retrieved 18 Dec. 2011). In the *Mabinogi* story "Lludd and Llefelys," a recurrent scream strikes terror in the hearts of the inhabit-

> Maddern suggests "... the dragons are probably metaphors for powerful forces in the land. When the land is disturbed (as with the clash between the Britons and the Saxons) the dragons awake." Personal communication, 24 Jan. 2012.

> In a slightly different version of the story, two jars were found in the pool, and inside the two jars were the eggs of the dragons that burst forth like butterflies from cocoons and began fighting as they always had—and maybe always will.

Present-day site of Castell Dinas Emrys

ants of King Lludd's British kingdom; it is the scream of two fighting dragons. Lludd's brother, Llefelys, King of France, tells Lludd "to dig a pit in the centre of Britain, fill it with mead and cover it with cloth. Lludd did this, and the dragons were imprisoned, wrapped in the cloth, underground at Dinas Emrys in North West Wales" (http://www.bbc.co.uk/wales/history/sites/themes/society/myths_lludd_and_llefelys.shtml, retrieved 18 Dec. 2011).

The legend of the collapsing tower that can only be stabilized by human sacrifice is not unique to Merlin and Dinas Emrys. In Celtic Scotland and Ireland, legends and archeological evidence point to voluntary (or not-so-voluntary) human sacrifices buried beneath the walls of important buildings. When St Columba's chapel on the Isle of Iona kept falling down, his faithful companion, Oran, willingly agreed to be buried beneath the foundations as a sacrifice (see *Powerful Places in Scotland,* pp. 38-41). The interred individual was believed to become a guardian spirit for the site. Perhaps the story of Vortigern's wisemen demanding the death of a child is a distorted memory of this earlier Celtic practice.

All is not myth and legend, however, on Dinas Emrys. The ruins of a late Roman fort and twelfth-century Norman keep can be seen at the top of the rocky, wooded hill, along with a pool. The pool is now a reed-filled hollow, but it may have originally been a cistern to ensure a supply of water on the hilltop. It is located quite near the rectangular foundation that was probably the base of a (the?) tower.

Who or what was Merlin/Myrddin? A man, a title? A seer who left behind a series of prophesies? A magician who transported Stonehenge from Ireland to the plains of Somerset? Although most people think of Merlin as the wizard/tutor/advisor to King Arthur, a closer reading of the surviving medieval texts tells a more complex story. There were

The "dragon pool," now overgrown with reeds.

at least three Merlins: Myrddin Wylit (Merlin the madman and prophet, AKA Merlin Caledonensis), the Roman-British warrior Ambrosius Aurelianus, and the composite figure Myrddyn Emrys (Merlin Ambrosius). It is possible these were historic figures whose stories blended over the centuries—and it's possible that several but not all of them existed.

> According to RJ Stewart, author of *Merlin: The Prophetic Vision and Mystic Life* (personal communication, 22 Jan. 2012), "The primal Merlin tradition is very simple: it refers to a title (Merddyn), not a name. This title was given to those who were within a tradition of 'crazy seership,' sometimes called *vates* in Latin. This is the root word for vaticination (prophecy) and, guess what, the Vatican (inherited from Roman paganism). The *vates* or mad seers were part of the ancient British Druidic structure, but were, so to speak, wild cards. Such traditions are known worldwide, and come under the modern label of 'crazy wisdom' that you find in many books. Probably the first substantial embodiments of this tradition in literature were those of Geoffrey of Monmouth, though there are partial texts and references before Geoffrey, but not much. After Geoffrey, the material blossomed in many directions, and the primal British tradition was substantially overplayed."

A waterfall on the path up to Dinas Emrys

Geoffrey of Monmouth first brought together disparate tales of the assorted Merlins in 1134-1138 in his *Historia Regum Britanniae (History of the Kings of Britain)*. In 1150 he continued the theme in *Vita Merlin (The Life of Merlin)*, a sort of "prequel." Monmouth created the Myrddin Emrys figure associated with King Arthur. For more details, go to http://en.wikipedia.org/wiki/Merlin or go to books by Dames, Markale, Stewart, and Tolstoy listed in this guidebook's bibliography.

When you visit Dinas Emrys, pay attention to the way the energy shifts. As we walked up the rocky path on the hillside, we passed through an "energy gateway" between two close-set trees, and Elyn saw a kind of shimmering in the air. The trail leads to the top of the hill, and you pass between the grass-covered ruined walls of the earlier fortifications. Keep walking and you will come to a fern-lined, rock-filled rectangular depression—the remains of Vortigern's tower? Stop and sense the energy.

Then continue past the vegetation-shrouded ruins to the hidden valley and the pool or cistern, a bit down the hill and to the left. Here the energy changes dramatically—or at least it did when we visited the site. Spend time amidst the twisted oak trees, covered with lichen, beside the reed-filled pool. The place had the feel of a faery glen or an enchanted forest. Don't be surprised if Merlin appears or the child Emrys comes riding by.

> Eric Maddern explains, "I don't think it's possible to assume an exact correspondence between what is on the ground and key elements of the story. Inevitably there have to be liberal doses of 'probably,' 'perhaps,' and 'maybe.' What is certain is that Dinas Emrys was used, off and on, from 300 or 200 BCE (as an Iron Age hillfort) right through to the thirteenth century CE. So, about fifteen hundred years. And it has featured as a sacred place in the stories of the Cymru for about a thousand years. ... So my hunch is that, over centuries, Dinas Emrys served as a meeting point and a place of ceremony and ritual. It is located centrally in northern Snowdonia, with three great valleys coming down from the north, two great valleys rising up from the south. I imagine people would have come there from all over northwest Wales—possibly even further afield—to seek wisdom, counsel, and courage, especially in times of danger. It is, I believe, what Joseph Campbell called an *omphalos*, a world navel, a sacred center." Eric Maddern, personal communication, 24 Feb. 2012.

Upstream from Dinas Emrys on the River Glaslyn is another mythic site: Llyn Dinas, where Vortigern is said to have hidden the throne of Britain underwater under a large and heavy stone. Legend also claims that the lake was the site of a battle between King Arthur's knight Owein and a giant. Some say that Merlin buried a treasure in the lake,

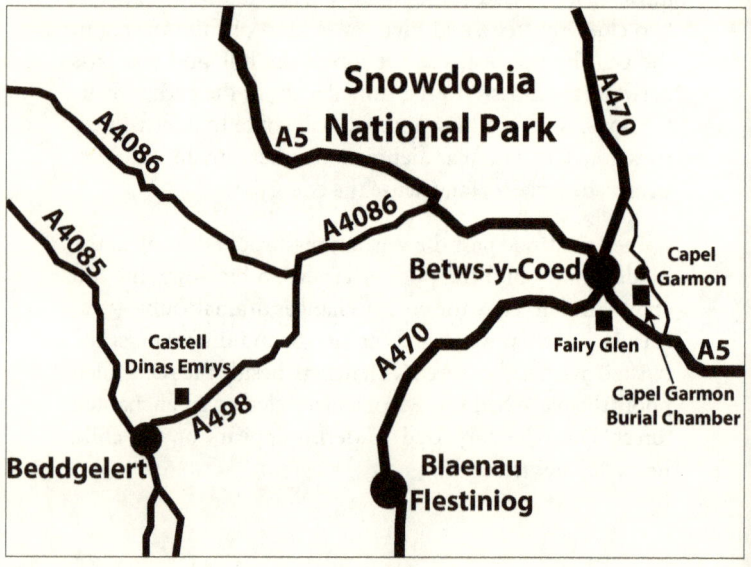

Area map

> "Wilderness reservations are best viewed as holes and cracks, as 'free spaces' or 'liberated zones,' in the fabric of domination and self-deception that fuels and shapes our mainstream contemporary culture." Thomas Birch.

but that is most probably a reference to treasure he supposedly buried beneath the nearby hillside.

Getting There

To reach Dinas Emrys: drive on A498 east of Beddgelert to the parking for Craflwyn Center National Trust Site. Inquire at the information center for a trail map. The trails were being reorganized in Summer 2012.

More to Experience
Snowdonia National Park

Dramatic Snowdonia National Park (Parc Cenedlaethol Eryri) is filled with impressive mountains, including Snowdon, the most-climbed mountain in Wales, glacier valleys, deep lakes, isolated Welsh-speaking villages, and picturesque hillsides dotted with grazing sheep and cattle. It is the oldest and largest of Wales' national parks (http://www.snowdonia-npa.gov.uk). Cadair Idris (see pp. 171-175) is at the southern edge of the park.

Snowdon can be ascended by anyone regardless of physical condition, thanks to the Snowdon mountain train that has been in existence in one form or another since the late 1800s. If you prefer to hike, six different trails lead up the mountain. The Sherpa bus network travels back and forth to these starting points.

While Merlin/Myrddin is associated with Dinas Emrys, King Arthur is associated with Snowdon. The Welsh name for Snowdon is Eryri, which means "Great Tomb," "Land of Eagles," or "Land of Snow." Legend says that Arthur slew the giant Rita Gawr and buried it at the summit. Although Arthur's court may have been at Caerleon (see pp. 50-51), local legend claims that Snowdon was his true home.

Legend also asserts that King Arthur and his nephew Mordred fought their final battle at Bwlch-y-Saethau (The Pass of the Arrows), between Snowdon Mountain and Y Lliwedd peak. It is claimed that Arthur died there of an arrow wound. The pass is 1300 ft above Llyn Llydaw, the lake into which, according to legend, Arthur's loyal companion Bedivere cast Arthur's sword, Excalibur. Of course, other sites in Cornwall and England also vie for these honors.

Legend states that after Arthur died, his body was brought to the Land of Apples or "Avalon" (*Afallach* in Welsh). Although the "Land of Apples" is often thought to be Glastonbury, some say that it is Bardsey Island, off the tip of the Llŷn Peninsula (see pp. 314-315), where once apples flourished. Black and Lloyd (2003) claim Avalon was the Realm of Afallon in northeast Wales. Others claim that Arthur never died but lies asleep with his knights in a Welsh cave, waiting to come to the aid of Britain in its time of greatest need.

Snowdonia National Park

> Some of Arthur's adventures are recounted in stories in the *Mabinogi*. In "Culhwch and Olwen," which dates from the tenth century, Arthur is a magical, folkloric figure chasing the boar, Twrch Trwyth, from Ireland to England. In "The Dream of Rhonabwy," Rhonabwy sleeps and dreams that King Arthur plays chess with Sir Owein, while men and ravens fight fiercely nearby. Arthur and Myrddin are also mentioned in the thirteenth-century *Llyfr Du Caerfyrddin (The Black Book of Carmarthen)*, the oldest surviving manuscript written entirely in Welsh.

Who was Arthur? Was he originally a Celtic god linked with Ursa Major, the "Great Bear" constellation (*Arth Fawr* in Welsh), or was he a brave Briton warrior? Or was he both? Historical evidence is scant and contradictory, but it appears that there was a historic figure on whom the legendary King Arthur is based. King Arthur is first mentioned around 800 CE in the Welsh monk Nennius' *Historia Brittonum,* where he is described as a sixth-century Briton hero who fought the invading Anglo-Saxons. Black and Lloyd (2003) make a case for Arthur being a Welsh battle leader who successfully fought the Saxons—and claim that almost all of Arthur's battles took place in Wales.

In 1134-1138, Geoffrey of Monmouth used Nennius' *Historia*, along with folklore and literary invention, as a basis for his opus, *Historia Regum Britanniae*. He added Guinevere, Merlin, Morgan la Fe, the Isle of Avalon, and medieval chivalry to the mix. Not content to leave well enough alone, the twelfth-century French poet Chrétien de Troyes added Lancelot and the Grail quest to the story. In the fifteenth century, Sir Thomas Malory wrote the English-language Morte d'Arthur and elaborated further. Over the centuries, the original story was expanded by numerous authors, including Alfred Lord Tennyson, and Arthur was turned into an idealized Christian knight and symbol of native Celtic Briton resistance.

Fairy Glen, Conwy Valley, Conwy

N53 04 31 W3 47 40

The Tylwyth Teg (the "Fair Folk," AKA the Welsh faeries) are said to live in the Fairy Glen, a secluded gorge on the River Conwy. A combination of rapids and waterfalls enliven the narrow ravine. Its wooded banks make for a pleasant stroll through an enchanting—and perhaps enchanted—glen. The wooded banks above the tumbling river are covered with an amazing amount of white quartz. Perhaps that accounts for the "fairy" in Fairy Glen, since quartz affects the resonance of the place. Imagine masses of quartz crystals vibrating, amplifying the energy of the rushing water that pummels the rock-lined riverbed. Some people find the Fairy Glen a lovely place to meditate and picnic; others experience intense, chaotic energy and flee.

Getting There

The Fairy Glen is located a short distance from Beaver Bridge on the outskirts of Betws y Coed. Take A470 towards Blaenau Ffestiniog and turn up the lane beside the Fairy Glen Hotel (see map on p. 250). From the car park, a loop path—20 minutes each way—leads to the glen. There

"Quartz is a hard crystalline mineral which is found abundantly all over the Earth in a variety of forms. It is the most common mineral on Earth, making up 12% of the Earth's crust by volume, and is used in a wide variety of applications including jewelry, scientific research, manufacturing, and building" (http://www.wisegeek.com/what-is-quartz.htm, retrieved 17 March 2012). It is found in sandstone as well as in granite and other igneous rocks. Quartz conducts electricity and is used in radios, radar, TV, watches, and computers. In watches, the quartz movement vibrates very rapidly in response to an electric charge, usually delivered from a battery. These vibrations are used to keep time.

White quartz in the Fairy Glen

are a small entry fee and parking charge, paid at the "honor box" at the car park. Be sure to pay: the owner is watching.

Betws-y-Coed (means "Sanctuary in the Woods") is an inland resort, especially popular for outdoors activities, including cycling, fishing, water sports, skiing, and hiking (http://www.betws-y-coed.co.uk). It lies at the confluence of four forested valleys, at the edge of the Gwydyr Forest Park, and within the Snowdonia National Park.

Getting There

Betws-y-Coed is located at the junction of A5 and A470 (see map on p. 250).

Capel Garmon Burial Chamber, Conwy

N53 04 22 W3 45 56

Capel Garmon Burial Chamber is a heavily reconstructed Cotswold-Severn-style burial chamber, built between 2500-1900 BCE. It is in a beautiful location with an impressive view. The megalith consists of three compartments, the central one covered with a large capstone. The surrounding mound is largely intact, including some of the original drystone walling. The wedge-shaped mound has a forecourt in the eastern end. White quartz pebbles were found there, suggesting a ritual function for the space. One unusual feature is a false portal behind the forecourt, perhaps intended to deceive both the dead and the living.

Getting There

Capel Garmon is located 2 mi SE of Betws-y-Coed, half a mile south of Capel Garmon village. It is reached by a five-minute signposted walk across farmland. (Cadw; unrestricted access).

"There is only one capstone remaining, but it is a fantastic piece of stone fourteen feet wide, and there are two false portals leading nowhere. These are believed to be for ceremonial purposes only. The present entrance was formed for use as a stable in the 19th Century; because of the disturbances, not many artifacts were discovered during excavation. However some sherds of late Neolithic (Beaker) pottery were found and some traces of bone were found in the passageway." http://www.walesdirectory.co.uk/Ancient_Sites/Capel_Garmon_Burial_Chamber.htm, retrieved 15 March 2012.

Anglesey (Ynys Môn), county of Anglesey

Hidden behind high reeds, accessible by a short dirt path, is a small sacred lake. When we were there, ducks and seabirds floated on its surface, and a light breeze gently brushed the air. Until the Romans conquered Ynys Môn, Druids came to this wind-rippled pond and deposited votive offerings, praying for success in battle. Ultimately, the gods refused to listen and the Celts were defeated. While we sat beside the peaceful shore, contemplating this ancient history of broken dreams, a fast-flying RAF jet took off from the nearby base, cracking the silence. The association of this lake with military prowess still remains. (Elyn)

Ynys Môn, the Isle of Anglesey, is known as the Druid Isle and "The Mother of Wales." Ripe with history, rich in resources, it is the largest Welsh island. Two bridges across the Menai Strait connect it to the mainland. At its narrowest, the strait is 270 yd wide. According to the medi-

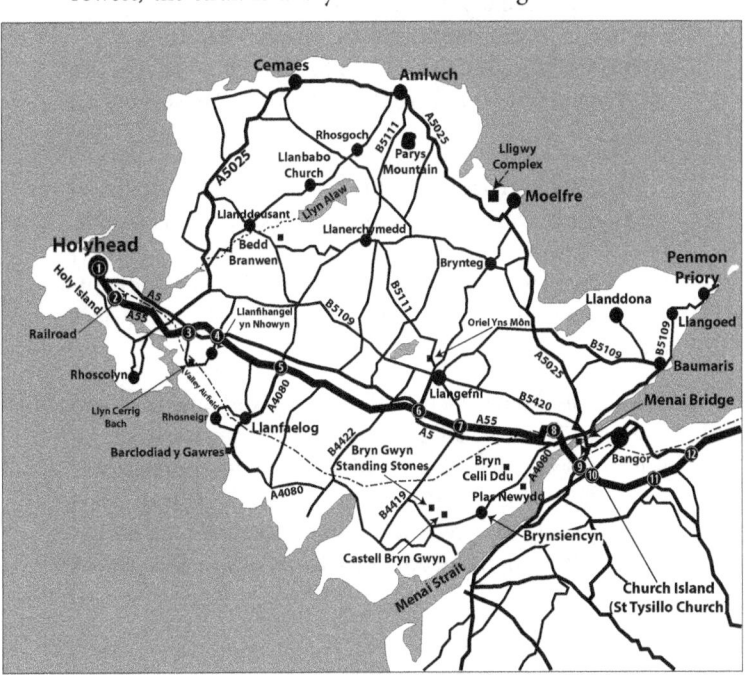

Anglesey

eval "Welsh Triads," at some time in the distant past, Anglesey was part of the Mainland—which in fact it was, 8000-12,000 years ago, when the sea level was lower. Here is more evidence of the accuracy of folk memory and legend.

Mesolithic hunters arrived between 8000 and 4000 BCE and spread across this abundant land. Starting around 2500 BCE, small farming communities began to appear, and they built many henges and stone circles on Ynys Môn. The Celts arrived in the seventh century BCE and dominated the island. Well situated at the apex of Celtic sea traffic, Anglesey "became the most important Druidic center in Europe" (Le Nevez et al., p. 442).

> "The Celts were not a fanatically religious people but the Romans saw Druidism as a serious menace - and Anglesey, spiritual home of the Druids, as the centre of that threat. The Romans were hostile to Druidism as it not only banded together individuals in a common focus but also allowed for an infrastructure of rebellion to flourish. So long as there were Druids in Britain, then rebellion and resistance would continue amongst the tribes and this, in turn, threatened the expansionism of the Empire itself." http://www.militaryhistoryonline.com/ancient/anglesey/default.aspx, retrieved 15 March 2012.

Ynys Môn/Anglesey was the last part of Wales to fall to the Romans. Determined to break the power of the Druids, in 60 CE the Roman General Gaius Suetonius Paulinus invaded the island. He conquered the Druids in a bloody, unrestrained campaign and proceeded to destroy the shrines and sacred groves.

After the Romans left in the fifth century, the Irish and later the Vikings invaded. But for many centuries, Anglesey was in a strong defensive position and under the control of the Princes of Gwynedd. In the thirteenth century, however, Edward I defeated the Welsh princes and built his last castle at Beaumaris on Anglesey to make sure they stayed defeated.

You could spend weeks experiencing powerful places on the island and enjoying its beaches. Almost the entire coastline of Anglesey is designated as an Area of Outstanding Natural Beauty, but many tourists never notice. Instead, they speed across the island to Holyhead to catch the ferry to Ireland. We have selected a few powerful places to get you started on your exploration.

Bryn Celli Ddu, Anglesey

N53 12 17 W4 14 20

Bryn Celli Ddu means "Hill Grove Dark" or "Mound in a Dark Grove," an indication of the mystery and power within this turf-covered prehistoric site. It has been called "the best passage grave in Wales," but it was more than a grave. It opens to the northeast, to the light of the summer solstice sunrise—the only such known alignment in Wales. It may once have had a roof-box to focus the sunlight's journey down the passageway, similar to the roof-box at Newgrange (see *Powerful Places in Ireland*, pp. 37-40), which focuses the winter solstice sunrise light.

In Irish mythology, the Dagda (father god of the Tuatha Dé Danann) mated with the great goddess Bóinne, who lived in Newgrange mound. Nine months later (magically, time had stopped, so it only seemed like a day), she gave birth to a son, Aenghus Óg. Perhaps the winter solstice light entering through the Newgrange roof-box and penetrating deep into the inner passage was a visual and symbolic substitute for this mythic sexual union. No such myth is known to be associated with Bryn Celli Ddu, but perhaps a similar intention was at work.

The site looked quite different in the late Neolithic, around 4000-5000 years ago. At that time, it was part of an extensive ritual and ceremonial landscape of which little remains. Bryn Celli Ddu began as a henge, an open-air ritual enclosure. It included a stone circle with 14 stones, surrounded by an exterior bank and an interior ditch. This construction had a diameter of 57 ft. Some 1000 years later, all except two of these stones were smashed: a replica of one survivor currently stands behind the mound and the other one is inside the chamber. Perhaps a new religion had taken over, resulting in a shift in ritual and belief system.

A passage grave was built over the circle-henge and covered by a large earthen mound. The walls were retained with kerbstones, and dry-stone walling stabilized the outer passage. During modern excavations, quartz pebbles, hearths, and an ox burial were found beneath the large forecourt.

Today, the reconstructed structure lies beneath a much-smaller-than-original turf mound. Outside the mound, in the southwest, is the replica of the 5-ft-high standing stone

Children entering Bryn Celli Ddu

found at the site. The original is in the National Museum in Cardiff. The stone is covered with zigzags and spirals, as if it was originally viewed from all directions. This stone was discovered lying on top of a pit behind the chamber. Perhaps it was used to sanctify the new passage tomb. In the pit were gravel, sand, clay, and a burnt bone and human ear bone, all that remained of a larger bone deposit—or maybe that was all that was buried, and the ear bone had special significance.

The reconstructed mound and the 27-ft-long entrance passage give the visitor the experience of entering into a dark, mysterious chamber, which is exactly what Bryn Celli Ddu is. Although an opening and recess have been created in the southwest wall to let light enter the chamber, originally this wall was buried within the much-larger earthen mound. There would have been no external light. (Bring a flashlight.)

Inside the chamber is an impressive standing stone. No one knows its purpose. It has an unusual texture, almost like a petrified tree trunk. Rupert Soskin has suggested that the megalith actually is a petrified tree trunk (see http://www.themodernantiquarian.com/forum/?thread=52982). According to Soskin, it has been impossible to have any invasive testing done, so perhaps the most that can be said is that "if the builders thought it was a stone tree it would have been magical to them" (Soskin, personal communication, 23 Dec. 2011).

The standing stone inside the chamber

It is unusual to find a freestanding monolith inside a megalithic chamber, although Steven Burrow, the archaeologist who discovered the summer solstice alignment, writes that similar pillars are found in passage tombs in Ireland and possibly near the chamber entrance at Barclodiad y Gawres (see pp. 267-271).

Bryn Celli Ddu has a rounded, feminine shape; it reminded us of a nurturing womb. This appearance contrasts strongly with the interior monolith, which resembles a huge lingam. Perhaps this is a clue to the original use of this sacred site: a balance of masculine and feminine, with the rays of the summer solstice sunrise penetrating the long entry chamber and entering "the womb" of the mound—the very place where the tall monolith stands off to one side. Was it a birthing room? A fertility chamber? A place linking life and death? We've been told the site is particularly powerful in March and is aligned with Venus. There is much to ponder in this mystery.

> Megalithic chambers, like other enclosed spaces, are resonance boxes. Modern researchers have revealed important acoustical properties in a number of ancient sites (see Hale 2007). One blogger hit the monolith at Bryn Celli Ddu and discovered that "When struck this stone emitted a bell-like tone, and as a musician I would say it was close to an e natural but this is really a guess. It reminded me of a Tibetan singing bowl that I own, having a similar long "clean" resonance. I have seen a similar stone deep within in an obscure and difficult to access sacred cave in Northern Thailand." Posted by Porkbeast, 12th July 2000ce, http://www.themodernantiquarian.com/site/352/bryn_celli_ddu.html, retrieved 19 Dec. 2011.

> Inside Cairn L in the Irish Loughcrew Hills, the rising sun at Samhain (early November) and Imbolc (early February), two Celtic-calendar cross-quarter days, strikes a freestanding white limestone monolith. The stone and cairn long predate the Celtic presence in Ireland, raising intriguing questions about the megalith builders' precursor to the Celtic calendar. Http://www.carrowkeel.com/sites/loughcrew/cairn11.html retrieved 27 Dec. 2011.

> We felt that the ancestors were still present in Bryn Celli Ddu, and I sensed that at least one of them, a fierce warrior with a threatening, upraised arm, was angry at our invasion of his "home." I heard him growl, "You didn't ask permission. You have no respect!" The vision was a powerful reminder that we must always ask before we enter a sacred place. (Elyn Aviva)

Before entering the chamber, ask permission. We sensed that the guardian spirit(s) were not pleased at having this sacred site turned into a tourist attraction. Treat it properly and with respect. Pay particular attention to the freestanding "petrified" stone in the chamber. When we were there, it seemed to radiate energy.

On the ridge to the north is a standing stone, a reminder of the extensive, intervisible megalithic landscape surrounding Bryn Celli Ddu. Unfortunately, little now remains.

Getting There

Bryn Celli Ddu is managed by Cadw; unrestricted access. On crossing the bridge over the Menai Strait, turn left toward Llanfairpwllgwyngyllgogerychwyrndrobwll-llantysiliogogogoch (yes, the town with the longest name). Take A4080 for approx. 2 mi and turn right at first crossroads. Park in the car park (see map on p. 257). The mound is reached by crossing over a stile and then walking ten minutes on a paved path from the parking area.

Bryn Gwyn Standing Stones and Castell Bryn Gwyn, Anglesey

Standing Stones: N53 10 40 W4 18 16

Castell Bryn Gwyn: N53 10 31 W4 17 44

The Bryn Gwyn standing stones (means "White Hill"), located on either side of a gate in a hedgerow between Brynsiencyn and Dwyran on Anglesey's southwest coast, are two of the tallest stones in Wales. Walking along the hedgerow, you won't see them until you are almost upon them, although they are visible across the field from the A4080, opposite Bryn Gwyn Hall. When you stand beside them, you realize how huge they are.

One is blade-like and over 13 ft high and 14 ft wide; the thinner side aligns east to west. The notches on top are the result of its having been used as a gable-end in an eighteenth-century cottage. The other standing stone is 10 ft high, 9 ft wide, and 6-8 ft deep, depending on where you measure. It has a bulky, trapezoidal shape, flat on top instead of pointed.

The two unmatched stones reminded us of the huge megaliths at Avebury, England, which some investigators think alternate masculine and feminine energies, depending on their shape (http://en.wikipedia.org/wiki/Avebury

The Bryn Gwyn Standing Stones

retrieved 23 Dec. 2011). The squatter standing stone has a small boulder at its base. If it is "female," perhaps this represents its "offspring"? (http://www.megalithic.co.uk/article.php?sid=716, submitted by AngieLake).

These immense, lichen-covered stones are part of what was a large ceremonial complex. From the Bryn Gwyn Stones, the midsummer sun rises over the center of nearby Castell Bryn Gwyn. The megaliths date from 2000 BCE. They are reputed to be part of a circular stone henge. "In 1723 Henry Rowlands described them as part of a ruinous circle of eight stones, some 16 meters across" (http://en.wikipedia.org/wiki/Bryn_Gwyn_stones). Recent excavations indicate that, although the other stones are no longer visible, Rowlands appears to have been accurate. (For a discussion on whether the stones were part of an alignment or a circle, see http://www.stone-circles.org.uk/stone/bryngwyn.htm.)

A public footpath runs past the stones from Bryngwynmawr on the A4080, continuing past Castell Bryn Gwyn, 306 yd (0.17 mile) to the NE; further to the NE, at Tre'r Dryw Bach another stone circle was recorded in the eighteenth century but has

> "...There is always a sense of comfort and calm about [Welsh standing stones] and a quiet feeling of ownership of the surroundings as though we are the ones visiting and they are the ones staying." Marcia Lieberman, journal entry June 1998, back cover, 2011.

long been cleared away. The path continues to Caer Lêb, another prehistoric site where there is nothing now to see. Further NE, two standing stones mark a minor bend in the Braint River (Avon Braint). Although many sites have been destroyed over the centuries, enough evidence remains to indicate that this was an important ceremonial area from the Neolithic into the early Christian era.

Castell Bryn Gwyn is located in a field close to A4080 between the villages of Dwyran and Brynsiencyn. The near-circular site has been occupied since 3000 BCE, perhaps beginning as a Neolithic henge. Later it functioned as an Iron Age site and then as a Roman fortification. It was not a hill fort—it is not on a hill—but it appears to have had earthen defense work. A high bank up to 8.5 ft high remains, surrounding a flat central area about 171-184 ft across. Outside the bank is a nearly obliterated external ditch. Perhaps it was used as a ceremonial center, and the "defense work" was intended to separate sacred from secular space.

Castell Bryn Gwyn

Getting There

To find the Bryn Gwyn Standing Stones, park in a lay-by on a bend on A4080 across from the mansion called "Bryn Gwyn" (see map on p. 257). You'll see a hiking/walking sign and a set of steps to climb over. Follow the path parallel to the road, to the left of the line of trees and hedges that divides the two fields. About 3 minutes walk along the hedge row you will see the stones to the right at a break in the hedges.

To get to Castell Bryn Gwyn drive on B4080 west of Brynsiencyn. On the left hand side of the road you will come to a Cadw sign for Castell Bryn Gwyn and a pull-off. Follow the path from there to the site.

Barclodiad y Gawres, Anglesey
N53 12 30 W4 29 51

Barclodiad y Gawres—"The Giantess' Apron-full"—is another important megalithic site on Ynys Môn. It is the largest Neolithic tomb in Wales and dates between 3000-2500 BCE. If you want to go inside, you must first arrange a tour or get the key (see below). Otherwise, you can look into the tomb, but only from the wrong side of a locked gate. It's in an impressive location, high on a cliff side, with pounding surf below.

A large, turf-covered concrete dome encircles the remains of this 5000-year-old cruciform passage grave/ritual chamber. It is likely that originally the passage grave was covered with a huge rock pile and no turf: hence the name, "The Giantess' Apron-full," referring to rocks carried—and dropped—by a giantess. For a Welsh legend, go to http://www.valleystream.co.uk/giants.htm.

The site is accessed from the north. Two metal gates lead into the mound, approached via an ample, stone-lined passage open to the sky. When we were there, the first gate was unlocked, so visitors could walk between two rows of tilting, moss-tinged standing stones. The second gate was locked, protecting the interior from unsanctioned visitors but enabling them to peer inside. Fortunately, we had a key.

Scattered in the center of the expansive dome are the bare remains of the cruciform passage grave. Three side chambers are set at the end of a straight passage, which opens into a large central chamber.

A massive engraved stone stands at the entrance to the central chamber, perhaps similar in concept to the monolith inside the chamber at Bryn Celli Ddu (see Burrow, p. 105). Over the years, investigators have identified six other pecked and incised stones with zigzag, chevron,

Entrance to Barclodiad y Gawres

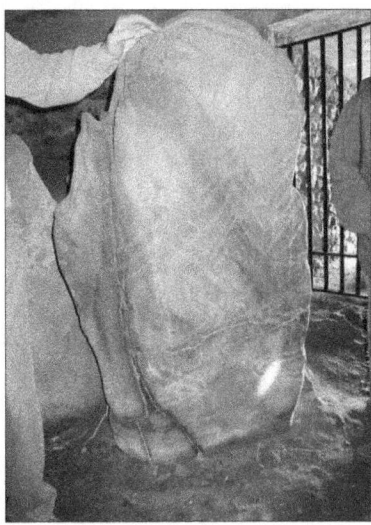
Incised stone at the entrance

and spiral designs, reminiscent of those found in Irish tombs. This suggests that ancient Irish colonizers built them both, or at least affirms that there was artistic communication between Wales and Ireland. These carvings (along with the stone at Bryn Celli Ddu) are considered the finest examples in Britain. Be sure to bring a flashlight if you want to see them.

Archaeologists made a surprising discovery in the central chamber. They excavated a hearth that had had a long-burning fire quenched with a stew of wrasse (a small fish), eel, whiting, frog, toad, grass snake, mouse, shrew, and hare, then covered with a layer of limpet shells and pebbles. Most of these are animals that we would not think of as edible, so the question is: why those creatures? The contents of this strange offering seem inexplicable.

In a side chamber archeologists found the cremated remains of two men. It appears that Barclodiad y Gawres was both a tomb and a place for ritual. Perhaps the burials were an intrinsic part of the rituals, or vice versa.

Elyn's first impression as she approached the entry to the mound was to feel "sorry" for the mossy green stones inside the locked metal gate. They seemed imprisoned and uncomfortable, separated from the other standing stones at the

> Rupert Soskin suggests "One possible link between these creatures [in the stew] is that they live in the margins of the natural world: in water, where man may drown; underground, where the dead are buried; or coming out at night, where the veils between living and dead seem to be lifted." Soskin, p. 87.

entrance to the mound. Inside the mound, Elyn felt increasingly ill at ease. While others in our small group crawled over and around the scattered megaliths, looking for carvings, taking photos, shining their flashlights in all directions, Elyn suddenly "heated up" as if she were on fire. Once outdoors she immediately felt better. Perhaps she was responding to energies that were trapped beneath the concrete dome, or perhaps to energies triggered by the disrespectful treatment of the sacred site.

> Even though today Barclodiad y Gawres is a jumble of fallen megaliths protected under a large cement dome, it is important to ask permission before entering and to wait for a response. Behave with respect. Clambering around the stones diminishes one's awareness of whatever energies may be present—and the spirit guardians of the place are not amused.

If you are able to enter Barclodiad y Gawres and Bryn Celli Ddu, compare your experiences. Both mounds have been reconstructed, but they have been reconstructed quite differently. At Bryn Celli Ddu, you seem to be inside the chamber as it was originally constructed, and the grass-covered mound completely covers the stone structure. At Barclodiad y Gawres, the interior space is much larger than the disarrayed stones, so you can walk around and over them.

The site is kept locked. Cadw offers guided tours on occasion. It may or may not be possible to get the key. Because of spray-paint vandalism, the visitation rules have been changed. To quote the Cadw plaque: "Accompanied viewing of the burial chamber internally is available on weekends and Bank Holiday from 12 – 4 pm, from 1 April to 31 October. To arrange a viewing please contact the Wayside Stores in Llanfaelog, approx. 1 mi away (tel. (0)1407 810153; mob. (0)7870 665605). To reach the shop, turn left out of the car park and continue along the A4080 to the Wayside Stores (AKA Storfa Wayside Shop), Llanfaelog. For current access details, contact Cadw at (0)845 0103 300." (Go to http://

cadw.wales.gov.uk/daysout/barclodiad-burial-chamber/visitor_information?skip=1&lang=en.)

Getting There

Park in the sandy parking lot close to the monument at Cable (Trecastell) Bay on A4080 and walk 500 yd (a 5-10 minute walk) up the sandy path into the dunes (see map on p. 257). You'll see the mound ahead of you on a promontory above Caernarfon Bay.

Lligwy Complex
N53 21 7 W4 15 17

The Lligwy complex in eastern Anglesey includes a burial chamber, a hut group, and a chapel. These diverse constructions provide an excellent opportunity to experience millennia of land use and habitation—Neolithic, Roman, and medieval—all during a short, pleasant walk through the countryside.

Lligwy Burial Chamber, Anglesey

Lligwy Burial Chamber resembles a strange eight-legged beetle, its squat uprights barely holding up the massive, 25-ton capstone. Approximately 2/3 of the chamber is underground. The capstone, marked with deep upright grooves that probably indicate how it was separated from bedrock, is 18 ft long by 15 ft wide, suspended over a natural fissure in the limestone rock. The capstone seems to hover over the pit, and it is probable that the chamber was excavated below the capstone—or that the capstone was pried out of the bedrock, lifted up, and then the pit was

Din Lligwy Burial Chamber

excavated. It is also possible that the capstone was dragged to the site, as suggested by the Cadw information plaques. There is no trace of the original rock or earthen mound, if there was one.

The unburned bones of between 15-30 people were found buried in the chamber and covered with a layer of limpet shells. Additional discoveries include animal bones, shells, flint implements, a bone pin, and pottery. The chamber was originally constructed during the Neolithic (3000 BCE); however, the most recent burial took place during the Bronze Age, 1000 years later, so it was in use for an extended period.

> "Studies of the cromlech at Lligwy (not to be confused with Din Lligwy), on the other hand, not only revealed no signs of a mound, but suggested that it was designed to provide its builders and later generations of visitors with a spring and autumn equinox alignment. This feature can still be appreciated today, on March 21st and September 21st, and this function would be rendered impossible had the megaliths been hidden by an earth and rocky cloak." Http://www.bbc.co.uk/wales/northwest/sites/anglesey/pages/cromlechi.shtml.

You can slide or back into the chamber through the original entry on the east. Inside, on the east, is a stone ledge. Was it an altar? A resting place for the dead? A place for "dream incubation" (the process of seeking visions and guidance by sleeping, perchance dreaming, in a particularly powerful place)? The interior of Lligwy burial chamber is an intriguing place, semi-subterranean but with light coming in through triangular gaps between the uprights.

Spend time in the chamber, sensing into the space, the energies. What does it feel like to be partly underground and underneath the massive capstone?

Din Lligwy Ancient Village, Anglesey

Din Lligwy Ancient Village or Hut Group is a Celtic and Roman settlement constructed close to the precipitous north edge of a limestone plateau. A small Iron Age farming community first inhabited Din Lligwy. It is an excellent example of native settlement during the late Roman occupation, the third and fourth centuries CE.

Din Lligwy Ancient Village

You approach Din Lligwy by a path that leads through the woods. Suddenly you come upon a clearing filled with stone foundations surrounded by a thick low wall. The modern entrance to the site is in the east, through a rectangular building inside the wall that may have been a barn and/or gatehouse. The original entrance was in the south.

The numerous well-built house/hut foundations probably date from the pre-Roman inhabitants. The walls and foundations are constructed from upright limestone slabs. Some of the foundations are circular (probably homes), others rectangular (probably workshops or barns). Evidence of an iron-working workshop has also been found.

Remains from the Roman fortified settlement include the massive pentagonal protective surrounding wall, now decreased in height. The wall would have been between 4 and 5 ft wide. It was constructed of two rows of limestone slabs, the interior filled with rubble. This surrounding protective wall is called a *din*—hence, "Din Lligwy." It enclosed approximately ½ acre. The defensive wall may have been built during the decline of Roman occupation, when marauding

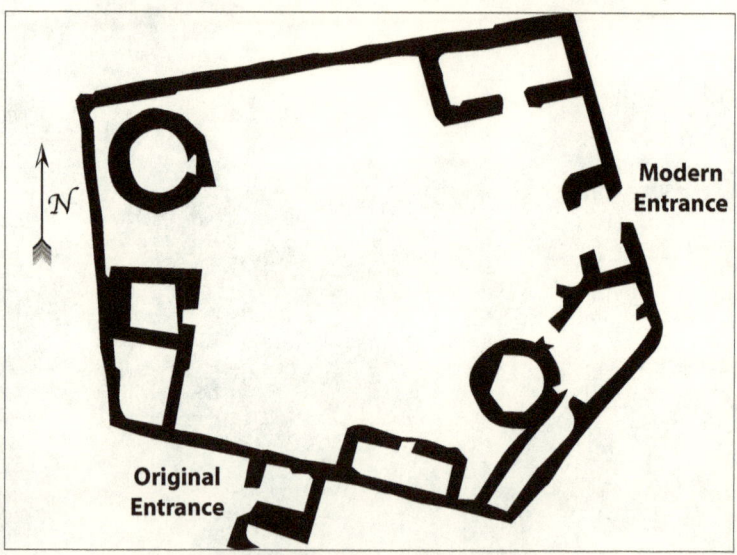

Plan of Din Lligwy Ancient Village

raiders were becoming prevalent, but it is doubtful whether it actually would have provided much protection. Perhaps it served some other purpose.

We (Gary and I) found the excavated settlement a surprisingly powerful place. Oddly peaceful, surrounded by mountain ash (rowan) and chestnut trees, it would be a lovely place to spend a day or two. The energy felt scrumptious, feminine, womb-like, protected, and safe.

Ynys Môn/Anglesey was the last holdout against the Romans. Some people have suggested that Din Lligwy was a Druid training center. If so, the initiates would have spent years living and studying—and performing ritual—in this location. Perhaps that accounts for the energy we felt.

Choose one of the circular huts and settle in on a comfortable ledge for a meditation. See what you discover.

Outer wall of Din Lligwy Ancient Village

Old Lligwy Chapel (Hen Capel Lligwy), Anglesey

Hen Capel Lligwy: Old Lligwy Chapel is a medieval church, now roofless, on a hill with an excellent view out to Lligwy Bay and, on a clear day, to the Isle of Man.

Originally built in the first half of the twelfth century, the upper parts of the walls were reconstructed in the fourteenth. In the sixteenth century, a small burial chapel and vault were added for the Pierce Lloyd family of Lligwy. The crypt is reached by a flight of rough stone steps. The church is entered through a doorway on the south. The large stone in the nave may have been the base of a churchyard cross. No more is known about the history of the church, including the saint to whom it was dedicated.

Old Lligwy Chapel

Entrance to the crypt

Although Hen Capel Lligwy stands alone in the middle of a field, it may originally have been in the midst of a village composed of wooden houses, now completely deteriorated. The village might even have been focused around Din Lligwy. The setting is attractive: scattered trees, rolling green hills dotted with sheep, the blue waters of the bay in the distance.

Din Lligwy is managed by Cadw; unrestricted access.

Getting There

Take the road signposted Din Lligwy from the roundabout on A5025 southwest of Moelfre (see map on p. 257). After passing Lligwy Burial Chamber, the road widens and there is room to park there (about 0.6 mi from A5025). Follow the footpath past Capel Lligwy.

Nearby Moelfre is a charming coastal village with several good cafes down by the harbor. It can be quite crowded.

Penmon Priory and St Seiriol's Holy Well, Anglesey

N53 18 21 W4 03 22

Penmon Priory and St Seiriol's Holy Well (Ffynnon Sant Seriol) are located on the easternmost tip of Ynys Môn. "Penmon" comes from the Welsh *pen*, meaning head, end, or promontory, and *Môn*, Welsh for Anglesey. The views are grand over the Menai Strait, with the hills of Snowdonia in the distance.

St Seiriol established a community here in the sixth century and became its first abbot. Danish raiders destroyed the original wooden buildings in the tenth century. The current church and cloister date from the twelfth and thirteenth centuries, when Penmon Priory came under the Augustinian Order. For a time, it was a thriving establishment.

The priory survived Edward I and expanded, but, like other British monasteries, it was dissolved in 1538.

The Bulkeleys of Beaumaris gained the property and enclosed much of the land. They converted the prior's lodging into a personal dwelling. In 1600 they built the impressive domed dovecote, with nesting room for 1000 birds, located next to the parking area. The medieval priory church has remained in use to the present day and is worth visiting.

Inside the priory church, note the checkerboard-patterned Norman Romanesque tower arch between the nave and the chancel. Its intriguing capitals might represent anything from fish to dragons to intertwined snakes. The walls of the south transept are decorated with a blind arcade of chevron-decorated stone arches. Above the arcade are several peculiar carvings, including a bearded man carrying an axe, which may represent Gofannon, the pagan god of blacksmiths, and a badly weathered, sandstone Sheela-na-gig with splayed legs. "The Sheela was thought to have originated on the west outside wall of the south transept, but

Entrance to Penmon Priory

is now fixed to the wall inside the south transept of the church" (http://www.sheelanagig.org/index.html#http://www.sheelanagig.org/SheelaPenmon.htm; also see this site for more information on other Penmon Priory carvings, including the capitals).

The church contains several other interesting objects. These include the boldly carved Norman pillar-piscine, dating to 1150, the current elaborately carved font, dating from 1000, and the tenth-century carved Penmon Crosses, whose interlacing and knotwork designs are clearly influenced by Scandinavian and Irish art styles. The smaller, better-preserved cross has one arm lopped off; at one time, the cross was used as a window lintel and was cut to fit the space. The amputation has destroyed its symmetry, but its interior location kept the complex carvings from disintegrating. Judging by the similar key patterns and panels of knots, it's likely that the original base of this cross is now used as a font.

Paths behind the church and opposite the domed dovecote lead to delightful St Seiriol's Well, a place of pilgrimage for centuries. The foundations of St Seiriol's original cell may be visible at the base of the limestone bluff to the left of the well house, but there is disagreement as to its exact location.

Originally, the well was known as Ffynnon Fair (Mary's Well). It was renamed St Seiriol's Well sometime after he arrived in the sixth century (Hughes, p. 181). The earlier name of Mary suggests that before

The south transept and the cross with the missing arm

the well was Christianized, it was associated with the Goddess or feminine energy.

The spring issues from the cliff behind, enters through the well house, and then flows into a large pond with ducks and water lilies, originally the monastic fishpond. When we were there, an elderbush to the right of the well had rags tied onto it, and the bottom of the well was covered with coins left as offerings.

> St Seiriol was known as the Pale Saint because once a week he would walk from Penmon Priory to Llanerchymedd to meet his friend St Cybi, who walked from Holyhead, where he had built a monastery within an old Roman fort. St Seiriol started out in the morning with the sun behind him and returned in the evening with the sun behind him, thus never receiving the direct impact of the sun's rays. St Cybi was known as the Golden or Tawny Saint because he started walking from the opposite direction, thus heading into the rising and setting sun.

The upper part of the well house is probably from the eighteenth century, but the lower section is much older, perhaps part of the priory's original chapel (which was built over the well, apparently). That might account for the serene atmosphere that surrounds the well—that and the fact that it has been sacred for millennia.

Find a place to sit down, perhaps on the bench next to the well house or on one of the inviting grass-covered,

> Graham Phillips (pp. 277-284) makes the intriguing but unverifiable suggestion that Sts Seiriol and Cybi were actually making a weekly pilgrimage to a holy well at Llanerchymedd, in the center of Ynys Môn, because next to the well was the burial place of Mary, mother of Jesus. Llanerchymedd Church is thought to be the oldest on Anglesey, and it is dedicated to the Virgin Mary. According to Phillips, her remains were later moved to Llanbabo church, and then moved again. Phillips suggests that Mary fled with Joseph of Arimathea to Ynys Môn to be far from Roman occupation. His story has a certain plausibility. The churches he mentions can still be visited. We found the energies around Llanerchymedd Church very unpleasant, however. The supposed well and grave are some distance from the church.

Inside St Seiriol's Holy Well

sun-warmed boulders scattered in the field, or at the base of the limestone bluff. Make yourself comfortable. Take time to center yourself. Open yourself to the environment, the holy well, and the garden. Breathe deeply and slowly. What do you feel? What do you experience? What memory do you want to take away from this sacred place?

We found the well and the area around it to be filled with loving, nurturing energy. When Elyn sat briefly on the stone bench/ledge beside the well, she felt as if her crown chakra had blown wide open.

Managed by Cadw; opening hours. Entrance is free but you have to pay to park at Penmon. The fee also lets you drive up the toll road for 0.75 mi to the easternmost point of Anglesey, within sight of Puffin Island, where St Seiriol established his original monastery.

Getting There

From Beaumaris take B5109 north for 1.7 mi, turn right at the T-junction, and continue along the lane to the priory car park (see map on p. 257). There is parking outside the priory but there is an option to travel further, on the toll road, toward the point and Puffin Island for a fee. The church is open throughout the day, all year.

More to Experience

St Tysilio Church, Church Island, Anglesey

N53 13 23 W4 10 18

The Church of St Tysilio is located on Church Island, Llandysilio, just over the Menai Bridge onto Anglesey. It is a tiny island, connected by a causeway to the shore. It is at the edge of the Swellies (pro. "swillies") stretch of the Menai Strait, between Telford Suspension Bridge (AKA Menai Bridge) and the Britannia Bridge. The Swellies are subject to strong, turbulent currents, reaching eight knots an hour. Church Island features an old cemetery, a war memorial, a huge yew tree, and the church.

Menai Strait and Britannia Bridge from St Tysilio Church on Church Island

Little is known about St Tysilio, but it is possible he was a Welsh missionary in Brittany in the late sixth and early seventh centuries. Inside the simple, fifteenth-century church, we felt a lot of buzzy energy, perhaps generated by the rushing waters of the Menai Strait. After all, fast-flowing water generates electricity, so it's no surprise that we felt a sort of "charge."

It would be interesting to stay in the church throughout the day, seeing what you feel as the tide ebbs and flows. It would also be interesting to compare the energies here with those in Llanfaglan Church (see pp. 292-294) on the mainland, located near the Menai Strait but not in it.

Getting There

The church can be reached in two ways. If you are on Anglesey heading to the Menai Bridge (not the Britannia Bridge), follow signs to Coed Cyrnol Park on Mona Road. If you are coming from the mainland via the Menai Bridge, keep going "straight" through the roundabout on A55 past Waitrose's shop and a Chinese restaurant. You'll see signs on the left for parking for Coed Cyrnol Park. Park in the lot, then follow the path down through the woodland to

The approach to Church Island along the Belgian Promenade

Church Island. Or, you might be able to park at the back of the parking lot behind the Anglesey Arms, right next to the Menai Bridge, and walk down a lane from the back of the lot. You'll soon reach the Belgian Promenade, a causeway built by refugees during WW I. At high tide, the promenade is wet and you have to walk along the top of the low barrier wall. Be sure to check tide times if you go this way. There are benches, and it's a pleasant place for a picnic (see map on p. 257).

Llyn Cerrig Bach, Anglesey

N53 15 32 W4 32 28

This small lake (today, a large pond) is located across from the RAF base. It is not easily seen from the road because it is hidden behind reeds, rushes, and gorse. This unassuming body of water was a sacred site for centuries. Numerous offerings—many of them weapons or objects, like chariots parts, associated with warfare—were deposited in the lake, apparently from 300 BCE to 100 CE. There is a theory that the offerings were deposited all at once by Druids desperate to defeat the invading Romans in 60 CE, but there is no clear evidence that this was the case.

Llyn Cerrig Bach

The offerings were discovered during WW II when the RAF was clearing the area. Some 150 offerings, most iron but some bronze and copper, were eventually hauled out of the bog at the southern end of the lake. They include iron slave chains, a trumpet, chariots and fittings, iron tools and bars, and swords, spearheads, and shields. The Llyn Cerrig Bach Horde is on display at the National Museum of Wales in Cardiff. See http://www.museumwales.ac.uk/en/2363/.

The now-shrunken lake is a peaceful place, somehow still sacred despite the centuries that have elapsed since Druids deposited offerings in its waters.

Getting There

Take A55 to the RAF Valley exit (Exit 4). Follow the road through housing and over a small railway bridge (see map on p. 257). The road swings around; on the left is the RAF base entrance with sentry; just beyond, on the right side of the road, is a plaque describing the votive finds; beyond that is the dirt path to the lake. You can park on the path. There is also a parking pull-off further on, on the left side, next to a sign declaring the area behind the fence is "Off Limits - Secrecy Act."

Bedd Branwen, Anglesey

N53 20 11 W4 27 46

Bedd Branwen, on the river Alaw near Llanddeusant, is the supposed burial place of Branwen, who died of a broken heart upon returning to Anglesey from Ireland. Tradition claims the site was "Branwen's Island," and in 1813 a tumulus was discovered there containing several urns and the cremated remains of a Bronze Age burial. Excavations in 1967 revealed that "the barrow had been erected around a central standing stone, which itself dated to before 1400 BCE. A low mound of earth originally surrounded the central stone, which it is thought would have remained visible" (Senior, p. 69). Bedd Branwen has been described as a ring cairn surrounded by the remains of kerbstones, with a stone in the center near what remains of a cist (see http://www.megalithic.co.uk/article.php?sid=5954). Unfortunately, today there is very little to see.

Bedd Branwen is located in a field near the SW tip of Llyn Alaw. It is south of the public footpath to Glanalaw house, reached from a minor road 0.6 mi east of Llanddeusant. To get there, you have to walk down a long lane. You must ask permission of the house owner to walk into the field.

Llanbabo Church, Anglesey

Llanbabo Church (Eglwys Pabo Sant) doesn't look very imposing from the outside. According to Graham Phillips, however, this may have been one of the churches where the remains of Mary, mother of Jesus, were kept. One

> It is "a good, scarcely altered simple Medieval church which retains a great deal of the Medieval fabric, including decorate fragments of probable 12th century date, and a fine later Medieval roof" (http://en.wikipedia.org/wiki/St_Pabo%27s_Church,_Llanbabo, retrieved 17 March 2012).

source says it was founded in the 460s and dedicated to Pabo, son of a Scottish chieftain, who died in 530 (http://www.anglesey-hidden-gem.com/llanbabo-church.html), but  this may be apocryphal.

The current building is a twelfth-century church. Its circular yard filled with gravestones is probably evidence of pre-Christian usage. A stone called the "Llanbabo Devil" (Diafol Llanbabo) was once embedded in the churchyard wall but is now in the church. It is thought to represent a Celtic deity.

Llanbabo Church

When we were there, the church was locked, and there was no contact information posted at the entrance. We had to content ourselves with wandering through the graveyard and looking for the nearby holy well.

We found the grey, lichen-covered stone church strangely unsettling. Over the entrance (on the south side) are broken chevrons and three crudely carved heads, perhaps referring to

Entrance to Llanbabo Church

the Trinity—or perhaps to something more ancient. The one on the left is quite worn; the one on the right looks feminine, perhaps the remains of a Sheela-na-gig; the one in the center is quite large. We felt we were in the presence of something ancient, primitive, and very powerful. Perhaps the heads are guarding something within, even if there is no longer anything to guard.

Getting There

The church is on a minor road between Llanddeusant and Rhosgoch, near the Llyn Alaw reservoir (see map on p. 257).

Oriel Ynys Môn, Anglesey

Oriel Ynys Môn is Anglesey's main heritage center and art gallery, just outside Llangefni. It has a permanent exhibition describing the island's culture and history, as well as temporary exhibitions and numerous special events. There is a café and shop (http://www.kyffinwilliams.info/eng/oriel_ynys_mon.html).

Getting There

Oriel Ynys Môn is just north of Llangefni on B5111 towards Llanerchymedd (see map on p. 257).

Plas Newydd, Anglesey

Plas Newydd, on the banks of the Menai Strait, dates back to the fifteenth century. It was the ancestral home of the Marquess of Anglesey. It is a fine gothic mansion open to the public. Plas Newydd Burial Chamber, a megalithic dolmen, is located on the grounds of the stately home. It is possible "some repositioning and reconstruction work was carried out when the estate gardens were landscaped in the 18th century" (McDonald, p. 104), so the chamber is no longer what or where it originally was.

Getting There

Plas Newydd is on A4080 north of Brynsiencyn (see map on p. 257). National Trust; for opening hours and fees, see http://www.nationaltrust.org.uk/plas-newydd/.

Parys Mountain, Anglesey

Parys Mountain resembles a lunar landscape. It is a nearly exhausted copper mountain that has been mined for over 3500 years. "…a Carbon 14 date from charcoal from the excavation of a spoil tip (in the 1980s) has led to claims for an Early Bronze Age origin for these workings" (http://www.coflein.gov.uk/en/site/33752/details/PARYS+MOUNTAIN+COPPER+MINES%2C+AMLWCH/). Later, the Celts extracted ore, followed by the Romans. In the eighteenth century, production became industrial; and in the 1780s, it was the world's largest source of copper.

Layers of slag lie scattered over the eroded surface, along with copper-tinted puddles and multicolored rocks. Its current blasted state is impressive, demonstrative of the damage caused by human mineral extraction—and indicative of the great importance of copper. There is a waymarked Industrial Heritage Trail; the leaflet is available from Amlwch Industrial Heritage Center in Amlwch, 1 mi to the north. Underground tours are sometimes scheduled (see http://www.parysmountain.co.uk/). For an excellent description of the mountain and copper mining, see McDonald, pp. 47-50.

Getting There

Parys Mountain is south of Amlwch between B5111 and A5025 (see map on p. 257). There is a path from the car park on B5111.

Holy Island, Anglesey

Holy Island (Ynys Gybi) and its drab town, Holyhead, are located just off the northwest tip of Anglesey but is connected by road and rail bridges. Holyhead (Caergybi) is named after St Cybi, and it was the site of a Roman fort before it was home to the sixth-century saint. Holy Island includes numerous nature reserves, beautiful scenery, archeological sites, megaliths, and beaches (http://www.visitanglesey.co.uk/en-GB/holy_island-1057.aspx).

We recommend that you plan to stay for several days, get an Ordinance Survey map, ask "the locals" about sites to see, and explore. Near South Stack Cliffs, for example, are the Penrhos Feilw standing stones. These two bladelike-standing stones are about 11 ft apart and 10 ft tall, oriented NNW. They are Holy-

> Neil McDonald (p. 65) thinks it a strong possibility that this site "was once part of a much larger sacred landscape... as this is a large area with evidence of settlements not far away on the mountainside and a chambered tomb less than a mile away."

head schist, rough and heavily textured. Legend says they were at the center of a stone circle.

Across from South Stack, on the southeast flank of Holyhead Mountain, are the Mountain Hut Circles (AKA Cytiau'r Gwyddelod, Holyhead Mountain Settlement, southwest), a collection of 50 circular dwellings, 20 of which are still visible. Some have internal stone benches and basins. A short walk will take you to a number of them; a longer, strenuous walk will take you uphill to an Iron Age fort. The settlement has been dated to the middle of the first millennium BCE.

Getting There

Holyhead is the western end of A55, which comes from the mainland. It is the ferry terminal for boats to Ireland and other destinations (see map on p. 257).

Driving toward the Llŷn Peninsula, Gwynedd

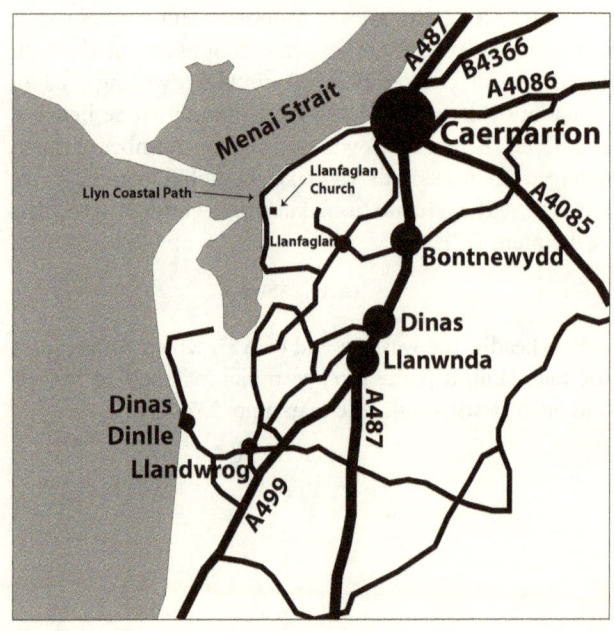

Area map

Llanfaglan Church, Gwynedd
N53 7 18 W4 18 42

Just beside the mouth of the Menai Strait is Llanfaglan Church, protected by towering beech trees and encircled by a stone wall in the middle of a green field. The church

Llanfaglan Church

is dedicated to a little-known Celtic saint, St Baglan ap Dingad, who may have been an abbot on Bardsey Island. It is an ancient church, built inside a raised oval enclosure, perhaps with standing stones incorporated into the surrounding wall.

The energy from the rushing Menai Strait is palpable, as is the wind. The church would have been a landmark on the old sea-lanes that went from northwest Wales to the south, as well as on the Pilgrims' Way to Bardsey Island.

The church is entered through a low, squat porch; the wooden truss dates to the fourteenth century. The church incorporates several fifth- or sixth-century engraved stones, another indication of its

> "The original nave dimensions make up a double square—another authenticator of Llanfaglan's antiquity—like those of the first Capel Beuno marked out in the floor at Clynnog Fawr" Hughes, p. 73. A double square is an important shape in sacred geometry: the square represents the element earth. The double square measurement is found in Solomon's Temple and in the King's Chamber in the Great Pyramid.

age. The interior is as it was in the eighteenth century, complete with box pews. A holy well, also dedicated to St Baglan, was located at the top of the field near the farm, a few hundred yards to the north. Unfortunately, it was dredged and infilled in the nineteenth century. The tradition was to throw bent pins in the well in hope of a cure.

The church was locked when we were there, but it felt like a powerful place. In 1991 the church was conveyed to the Friends of Friendless Churches, which works for its preservation. To obtain the key, contact Mr Bayles, White House, Llanfaglan; tel. (0)1286 673003; Mr Huw Jones, 4 Uwch Menai, Saron, tel. (0)1286 831335; or Mr Ifor Williams, Gwelfa, Llanfaglan, tel. (0)1286 676905.

Getting There

Situated 0.5 mi NW of Llanfaglan, in an isolated situation in a field some 160 yd east of the Llyn Coastal Path, which is a minor road that runs along the edge of the Afon Gwyrfai estuary (see map on p. 292).

Dinas Dinlle, Gwynedd
N53 5 4 W4 20 10

We often talk about "thin places," where the veil between worlds and realities becomes transparent, where you feel as if, if you take one more step, you will walk through into another realm. Here, at Dinas Dinlle, surrounded by beach tourists, it may be hard to imagine that this is such a place. But if you listen hard and long, sinking into quiet, you might almost — almost—see Gwydion the Magician strolling along the shore, and Dylan shape-change into a fish as he jumps into the sea,

> Caer Arianrhod is Welsh for the Corona Borealis constellation, and this connection links Arianrhod to "the Greek goddess Ariadne, whose silver circlet became that group of stars in Greek mythology. We thus perhaps have here an early religious site, the home or 'castle' of the local version of a pan-European goddess." Senior, pp. 12-13.

and his mother Arianrhod spinning in her spinning castle, the wheel of time, sunken under the near-transparent waters. (Elyn)

Driving toward the Llŷn Peninsula from Caernarfon, you'll see a large green mound rising beside the shore, south of the mouth of the Menai Strait. Part of this steep hill has disappeared into the sea. A wooden-plank path leads up to the top, past intriguing ridges and indentations. Something about it doesn't look natural—and that's because it isn't. Dinas Dinlle is a double-rampart Iron Age fort, constructed on top of a glacial deposit conveniently overlooking a maritime landing place. The oval-shaped fortification is about 164 yd by 120 yd. It was probably constructed around 500 BCE and was later used by the Romans until after the third century CE.

View of Dinas Dinlle from the nearby parking lot

Dinas Dinlle is described in the Fourth Branch of the *Mabinogi*, "Math, son of Mathonwy," as the home of Gwydion the magician. It was here that he raised his son/nephew, Arianrhod's rejected son, Lleu Llaw Gyffes (see pp. 240-242). The name may mean "the Fort of Lleu": *din* means fort, and *lle* may derive from Lleu. The hilltop fort looks out at the Yr Eifl and Gyrn mountain ranges, as well as at Caer Arianrhod to the south.

Between Dinas Dinlle and Pontllyfni, a short distance offshore, is a reef of stones known as Caer Arianrhod, the castle of Arianrhod, also mentioned in the Fourth Branch. This feature might be the remains of a stone circle or an ancient castle—or, more likely, a glacier-deposited lump of rocks. Whatever it is, it is visible at low tide.

South of Dinas Dinlle, between Pontllyfni and Aberdesach, is Trwyn Maen Dylan, which translates as "the Headland of Dylan's stone." On the beach below is a large boulder, sometimes submerged, known as Maen Dylan or Dylan's

View to the sea from the top of Dinas Dinlle

Stone. This stone is associated with Arianrhod's other rejected son, Dylan Eil Ton (Dylan, Son of the Waves), who was named by his great-uncle Math. As soon as the child was baptized, he leaped into the sea, returning to his true element. Later, his uncle Gofannon inadvertently killed him. Legend says that here, at this tide-washed boulder, Dylan plunged into the water.

Climb to the top of Dinas Dinlle. Scan the shoreline. Imagine that you are entering into a mythic realm. Imagine that Gwydion the magician strolls proudly along the beach, that Arianrhod spins in her revolving castle under the sea, and that the child Dylan swims like a fish in the rippling waters.

Getting There

Drive on A487 south of Caernarfon, turning at the Llandwrog exit. Continue on the minor road to Dinas Dinlle (see map on p. 292).

Plank path on Dinas Dinlle

Llŷn Peninsula, Gwynedd

Crossing to Bardsey Island (Ynys Enlli), two miles from the tip of the Llŷn Peninsula, is a dangerous undertaking. If you succeed in reaching the whale-shaped island, you may be stranded for days. But you would have good company. Some 20,000 saints reportedly lie buried there—along with Merlin, who is said to guard the thirteen talismans of Britain, hidden on this wind-swept bit of land. We're told that Bardsey is a magical place, and it must be if Merlin is there. But we were only able to see the island from the shore. The churning sea was too difficult for us to cross. (Elyn)

The Llŷn Peninsula, like Ynys Môn, is filled with powerful places. It is about 25 mi long and averages 8 mi wide. It is much less developed than Ynys Môn and remains (like Ynys Môn) a stronghold of Welsh language and cultural identity. For centuries, the Llŷn was a thoroughfare for pilgrims heading to holy Bardsey Island. The Romans came close to the Llŷn, establishing an important regional center at Segontium, near modern-day Caernarfon, but it appears they penetrated no further. Thus the Llŷn remained undeveloped, indigenous, and self-contained.

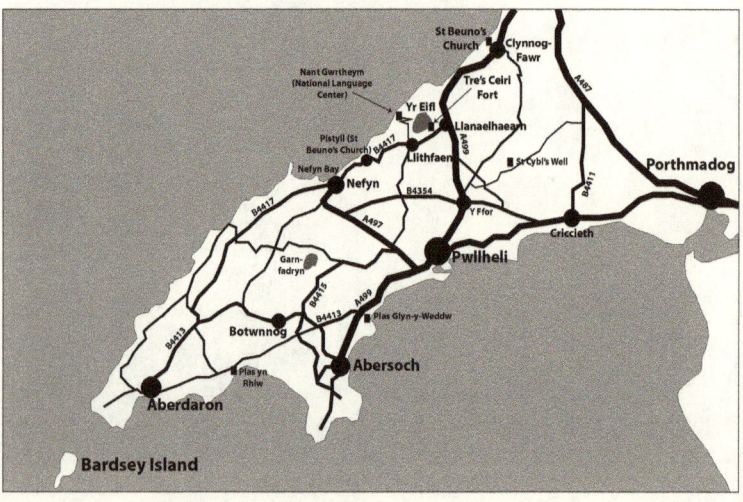

The Llŷn Peninsula

St Beuno's Church, Clynnog Fawr, Gwynedd
N52 57 8 W4 29 24

St Beuno's Church at Clynnog Fawr is located at the entrance to the Llŷn Peninsula. Its size seems to overwhelm the tiny community beside it. At one time, however, this was one of the most important churches in North Wales. Originally founded by St Beuno in the seventh century, it was dramatically expanded in the late fifteenth or early sixteenth century to become the large church you see today. A barrel-vaulted passageway in the church leads to the sixteenth-century chapel probably built over St Beuno's cell.

In the Middle Ages and later, this was an important pilgrimage shrine en route to Bardsey Island. In addition, the church was famous for its curative holy well and the miracle-working tomb of St Beuno. The seventh-century saint's healing power was called upon for epileptic children, sick animals, and general ill health.

"Throughout the Middle Ages epileptic children, as well as men and women seeking physical cures, would travel far and wide to bathe in the sacred well next to St Beuno's great monastery, and final resting place, at Clynnog Fawr. … After being washed, the sick pilgrims would sleep on, or next to, the holy abbot's Shrine – and those who succeeded in dozing off were said to be certain of a cure. St Beuno was also a very popular patron of sick animals, and many farmers from all over Wales and the borders would bring votive offerings to his church, seeking healing or health for their livestock. … Indeed, it can be said that many visitors and pilgrims still come to Clynnog Fawr, seeking the intercession of the saint either for themselves, friends and relatives, or a beloved pet." http://areluctantsinner.blogspot.com/2010/04/st-beuno-patron-of-epileptics-and-sick.html, retrieved 24 Dec. 2011.

Exterior of St Beuno's Church, Clynnog Fawr

When we visited, St Beuno's Church felt empty, like a long-vacant house. It was filled with light from many windows, and the walls were plastered white, so it wasn't dark

Interior of St Beuno's Church, Clynnog Fawr

and dreary inside. But it felt empty. We weren't sure what was missing, but something seemed to be. Perhaps the church is an example of how, without ongoing interaction, even a venerated holy place may become flat and dull, losing its energy. However, you may have a different experience.

The holy well is located 200 yd WSW of the church, on the old road as you walk out of town. The well is a walk-in structure with stone seats. Unfortunately, we could not get in because a padlock had been attached to the gate. Although some years ago the well was open and well cared for, it was now inaccessible and in a state of neglect.

Getting There

Clynnog Fawr and St Beuno's Church are on A499 south from Caernarfon. Drive on A487 to the junction with A499 and continue south (see map on p. 298).

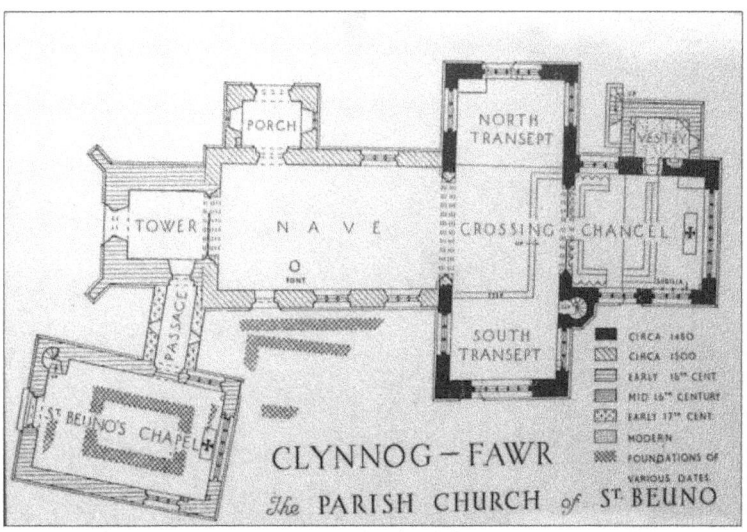

Floor plan of the church

Nant Gwrtheyrn, Llŷn Peninsula, Gwynedd
N52 58 32 W4 27 29

Nant Gwrtheyrn is a deep, narrow slit in the land, leading down to the sea. The Nant valley is surrounded on one side by Yr Eifl (the Eifl Mountains) and the other by Nefyn Bay. Overlooking the valley is Tre'r Ceiri, with its impressive prehistoric hillfort remains, including over 150 stone huts, proof that the area has been inhabited since the Iron Age. The Celts were there, as well as the Romans, and then medieval princes, and, later still, modern quarrymen and their families. The legends that resonate in the valley span millennia.

Nant Gwrtheyrn

The sinuous road that descends abruptly from the top of the valley is lined with dark, looming trees and thick clumps of rustling bracken ferns. The further you descend into the valley, the more you feel that you are entering a place filled with unseen creatures and shifting energies. Once you reach the bottom of the valley near the sea, however, the atmosphere lifts.

In 1878 Nant Gwrtheyrn village was established for workers in the nearby Port Nant granite quarries. The granite "square stone sets" were shipped directly from the port to pave British streets. By the end of WW II there was no more need for the stones, and by the late 1950s the village was deserted, the houses derelict, and the one-time quarrying village was an official "lost village" and the steep, corkscrew road unpaved. In 1978 it was bought by a charitable trust and transformed into The Welsh Language and Heritage Center, specializing in residential Welsh-language immersion courses (http://www.nantgwrtheyrn.org). Our guide, Hilary Wylde, told us that when she studied Welsh at the center, she sometimes had to walk into and out of the Nant because the road surface was quite hazardous in bad weather. It has been improved since.

The atmosphere of the valley is thick with legends. According to one version, when the Romans withdrew from the British Isles, they left their stewards, the Gwrtheyrnion, in charge. According to this version, Gwrtheyrn Gwrthenau (AKA Vortigern; see pp. 244-245) was a despot who employed Saxon soldiers to retain power but they turned against him. In 450 CE he fled first to Dinas Emrys and then to Nant Gwrtheyrn. Why there? Perhaps because the valley was a rich source of iron, used in weaponry, or perhaps because his wise men/Druids told him to flee there.

Legend says he built a castle in the Nant and was buried in a nearby tumulus called Bedd Gwrtheyrn, "Vortigern's grave," at nearby Castell Gwrtheryn. Other legends claim

Gwrtheryn jumped off a nearby cliff in despair for his betrayal of the Briton cause. In another version, "God sent fire from Heaven to burn Gwrtheyrn during a storm only for him to be killed, together with his son Gwrthefy, whilst escaping from ... one of the local leaders" (Clowes, p. 14).

Another legend says lightning struck Gwrtheryn's castle and destroyed it. A nearby area is called Carreg Ddu ("Black Rock"), where the stones appear to draw lightning. Perhaps this has something to do with the high iron content of the igneous cliffs. So many stories revolve around Gwrtheryn/Vortigern that there might be some kernel of truth in the sum of them.

Long after Vortigern's death, according to the local legend, three monks came to the Nant on their way to Bardsey Island. They were not made welcome, and they cursed the village three ways: no land there would ever be sacred and hence nobody was ever buried in the valley; the Nant would succeed three times and fail each time; and there could be no marriages among families living in the Nant.

Mining tools in the museum at Nant Gwrtheyrn

Memorial to Rhys and Meinir

And indeed, even when the village was thriving, the dead were never buried in the Nant. Instead, they were laboriously hauled up the sides of the valley on a sled and buried in nearby towns (Clowes, pp. 14-15).

Another tale recounts the tragic wedding day of Rhys and Meinir, two young people from the Nant. Some 400 years ago they fell in love, even though they were cousins—in other words, members of the same family. Remember the curse? Everyone was happily looking forward to the wedding. That day, according to the local custom, Meinir hid and the groom-to-be with his friends went to find her and bring her back to the church. But they couldn't find her. Rhys searched for months, finally going mad with grief. Some years later, lightning split an old oak tree. Inside were Meinir's skeleton and the remains of her wedding dress. Apparently she had fallen into the hollow tree and could not escape. Once again, the monks' curse had fallen on the people of the valley. (Adapted from Clowes, pp. 15-16). A modern metal and oak-tree sculpture called "Meinir's Tree" commemorates the tragic couple.

The Nant is a place steeped in legends and mystery. Imagine Vortigern fleeing his enemies, racing for safety—finding the valley and descending into its depths. Imagine him wandering the steep cliffs, anguished by the harm he had caused and knowing that, although his advisors had supported the decision, he would bear the blame throughout history. Imagine the monks cursing the valley. Imagine, just imagine....

If you don't mind the drive down and up, the valley is a pleasant place for a short holiday. There is an excellent heritage center, a café/restaurant that also caters wedding feasts, and an office with a good supply of Welsh-language books and teaching materials. The village buildings have recently been refurbished and expanded to offer B&B and four-star self-catering accommodations. Hiking paths along the coast enable visitors to walk part of the pilgrims' route to Bardsey Island (Ynys Enlli). There is also a 3-mi-long nature trail.

Getting There

The 2-mi-long, precipitous road has 2 very sharp hairpin turns, one of which seems to point directly to the sea below. Going down the road only takes 5 minutes—unless you meet traffic: it is a one-lane road with frequent pullouts. Drive on A499 south of Caernarfon to the Llanaelhaearn roundabout and turn toward Nefyn (B4417). In Llithfaen, turn right opposite the shop and post office. Continue 2 mi, past houses and a car park on the left. The road will become narrower before descending to the village (see map on p. 298). Better yet, walk. They say it takes 20-30 minutes descending on foot, 40-50 minutes ascending.

St Beuno's Church, Pistyll, Llŷn Peninsula, Gwynedd

N52 57 8 W4 29 24

St Beuno's Church in Pistyll, on the north coast of the Llŷn Peninsula, doesn't look like much, but it packs a powerful energetic wallop. The unadorned, lichen-covered

Hilary in St Beuno's Church, Pistyll

grey stone building was an important staging point for medieval pilgrims to Bardsey Island. Nearby was a hospice for pilgrims, and the local monks grew hops and fruit. Perhaps the berry bushes around the church survive from that time.

The monks inherited the healing tradition from St Beuno (see p. 299), and some of their medicinal herbs are still found growing in the churchyard. Beginning sometime after 1950, the Friends of St Beuno's Church have strewn the floor with rushes and sweet-smelling medicinal herbs at Christmas, Easter, and Lammas.

The church is located on the downside of a slope, between a stone wall and a grove of trees, with a view of the sea. It was built upon a mound—perhaps the site of a previous, pre-Christian holy site, although there is no evidence. Originally founded in the seventh century by St Beuno, most of the church dates from the twelfth century. The steps jutting out from the base of the south wall may have been the original seventh-century entry. The cornerstone visible in the eastern part of the north wall is also from the original church. The church had a thatched roof until it was changed to slate in the nineteenth century. Nearby is a monastic fishpond.

Today, the interior walls are unadorned stone; the ceiling is wooden staves, some of which form an arch over the single nave. The solid, twelfth-century font has a Celtic design of intertwining strands, similar to the "endless knot" pattern.

Centuries ago there was a leper colony and hospital near the church. The lepers were kept outside the church but were able to see Mass and the elevation of the Host through the deep-set leper's window (called a "squint") to the left of the altar.

> St Beuno was born into Welsh royalty in 545. He became a wandering hermit until at last he settled down in what is now Caernarvonshire. He founded many churches along the western coast of Wales, including one on the Holy Island of Bardsey. Some eleven ecclesiastic establishments are credited to him, including Clynnog Fawr (see pp. 299-301). St Beuno restored his niece, Saint Gwenffrewi (Winefride), to life after Prince Caradoc decapitated her for refusing his amorous advances (see pp. 321-322).

Gary dowsed a water line up the nave, a water line crossing it at the altar, and a fire line crossing near the altar. There was also an energy vortex a bit off-center from the crossing.

When we visited the church, the floor was strewn with rushes. It seemed small, unassuming, modest, but like much of Wales, it doesn't reveal itself at the first glance, and never to a casual visitor. A group of tourists descended on the place, walked through while talking, looked around, took some photos, and left without even experiencing this powerful place.

After they had left, we (Elyn, Gary, and Hilary) sat in the wooden pews and meditated, dropping deeper and deeper, and the space opened up in a most surprising way. Elyn felt sadness in the church, perhaps because of the leper colony, and a need for healing. It was good that friends of the church are

Baptismal font in St Beuno's Church

putting herbs and rushes on the floor and showing their affection for the place. There were also much deeper energies to experience. Spend time meditating in the church and see what you discover.

Getting There

Pistyll is on B4417 west of Llithfaen. Detailed directions to Llithfaen can be found on p. 306 (see map on p. 298).

Garnfadryn (Carn Fadrun), Llŷn Peninsula, Gwynedd

N52 53 9 W4 33 39

The heart of the Llŷn Peninsula landscape, both geographically and perhaps mythically, is the flat-topped mountain Garnfadryn or Garn Fadrun, located toward the end of the Llŷn peninsula. It is an impressive site, with the remains of a Bronze Age cairn and ruins of an Iron Age hillfort, huts, and other structures, including a medieval castle. The view from the top is outstanding. A large flat stone on top is known as Arthur's Table and is associated in legend with the Stone of Destiny under the Coronation Chair in Westminster Abbey.

The word *Madryn* comes from the same source as *Modron*. Gon Madrin means Cairn or Stones of Modron, the Mother Goddess, the ancient creatrix of the land, goddess of fertility. She is equated with Greek Demeter and Irish Danu, as well as with the Morrigan—and even with Morgan la Fey in Arthurian legend. She is often said to be the daughter of Afallach, king of the Otherworld. Modron was the mother of Mabon, according to the *Mabinogi* tale "Culhwch and Olwen," and she is said to be the mother of Owain in the "Welsh Triads."

In one local legend, Madryn was the daughter or granddaughter of Vortigern, and she gave birth to Ceidio, who was "hidden from the enemies of religion"—the Christians. A nearby farmstead still bears the name of Ceidio Bach (Little Ceidio).

The ancient energies are strong in this peninsula, and they have left their mark on the place names. Sometimes there is not much to see, and only the name remains to evoke the power of place—that, and the special feeling one gets walking on the land. Sometimes there's a story that, in the telling, stirs the ancient landscape into life. Coastal walking trails link many of these sites. Go to http://www.ccw.gov.uk/enjoying-the-country/visiting-the-coast.aspx for detailed information.

> "Afallach is also a Welsh god of the Otherworld and of healing, son of Nudd and brother to Gwyn ap Nudd. His island is called [in Welsh] Ynys Afallach, 'Isle of Apples.' Related linguistically is the Irish Emhain Abhlach, 'Plain of Apples,' the home of Manannán mac Lir, trickster god of the sea and Otherworld." http://www.maryjones.us/jce/avalon.html, retrieved 23 Dec. 2011. Some think that Bardsey Island might be Avalon (see pp. 314-315).

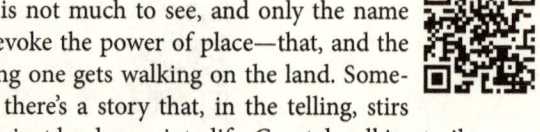

St Cybi's Well, Llangybi, Llŷn Peninsula, Gwynedd

N52 56 41 W4 20 24

Llangybi means "Cybi's Church or Enclosure." Just north of Llangybi is an area replete with dolmens and other megalithic remains. Here you will find St Cybi's Well (Ffynnon Gybi). St Cybi created—or more likely Christianized—the well in the sixth century. He also established a religious community at Holyhead on Ynys Môn, from whence he would walk weekly to meet his friend St Seiriol (see pp. 277, 280).

Legend says that St Cybi struck his staff on the ground and the holy well waters sprang forth. The well became famous for curing warts, blindness, scurvy, rheumatism, and for foretelling the romantic intentions of men. On the eve of Beltane, women dropped handkerchiefs, feathers, or even bits of bread "into the larger of the two pools and closely studied the direction in which they floated—southwards indicating their lover's future constancy, northwards his potential for infidelity" (Cope, p. 97).

St Cybi's Well includes two separate chambers: an ancient stone-walled spring and a large, more modern well house, unique for its beehive vaulting. The larger chamber was used for bathing or submersion. There was also a privy, wisely located downstream from the healing well. The well guardian's cottage was built around 1750, but the age of the other buildings is uncertain.

Approaching St Cybi"s Well

One of the treatments recorded in the eighteenth century was drinking well water and seawater in equal measures, then bathing in the well, and then spending the night in the adjacent cottage. "This act of incubation was thought to attract the saint back to his well to activate the healing process" (Cope, p. 97).

Sign on the path to St Cybi's Well

Like many Welsh holy wells, Ffynnon Gybi retains its sense of sacredness. Spend time sitting beside the waters, taking in the fresh and pleasing atmosphere. How does this well compare to others you have experienced, such as St Non's in Pembrokeshire, St Seiriol's at Penmon Priory, and Ffynnon Wnda at Llanwnda?

Getting There

The path to the well crosses several fields and runs beside a stream. It can be very muddy in wet weather, so wear appropriate footwear (wellies). It takes approximately ten minutes to walk there from Llangybi church. One route involves clambering over a stile at the back of the cemetery and following the fence line. Managed by Cadw; generally unrestricted access.

More to Experience
Aberdaron, Llŷn Peninsula, Gwynedd

The fishing village of Aberdaron is 2 mi before the tip of the Llŷn. Beginning in the sixth century, it was the last stop for many pilgrims heading to Ynys Enlli (Bardsey Island). The fourteenth-century Y Gegin Fawr (The Big Kitchen) served as a gathering place for pilgrims; now it serves as a café for tourists. The twelfth-century, double-naved church of St Hywyn was also an important stop for pilgrims before they set off to cross the treacherous strait. RS Thomas (1913-2000), one of Wales' greatest modern poets, was minister there until he retired in 1978.

Getting There

Drive on A499 past Pwllheli to Llanbedrog. Turn on B4413 and drive to the end of the penninsula (see map on p. 298).

St Hywyn Church, Aberdaron

Bardsey Island (Ynys Enlli), Llŷn Peninsula, Gwynedd

Bardsey Island (Ynys Enlli) is aptly named the Island of the Currents. The wild, whale-shaped island is located 2 mi from the tip of the Llŷn. The nearness is deceptive, however. The churning waters are unpredictable and dangerous to cross.

The island became a pilgrimage site in the sixth century when St Cadfan established his monastery there, although it is probable that it was a holy site long before Christians claimed it for their own. In the Middle Ages, three visits to Ynys Enlli were the equivalent of one pilgrimage to Rome.

> "Of all the islands which fringe the Welsh coast, Bardsey is the most sanctified. Here is a real Isle of the Blessed in the West, an island for the dead situated at the end of a peninsula along which a concentration of spirit paths and ancient pilgrims' ways run." Main, p. 21.

Bardsey Island is said to be the Isle of 20,000 saints—meaning holy people and pilgrims, not canonized saints—many of whom came to die upon the holy land. Others were transferred after death by boat across Cardigan Bay. Some say Myrddin lies sleeping there in a glass castle, guarding the Thirteen Treasures of Britain. Some claim Bardsey is the Isle of Avalon, and the mortally wounded King Arthur was transported there. According to Main (p. 25), "Welsh Druidical tradition places

> The legendary Thirteen Treasures of Britain are: Arthur's Cloak of Invisibility, the Sword of Rhydderch Hael, the Hamper of Gwyddno Garanhir, the Drinking Horn of Bran, the Chariot of Morgan, the Halter of Clydno Eiddyn, the Knife of Llawfrodedd, the Cauldron of Dyrnwch, the Whetstone of Tudwal Tydglyd, the Red Coat of Padarn, the board game Gwyddbwll, the Ring of Eluned, and the dish of Rhygenydd. There may be two more, mentioned in the "Welsh Triads": the Crock of Rhygenydd and the Mantle of Tegau Gold-Breast.

this Island of Apples off Cardigan Bay in the direction of Ireland."

A few buildings, a lighthouse, Lord Newborough's Crypt, a ruined twelfth-century Augustinian abbey, and numerous unmarked graves are all that remain on the island. Most people come to the island for a day to see the birds, especially the breeding shearwaters. Hilary Wylde spent several weeks there over the years, and she describes it as a very mystical and powerful place: "A real Celtic Otherworld with the haunting sound of the singing seals."

There are no facilities on the island, although some houses are rented out by the week. If you decide to spend a week instead of just a day, you'll need to bring all your food and other supplies, and book well in advance. If you are fortunate enough to make it across the strait, let us know what you discover.

Contact http://www.bardsey.org for rental information; Boat trips can be arranged from Aberdaron (http://www.bardseyboattrips.com) or from Pwllheli or Porth Meudwy (from there it is a 20-minute ride) (http://www.enllicharter.co.uk/ or http://www.enlli.org). Like any good pilgrimage, the journey is often as important as the goal.

Plas Glyn-y-Weddw Gallery, Llŷn Peninsula, Gwynedd

Plas Glyn-y-Weddw Gallery at Llanbedrog, near Pwllheli, is the oldest art gallery in Wales. Plas Glyn-y-Weddw is housed in a Victorian-gothic mansion, set in picturesque grounds with views of Cardigan Bay and Snowdonia. The gallery includes contemporary works, varied art exhibits, and a permanent collection. The conservatory has a very good tearoom. Accommodation is available in the rear wing of the building (http://www.oriel.org.uk).

Getting There

Plas Glyn-y-Weddw Gallery is on A499 between Pwllheli and Abersoch (see map on p. 298).

Entrance hall of Plas Glyn-y-Weddw Gallery

Plas yn Rhiw, Llŷn Peninsula, Gwynedd

Plas yn Rhiw House and Gardens (pro. "Plahs uhn Rhe-oo") are managed by the National Trust. The part medieval, part Tudor, part Georgian manor house is surrounded by lovely grounds, including ornamental gardens. It's a nice place for a short break during the day. Entry fee; opening hours; http://www.nationaltrust.org.uk/plas-yn-rhiw/.

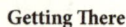

Getting There

Plas yn Rhiw is 11 mi SW of Pwllheli on a minor road off B4413 (see map on p. 298).

Gop, the North Coast (Denbighshire)
N53 18 36 W3 21 54

Gop is an artificial mound on top of a hill made higher by human effort. "See us!" "All this is ours," the builders of Gop seem to declare. But Gop is more than a point of reference from a distance—it is a powerful place, filled with Earth energies and the presence of the Dark Mother. Meditating in the concave center, I felt a rush of energy surround me. "Don't be afraid," it whispered. "There is nothing to fear in death." Although the wind blew fierce and wild across the top of Gop, I felt warm, surrounded by silence, in the calm eye of the storm. (Elyn)

Gop is Wales' largest and Britain's second largest artificial Neolithic mound (Silbury is the largest). It is also known as Carn Gop, Bryn-y-Saethau, and Gop-y-Goleuni. Built between 4000-3000 BCE, it is made of stone, covered with turf. It is a "huge, steep-sided smooth dome, with a large hollow in its center" (Senior, p. 82). The oval mound is on top of a hill 800 ft above sea level, with excellent views in all directions. It is approximately 300 ft by 240 ft, and 40

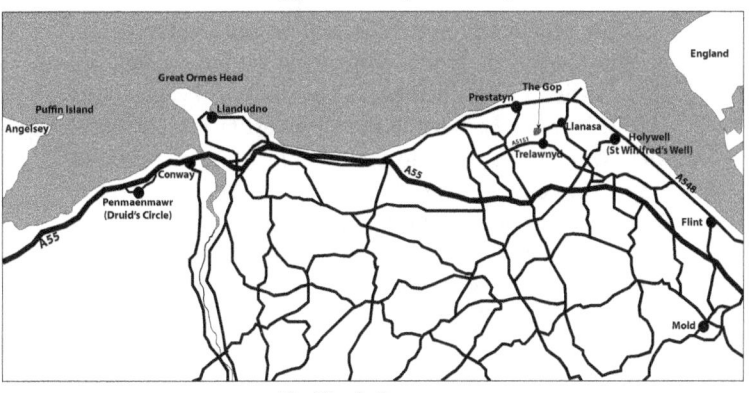

The North Coast area

ft high. It has not been fully excavated, but no burials have been found within.

Elyn "got" that Gop was used for seasonal ritual and ceremony. Gary "got" that it was a marker of great importance, visible from a great distance. It is reached by walking up a forest path. Don't forget to ask permission as you walk through the woods. Elyn had the distinct feeling partway along the path that she was walking not through a "thin" place but through a "thick" place, as if there was energy pushing back against her. After she asked permission to enter, the energy shifted. She had to ask permission more than once. She was quite surprised, since this occurred some distance before reaching Gop. Be attentive. Be respectful. See what happens.

> "It is possible that both the cave and cairn at Gop were part of a deliberately constructed landscape associated with death and the spiritual life of the local people."
> Burrow, p. 83.

Elyn approaching Gop

Below the massive cairn, in a limestone outcropping, is Gop Cave. Nineteenth-century excavations revealed a stone-walled burial chamber at the back of the cave, and at least fourteen bodies and numerous artifacts were found there. The bodies dated to the Neolithic. Legend says that Gop is the burial place of Bodicca (Boadicea), the brave Celtic warrior queen who fought against Suetonius Paulinus, the Roman governor of Britain, but there is no historic evidence of Bodicca or Paulinus having fought that battle in Wales or of her being buried there.

Elyn meditating inside Gop

Gary exploring the cave below Gop

Getting There

The site overlooks the Clwydian Hills, 4 mi SE of Prestatyn. It is accessed from a path above Trelawnyd on A5151 (see map on p. 317). Drive into Trelawnyd and turn up High Street at the community building with the clock tower; the turn is also marked with a sign to Llanasa. Follow the lane up and around, curving to the right and uphill toward the forest. You'll pass a large tree, a farm gate, and a stone wall on the left with a metal gate and some walking arrows on the post. Park off the road just a bit ahead. The path may be muddy and slippery, so hiking sticks are useful.

It is a gentle uphill walk of about 100 yd (perhaps 10-15 minutes in all). Walk up the path and through a gate. Immediately after, go through (or over) the gate on the left. A signpost there is engraved "Bryn Gop," but it is hard to read. The path forks; take the narrow path to the left through the woods.

After a short walk, you'll see Gop ahead of you. As you walk up to Gop, a barely visible path on your left leads down the hillside through the bushes. If you follow the path downhill, look to your right and aim toward two low, lumpy "mounds." The limestone outcropping and cave are just above that, directly below Gop. Be careful—the path may be slippery.

More to Experience
St Winifred's Well, Holywell, Flintshire

N53 16 41 W3 13 25

St Winifred's Well in Holywell (Ffynnon Gwenffrewi at Treffynnon) is in a dramatic location at the bottom of a wooded hillside. It has been a Christian site for over 1300 years. Before that, the waters were used by the Romans to relieve rheumatism and gout. Even before then, it was an important site, though we lack written documentation. This long history contradicts the Christian origin story that the spring burst forth in 660 CE at the spot where St Non's decapitated head came to rest.

According to the Christian origin story, in 660 CE (or thereabouts) Caradoc, a chieftain's son, decapitated the young virgin Gwenffrewi (AKA Winefride, Winifred, or Wenefred) for rejecting his unwelcome advances. The icy-cold spring sprang forth from the ground where her head fell. Fortunately for her, her miracle-working uncle, St Beuno, was nearby. He put her head back on her body, said prayers, and sprinkled her with the holy well water. She revived and be-

"This holy site is the oldest unbroken place of Christian pilgrimage in Britain - successfully surviving the Reformation, and nowadays called the 'Lourdes of Wales.' It is also the site of what legend claims to be the first British convent for women. Over the centuries many pilgrims and patrons as diverse as Lady Margaret Beaufort (Countess of Richmond, and mother of King Henry VII) and William Shakespeare (whose father called on St Winifred as a heavenly witness to his last will and testament) have been attracted to Holywell." http://areluctantsinner.blogspot.com/2010/04/st-beuno-patron-of-epileptics-and-sick.html, retrieved 28 Dec. 2011.

came abbess at Gwytherin Convent, a local monastic community near Llanrwst. St Winefride's became the center of a major popular cult, one strong enough to survive the Reformation.

> Inspired by the miraculous springing forth of the fountain, the poet Gerard Manley Hopkins wrote: "this dry dene, now no longer dry or dumb, but moist and musical/ With the uproll and the downcarol of day and night delivering/ Water which keeps thy name…" "St Winefride's Well."

The well is probably the Holy Head mentioned in the fourteenth-century poem *Sir Gawain and the Green Knight*. The elaborate well building visible today ("grandest well building of all of the wells in the British Isles," according to Cope, p. 213) was constructed around 1500. It includes the star-shaped well in the crypt, the large main bathing pool, and the chapel built above the crypt. The chapel key is available at the ticket office. The spring rises in the open crypt and flows out into the large exterior bathing pool. Modern-day pilgrims kneel and pray beside Maen Beuno (St Beuno's Stone) at the base of the steps in the frigid pool.

St Winifrede's Well

The on-site museum provides documentation of miraculous cures and contains numerous relics. Next to the chapel is the Parish Church of St James, built in 1770. It probably stands on the site of the original seventh-century chapel constructed by St Beuno.

Annually, some 30,000 pilgrims visit "The Lourdes of Wales." Healing pilgrimages take place, particularly during the summer and on St Winefride's Day, the near-

est Sunday to June 22. Arrangements to bathe are made with the custodian. Entry fee; opening hours (http://www.saintwinefrideswell.com).

Although the setting is impressive, and the ancient holy well should be a powerful place, we were unable to "get through" the institutionalized religiosity of the place. Cheap plastic rosaries were draped across the metal fence beside the chapel, a Welsh version of the Celtic "rag" or "clootie"-draped trees found beside holy wells throughout Ireland and Scotland.

Getting There

Holywell is 4 mi NW of Flint, on A548, the North Coast road (see map on p. 317).

The Great Orme, Llandudno, Conwy

The Great Orme (Y Gogarth) and Great Orme Copper Mine are located just outside Llandudno, on the northern coast. The Great Orme is a massive limestone headland with wonderful views (http://www.conwy.gov.uk/countryside). There are a few Neolithic sites on the hill, but the Bronze Age settlement was more extensive.

It had been thought that the Romans were the first to exploit the mines, but in the 1980s, excavations uncovered 4000-year-old animal bones used as scrapers (http://www.greatormemines.info). This is when Bronze Age people began to smelt the contents of the hill. They had discovered that the copper at Great Orme was available in a form easily extracted using simple tools.

At one time, Great Orme was the most important copper mine in Europe, if not the world. Great Orme Mines are the oldest metal mines open to the public anywhere. Exhibits, self-guided tour; entry fee. Note: the mines are closed during winter months, so be sure to check the schedule.

The area can be explored on foot, by car (including the thrilling Marine Drive, with its panoramic views), and by the Victorian Great Orme Tramway (http://www.greatormetramway.com).

Llandudno has managed to maintain an up-market Victorian resort atmosphere. There is even an Alice in Wonderland connection. Lewis Carroll modeled Alice on Alice Liddell, whose family summered in Llandudno in what is now the St Tudno Hotel; hence the White Rabbit statue on the seafront.

Getting There

Great Ormes Head and the town of Llandudno are just off the A55, which crosses Wales on its way to Angelesy and the ferries to Ireland (see map on p. 317).

Druids' Circle, Penmaenmawr, Conwy

The fancifully named Druids' Circle (Y Meini Hirion; means "Long Stones") on Penmaenmawr Mountain is worth the long trek up the hill. It is considered "the finest example found in Wales and .... among Britain's most notable prehistoric monuments" (Julian Heath, p. 95). It sits beside an ancient Bronze Age trackway running from Bwlch-y-ddeufaen to Conwy, now incorporated into the North Wales Path. Located on a broad plateau in the middle of moorland, there are magnificent views of Penmaenbach, the Great Orme, and Snowdonia.

> "The Druids' Circle probably formed the central focus of an important religious sanctuary or 'cult center' and people from both near and far probably came to perform rituals and ceremonies at the circle and the sites nearby." Julian Heath, p. 95.

To the NW is the igneous outcrop Graig Lwyd, protruding from the eastern end of Penmaenmawr headland. Graig Lwyd was a major source of stone for

> "One of the stones has an obvious ledge on it and is known as the Stone of Sacrifice, though a legend states that if a baby less than a month old is laid on the ledge briefly it will have permanent good luck! Another stone is badly shattered and tradition has it that it was once dragged away from the circle and rolled down the hillside you have just climbed up, where it shattered, only to be miraculously restored to its position by the following morning." http://www.walkingbritain.co.uk/walks/walks/walk_b/2497/, retrieved 25 Dec. 2011. (This link provides a detailed walking guide.)

axe making from around 3000 BCE. This was once one of the most important axe-making "factories" in Europe; examples have been found in Cornwall and southeast England. It is possible that the Druids' Circle was a trading center for stone axes quarried and shaped at Graig Llwyd (Julian Heath, pp. 96-97). Graig Lwyd is now the site of a modern stone quarry.

The stone circle currently consists of 30 stones of different sizes set in a low, stony bank. The entrance was in the SW, probably  originally flanked with portal stones. The diameter of the bank is approximately 80-85 ft. Two of the portal stones may have marked the moon setting in its most southerly direction. A number of cremated remains of children, aged 11-12, have been found at the site.

Getting There

Driving on A55 from Llandudno, take the minor road (which used to be A55) into Penmaenmawr. Turn left at the traffic light in the village center. The car park is almost immediately on your right.

Castell Dinas Brân, Llangollan, Denbighshire
N52 58 47 W3 9 11

The hilltop remains of the Dinas Brân Iron Age castle are impressive, even from a distance. Stark, outlined against the sky, they summon up images of martial power. Clearly, this was the seat of kings—or princes, at the very least. We made our way up the hill to the mythic seat of the giant Brân the Blessed, god of sun, writing, arts, and war, possessor of a magic cauldron, the son of the sea god Llŷr and grandson of Belenos, the Sun God. According to Mara Freeman, Dinas Brân may be the legendary Castle Corbenic of the Grail legends, the abode of the Fisher King and the birthplace of Sir Galahad. (Elyn)

Castell Dinas Brân is a romantic ruin, perched on top of a 308 m (1,010 ft) high hill above Llangollan. Although the giant Brân lived at Harlech (see p. 181; and see the Sec-

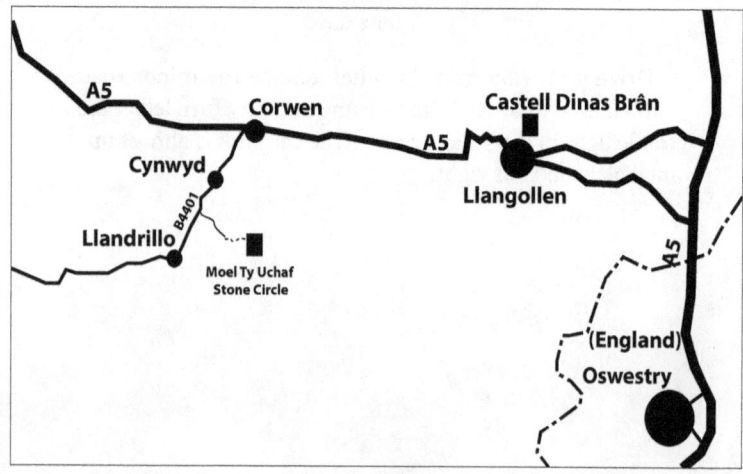

Area map

Approaching Castell Dinas Brân

ond Branch of the *Mabinogi*, "Branwen, Daughter of Llŷr") he apparently also lived here. At any rate, Castell Dinas Brân is named after him.

Originally it was an Iron Age hill fort. In the thirteenth century, Prince Gruffydd ap Madoc built a castle on the site. The site commands the entire region, providing a clear view of the River Dee (Afon Dyfrdwy) below and the hills in every direction. Strategically, it must have been an important place, but the fortification was only in use from the early 1260s to 1277, when it was destroyed and not rebuilt.

Hilary Wylde likened Dinas Brân to a kind of Welsh Mount Olympus: the possible seat of Brân the Blessed, the creator god who was too big to fit into a house. His Welsh name, Bendigeidfran, means "Blessed Raven." The locals sometimes refer to the ruins as Crow Castle. It is a place of power, seeming to focus the energy of surrounding hills.

Llangollen itself is an attractive and historic town, worth a visit and perhaps a short stay. It was located on the London to Holyhead stagecoach route in the eighteenth and nineteenth centuries. Don't miss visiting Plas Newydd, the house of the celebrated Ladies of Llangollen, an eccentric late-eighteenth, early-nineteenth century Anglo-Irish couple. Llangollen is the seat of the International Music

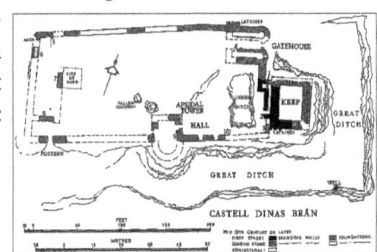

Site plan of the castle

  Eisteddfod, held in July, followed by the Llangollen Fringe, and is extremely busy at those times (http://www.international-eisteddfod.co.uk; http://www.llangollenfringe.co.uk). We recommend visiting at less popular times or else making reservations many months in advance.

Getting There

Llangollen is on the main A5 highway from London to the northwest coast and Angelsey (see map on p. 326). There are two ways to get to Castell Dinas Brân. Both require walking. The first is a gradual footpath that begins in Llangollen. It leads from Canal Bridge and runs beside Ysgol Dinas Brân. After passing several cottages, it reaches the lower slopes and becomes a zig-zag path to the summit. The second path is shorter but steeper. It can be reached by car from Llangollen and requires driving on a steep and narrow road. From just east of Llangollen, turn north off A539 at Trevor Uchaf at the Sun Terrace Bar. Continue to drive westward under Eglwyseg Rocks. Just east of the pub-

Interior of Castell Dinas Brân

lic footpath is a small pull-off for cars. Walk down the small lane running south. You'll see the trailhead, marked "Castell Dinas Brân," leading up the hill. This second route can also be approached from A539 west of Llangollen. Turn up a minor road at Pentrefelin and drive eastwards under Eglwyseg Rocks to the same parking area. The walk to the castell takes 15-25 minutes, depending on your fitness level. See http://www.cpat.org.uk/educate/guides/dinasb/dinasb.htm.

More to Experience

Moel Ty Uchaf Stone Circle, Denbighshire

The stone circle known as Moel Ty Uchaf ("High Bare House") is located in the Berwyn Mountains, on a hill above Llandrillo. It overlooks the Dee Valley.

This is "one of Wales' most famous prehistoric sites and represents the remains of a cairn circle, though unfortunately no traces of the inner cairn now survive" (Julian Heath, p. 107). The kerbstones are located on top of a hill. There are wonderful views. The 41 contiguous boulders, all about 5 ft high, form an almost perfect circle that is 39 ft in diameter. There are two gaps, one of which was presumably the original entrance. A well-preserved cist-grave, no longer covered by its cairn, is visible in the center. The original entrance to the cairn probably faced SSW. There is an outlier stone to the NNE. Another stone circle is located further along the footpath into the hills, and close to that a small standing stone. See http://www.cpat.org.uk/walks/ for detailed hiking information for Moel Ty Uchaf Stone Circle and Berwyn Burial Cairns.

We have been told the stone circle is energetically very powerful. Robin Heath found eclipse year, solar year, and lunar year measurements built into the circle. Laurence Main records that many "spirit paths" converge or radiate from Moel Ty Uchaf. Earth tremors, strange "earthlights," and possibly a downed flying saucer are also associated with the site (see Main, pp. 36-38).

Getting There

Follow A5 out of Llangollen towards Corwen. Where the road passes through Corwen and turns right toward the river, turn left onto B4401. Just past Cynwyd, look for a red telephone box located on the corner of a lane. Turn up that lane and follow it until you reach a gate, and park just beyond it (see map on p. 326). Follow the footpath up the hill until the stone circle comes into view (http://www.isleofalbion.co.uk/sites/28/moel-ty-uchaf.php).

Afterword

We hope you will visit many powerful places in Wales. As we have said, "it be deep." On the one hand, its natural beauty is obvious, abundant, and exuberant. It is a land filled with beaches, hills, and valleys that delight the eyes and nourish the heart. On the other hand, many of its powerful places are not "showy" and do not reveal themselves quickly. It is a country where you must slow down and stay awhile, sinking into the landscape and the stories of the land.

Learn to look at powerful places in Wales from all directions, all angles. Practice seeing a sacred site with both historic and mythic eyesight, experiencing the layers built upon layers. Bronze Age megaliths incorporated into a farmer's fence tell a story. So do a bubbling well sheltered under lichen-covered stones, an ancient yew, hollowed-out with age, shading what is now a churchyard but was once a burial mound, and a brooding mountaintop obscured by drifting fog.

Don't forget the people. It is their land, and they can help you enter into its mysteries. The Welsh are survivors: determined, fierce in their heritage and yet gentle and welcoming if you come with an open mind and a friendly smile. They take their traditions seriously—and if you do too, they'll take you seriously. The Welsh go deep. We found them rooted in their land, connected to the earth, the energies, and the stories that still live with them and through them.

Perhaps the best way to sum up Wales and the Welsh is the stirring national anthem. Better yet would be to hear it

---

"It's entirely conceivable that life's splendor surrounds us all, and always in its complete fullness, accessible but veiled, beneath the surface, invisible, far away. But there it lies, not hostile, not reluctant, not deaf. If we call it by the right word, by the right name, then it comes. This is the essence of magic, which doesn't create but calls." Franz Kafka, from his diaries, cited by Roberto Calasso.

sung by a Welsh male voice choir, with the audience standing and singing along, tears in their eyes:

The land of my fathers is dear unto me,
Old land where the minstrels are honored and free:
Its warring defenders, so gallant and brave,
For freedom their life's blood they gave.

Land!, Land!, True I am to my land!
While seas secure, this land so pure,
O may our old language endure.

O land of the mountains, the bard's paradise,
Whose precipice, valleys lone as the skies,
Green murmuring forest, far echoing flood
Fire the fancy and quicken the blood

For tho' the fierce foeman has ravaged your realm,
The old speech of Wales he cannot o'erwhelm,
Our passionate poets to silence command
Or banish the harp from your strand.

(http://en.wikipedia.org/wiki/National_Anthem_of_Wales)

Pronunciation Guide

(Many thanks to Gwen Saunders Jones and Huw Tegid of Menter Iaith Môn [Isle of Anglesey] for their painstaking work on the words in this pronunciation guide. The following pronunciations may have a slightly "North Walian" [northern] dialect slant. If there are any errors, they are the responsibility of Aviva and White.)

With the exception of some place names, the stress/accent is always on the penultimate syllable.

Aberdyfi/Aberdovey (pro. "aber-DUV-ee")

Aberhonddu (pro. "aber-HON-thee"—"dd" pro. like a hard "th" as in "then")

Aberteifi (pro. "aber-TEI-vee")

Aberystwyth (pro. "aber-IST-with"—a soft "th" as in "think")

Afon (pro. "AV-on")

Afon Dyfi (River Dovey) (pro. "AV-on duv-ee")

Afon Gwaun (pro. "AV-on gwine")

Annwn (pro. "ah-NOON")

Arianrhod (pro. "ah-ree-AN-rhod"—try and gently trill the "r" a bit like in Spanish; "rh" as in rhodedendron: the "o" is long as in road)

Barclodiad y Gawres (pro. "bar-CLOD-ee-add er GOW-rez")

Beuno (pro. "BAY-no")

Betws-y-Coed (pro. "betoos-er-coyd")

Blodeuwedd (pro. "blod-EYE-weth"—the "eye" like your eyes; soft "th" as in "think")

Branwen (pro. "BRAN-wen")

Bryn Myrddin (pro. "brin MUR-thin"—a hard "th" as in "then")

Bryn Celli Ddu (pro. "brin KEll-ee thee"—the 'll' is a voiceless, blown "l"; the "th" is hard, as in "then")

Bryn Gwyn (pro. "brin gwin")

Cadw (pro. "KA-doo")

Caerfyrddin (pro. "kaeer-VER-theen" —"dd" pro. like a hard "th" as in "then")

Carningli (pro. "karn in-glee")

Carreg Ddu (pro. "kareg thee"—"g" is hard, like "give"; "dd" pro. like a hard "th" as in "then")

Castell (pro. "KAS-tell"— the "ll" is a voiceless, blown "l")

Castell Dinas Brân (pro. "KAS-tell DI-nas brahn"— the "ll" is a voiceless, blown "l")

Castell Dinefawr (pro. "KAS-tell deen-EV-oor"—the "ll" is a voiceless, blown "l")

Castell Henllys (pro. "KAS-tell HEN-lleese"— the "ll" is a voiceless, blown "l")

Ceidio (pro. "KEYE-deeo")

Ceredigion (pro. "kere-DIG-eeun"—"g" as in "goat")

Ceridwen (pro. "ker-RID-wen")

Clynnog Fawr (pro. "KLI-nog VOW-er")

Croeso i Gymru (pro. "kroyso ee gum-ree")

Cwm (pro. "koom")

Cwm Cych (pro. "koom kee-ch"—"ch" as in Scottish "loch")

Cwm Gwaun (pro. "koom gwine")

Cymru (pro. "KUM-ree"—as in "come")

Dewi Sant (pro. "DE-wee SANT"—"de" as in "den"; could also be "DEW-ee," still with "de" as in "den")

Dinas Dinlle (pro. "DIN-as DIN-lleh"— the "ll" is a voiceless, blown "l")

Dolgellau (pro. "dol-GEll-ah-ee" — the "ll" is a voiceless, blown "l")

Dyffryn Ardudwy Burial Chambers (pro. "diff-rin ard-DUD-wee")

Eglwys (pro. "EG-lewis")

Eglwys Gadeiriol Llandaf (pro. "EG-lewis ga-DIRE-eeol LLAN-dav"— the "ll" is a voiceless, blown "l")

eisteddfod (pro. "aye-STETH vod"); the plural, eisteddfodau (pro. "aye-steth-vuh-dye"—"dd" pro. like a hard "th" as in "then")

Eryri (pro. "eh-RUH-ree")

Ffynnon (pro. "FUN-on")

Ffynnon Antwn (pro. "FUN-on AN-toon")

Ffynnon Gwenffrewi (pro "FUN-on gwen-FRE-wee")

Ffynnon Rhinweddol (pro. "FUN-on rhin-OOETH-ol"— "dd" pro. like a hard "th" as in "then")

Ffynnon Wnda (pro. "FUN-on OON-da")

Ffynhonnau Eglwys Gumfreston (pro. "fun-hon-aee eg-lewis gum-VRES-ton")

Foel Eryr (pro. "VOY-el AIR-eer")

Foel Feddau (pro. ""VOY-el VETH-aee"—"dd" pro. like a hard "th" as in "then")

Garnfadryn (pro. "ga-run-VAD-reen." This is the same pronunciation as the next name, but Garnfadryn is the name of a village)

Garn Fadrun (pro. "ga-run-VAD-reen"—name of a fort)

Goodwick (pro. "GOOD-ick)

Gors Fawr (pro. "gors VAW-er")

Govan (pro. "go-van")

Gumfreston is an English name for the village; the "f" is closer to "f" in France than "v" in Venice.

Gwaun (pro. "gwine")

Gwyndaf (pro. "gwin-dav")

Gwrtheyrn (pro. "nant GOOR-th-ay-rn" (soft "th," as in "think")

Hen Capel Lligwy (pro. "hane ca-PEL LLIG-wee"— the "ll" is a voiceless, blown "l")

llan (pro. "llan"— the "ll" is a voiceless, blown "l")

Llandeilo (pro. Llan-DAY-lo"—the "ll" is a voiceless, blown "l")

Llandudno (pro. "Llan-DUD-kno"— the "ll" is a voiceless, blown "l")

Llanfaglan (pro. "Llan-VAG-lan"— the "ll" is a voiceless, blown "l")

Llanfihangel (pro. "Llan-vee-HANG-el"—the "ll" is a voiceless, blown "l")

Llangollan (pro. Llan-GOLL-en"—the "ll" is a voiceless, blown "l")

Llangybi (pro. "Llan-GUB-ee"— the "ll" is a voiceless, blown "l")

Llanllawer (pro. "Llan-LLOW-er"— the "ll" is a voiceless, blown "l")

Llansteffan (pro. "Llan-STEF-an"— the "ll" is a voiceless, blown "l")

Llanthony is pronounced like the English "AN-thony" but beginning with the voiceless, blown "l".

Llanwnda (pro. "Llan-OON-da"— the "ll" is a voiceless, blown "l")

Llech y Drybedd (pro. "Llech uh DRUH-beth"— the "ll" is a voiceless, blown "l"; "dd" pro. like a hard "th" as in "then")

Lleu Llaw Gyffes (pro. "Llay llow GUH-fes"— the "ll" is a voiceless, blown "l"; "llow" rhymes with "how")

Lligwy (pro. "LLIG-wee"—the "ll" is a voiceless, blown "l")

Llŷn (pro. "lleen"— the "ll" is a voiceless, blown "l")

Llyn y Fan Fach (pro. "llin uh van vach"— the "ll" is a voiceless, blown "l")

Mabinogi (pro. "mabin-OG-i")

Maen Ceti (pro. "MINE KET-ti")

Meddygon Myddfai (pro. "me-THUH-gon MUTH-veye"—"dd" pro. as a hard "th" as in "this")

Melangell (pro. "me-LAAN-gell"— the "ll" is a voiceless, blown "l")

Modron (pro. "MOHD-ron")

Moel Ty Uchaf (pro. "moyl tee EECH-ay"—"ch" like the Scottish "loch")

Mwnt (pro. "moont")

Myddfai (pro. "muth-veye"—"dd" pro. like hard "th" as in "this")

Mynachlog-ddu (Pro. "muhn-ACH-log th-ee"—"ch" like the Scottish 'loch'; "dd" pro. as a hard "th" as in "this")

Mynydd (pro. "muhn-ith"—"dd" pro. like hard "th" as in "this")

Mynydd Carningli (pro. "MUHN-ith carn ING-lee—"dd" pro. like hard "th" as in "this")

Mynydd Dinas (pro. "MUHN-ith DIN-as"—"dd" pro. like hard "th" as in "this")

Mynydd Ddu (pro. "MUHN-ith thee"—"dd" pro. like hard "th" as in "this")

Mynydd Parys (pro. MUHN-ith PAR-is"—"dd" pro. like hard "th" as in "this")

Mynydd Preseli (pro. "MUHN-ith preseli"—"dd" pro. like hard "th" as in "this")

Myrddin (pro. "MER-thin"—rhymes with "Merlin"; "dd" pro. like hard "th" as in "this")

Nant Gwrtheyrn (pro. "nant GOOR-th-ay-rn" (soft "th" as in "think")

Parc y Merw (Meirw) (pro. "park uh me-eeroo")

Pennant Melangell (pro. "pennant me-LAAN-gell"— the "ll" is a voiceless, blown "l")

Pistyll (pro. "PIS-till"— the "ll" is a voiceless, blown "l")

Pistyll Rhaeadr (pro. "PIS-till RHAY-udder")

Plas Glyn-y-Weddw (pro. "plahs glyhn uh WETH-oo"—"dd" pro. as a hard "th" as in "this")

Plas yn Rhiw (pro. "plahs uhn RHE-oo"—"rh" like "rhod-edendron")

Pwyll, a character in the Mabinogi (pro. "poo-ell"— the "ll" is a voiceless, blown "l")

Pwllheli (pro. "pooll-HEL-ee"—the "ll" is a voiceless, blown "l")

Rhaeadr Ddu (pro. "RHAY-udder thee"—hard "th" as in "this")

Rhiannon (pro. "rhee-AN-on")

Siambr Gladdu Tinkinswood (pro. "sh-amber gla-thee tinkinswood"—"dd" pro. like hard "th" as in "this")

Tre'r Dryw Bach (pro. "tray-r dreeoo bach"—"ch" as in Scottish "loch")

Tyddewi (pro. "tee-THEW-ee"—"dd" pro. like "th" as in "this")

Tywi (pro. "tuh-wee")

Y Frenni Fawr (pro. "uh VREN-nee VOW-er")

Ynys Môn (pro. "in-is mawn")

Ynys Gybi (pro. "in-is GUH-bee")

Ynys Dewi (pro. "in-is DE-wee")

Ynys Enlli (pro. "in-is EN-llee"— the "ll" is a voiceless, blown "l")

Glossary

alignment A row of standing stones.

Anglican Christian churches with historical connections to the Church of England, established in the 1534 by Henry VIII in a breakaway from the Roman Catholic Church.

anima loci The "place-soul." The essential "personality" of a place. The sense of sacredness of a particular hill, spring, standing stone, etc.

archeo-astronomy The science of exploring the relationship between the positioning and orientating of megalithic constructions (dolmens, alignments, pyramids, etc.) and astronomical events (solstice, equinox, eclipses, etc.), including the study of related mythology, celestial lore, and astronomical practices.

auroch Large, wild, now-extinct ancestor of modern domestic cattle. Inhabited Europe, Asia, and North Africa.

axis mundi (world axis) A symbolic representation of the vertical "center" of the world; the cosmic axis or world pillar, where the heaven (sky) connects with the earth and access is possible between lower and higher realms. May be a tree, a pillar, etc.

barrow A mound of earth, turf, or peat covering a burial.

BCE Before the Common Era (contemporary replacement for BC, which stands for Before Christ).

Beltane The Celtic May Day festival (May 1). A Celtic cross-quarter day, since it falls approximately halfway between a solstice and an equinox. The cross-quarter days were important feast days in traditional Celtic societies.

bluestones See dolerite.

Bronze Age An age that began with metalworking, specifically the smelting of copper and tin to make bronze. In Britain, the Bronze Age lasted generally from 2100–750 BCE; in Wales, from about 2100 BCE - 650 BCE; in Scotland, it began just before 2000 BCE; in Spain, from 2200 - 750 BCE; in Brittany, from around 1900 - 800 BCE. The Bronze Age is associated with various types of cairns, sometimes built inside Neolithic henges or tombs.

burin A common Stone Age tool, similar to a chisel. Was used for engraving and for carving pieces of bone, wood, and antler.

cairn A human-made pile of stones, often in a conical form. They may be of recent construction or very old. Also refers to a megalithic tomb covered with small stones. Those we describe in this book were constructed in Neolithic times.

canon Member of a Catholic religious order (e.g., Augustinian), ordained as a priest. May live a life of poverty, chastity, and obedience without withdrawing from the world.

capstone The horizontal flat topstone that serves as a roof on a dolmen or cromlech.

carn A Welsh word for upthrusting summits, as in Carningli or Carn Enoch.

castell Stone fortification

Celt A nineteenth-century term used to describe any of the European peoples who spoke, or speak, a Celtic language. The term is also used in a wider sense to describe the modern descendants of those peoples, notably those who participate in a Celtic culture.

A member of a group of Indo-Europeans found in Germany and France in the Second Millennium BCE. The six territories recognized by the Celtic League and Celtic Congress as Celtic Nations are Brittany, Cornwall, Ireland, Isle of Man, Scotland, and Wales. Limiting the territories to these six is disputed by people from England, Asturias and Galicia in Spain, and several other European countries that also retain some Celtic cultural traits. Celts settled in Scotland beginning around 1000 BCE, in Wales around 600 BCE, and in Spain by the 6th century BCE. However, modern DNA testing is challenging some of these assumptions.

CE Common Era (contemporary replacement for AD, which stands for Anno Domini—in the Year of the Lord).

cist Stone-lined burial pit covered with a capstone, or a smallish stone box made to contain bones; may be what remains of the interior of a larger megalithic construction.

chalybeate (Spring) water heavy in iron content, often leaves a rust-red deposit and tastes of iron. Thought to have health-giving properties.

crannog A partly or entirely artificial island constructed in a lake, river, or estuary, dating back to 3000 BCE in Scotland and 1200 BCE in Ireland. The Welsh Crannog on Llangorse Lake dates to 916 CE. Crannogs were much more common in Scotland and Ireland than Wales. People built dwellings on them and lived on them for various reasons, including defense, convenience, prestige, and hermetic isolation.

cromlech Welsh word for megalithic tombs; in the past (and still today in several other countries), the same megalithic structures were called dolmens.

crypt A subterranean chamber or vault, especially one beneath the main floor of a church.

dinas Earthen fortification

dolmen A type of single-chamber megalithic (large stone) construction, usually consisting of three or more upright stones supporting a large flat horizontal capstone. Most date from the early Neolithic period (4000 - 3000 BCE). Although often used for burials, they were also ceremonial or "power" centers. They were initially covered with earth or small stones to form a tumulus or cairn, but in many cases that covering has weathered away. In Wales a dolmen is now usually referred to as a cromlech, a Welsh word for megalithic tombs.

dolerite A dark igneous rock. The famous bluestones in Stonehenge are a kind of spotted dolerite. When wet, the stone appears to be blue. Many of the examples at Stonehenge originally came from the Preseli Mountains in Wales, but how they reached Salisbury Plain is still a mystery.

dowse To search for underground water, metal, etc., by the use of a divining rod or pendulum. Dowsers: people who dowse.

Druid A member of the priestly and learned class active in Gaul, and perhaps in Celtic culture more generally, during the final centuries BCE. They were suppressed by the Roman government from the 1st century CE and disappeared from the written record by the 2nd century, although there may have been later survivals in Britain and Ireland. Their teachings were passed down orally and so very little is verifiably known about them.

eisteddfod (pl., *eisteddfodau*) a festival honoring Welsh music, performance, visual arts, and literature, which dates back to the twelfth century. Eisteddfodau are held throughout Wales.

eremitic Christian tradition, originating with the Egyptian Desert Fathers, of isolated, ascetic retreat and solitude, although sometimes practiced in community. Related to the word "hermit."

equinox The day (twice each year) when the tilt of the Earth's axis is inclined neither away from nor towards the Sun. The day when the night and day are nearly equal in length.

Estuary A body of water formed where rivers and streams flow into the ocean, causing freshwater to mix with seawater. An important place of transition, an estuary is influenced by tides, ocean waves, storms, and winds, but also partly protected because of nearby land or barrier islands.

faery A (perhaps) mythical being or spirit. Faeries are sometimes described as the wee folk, the good folk, or other euphemisms. We use the spelling "faery" to distinguish these powerful beings from the trivialized, popularized, romanticized "fairy."

geomancy An art that analyses the subtle earth energies that ebb and flow throughout the landscape, influencing health and wealth; home, garden, and office alike.

gorsedd (pl., *gorseddau*) A community gathering of modernday bards to promote literature, poetry, and music. Usually refers to the Welsh Gorsedd Beirdd Ynys Prydain, "The Gorsedd of Bards of the Island of Britain," although others exist in Cornwall and Brittany.

henge A large, nearly circular or oval prehistoric earthworks composed of a boundary ditch and an external bank.

Ice Age A geological period of long-term reduction in the temperature of the Earth's surface and atmosphere, resulting in an expansion of continental ice sheets, polar ice sheets, and alpine glaciers. The last Ice Age ended around 10,000 years ago in Europe.

igneous rock Comes from the Latin igneus, meaning fire. Volcanic in origin, formed from cooling, solidified molten magma. Igneous intrusive rock has solidified below the surface; if it solidified above the surface, it is called extrusive (volcanic) rock.

intervisibility Visible to each other. Megalithic sites were often constructed to be within sight of each other.

Iron Age The period after the Bronze Age, during which tools and weapons were primarily made of iron or steel, replacing bronze. The period began in Scotland around 700 BCE and in Wales perhaps as early as 650 BCE, although the earliest datable settlement, found on the Llŷn Peninsula, dates around 400 BCE. There is a paucity of evidence of burials but much evidence of defensive and domestic sites.

kerbstone A stone on the perimeter of a cairn or mound that forms part of the kerb; the stone footing or wall surrounding the site.

ley line "Line of sight" straight path, track, or line that can be drawn on a map that appears to run through several ancient and/or medieval sites, suggesting an intentional alignment. May also refer to "spirit paths" or "energy" paths that can be dowsed.

llan Originally, an enclosed piece of land, probably indicating a tribal enclosure. Later, the term became associated with a church and the surrounding parish built in this enclosure. Occurs frequently in Welsh place names, indicating the origin of the town as a sacred space, although sometimes the *llan* derives from another word, such as *glan* or *nant*.

Mabinogi, Mabinogion Medieval Welsh masterpiece, first written down in the late eleventh or early twelfth century, although it circulated in oral form much earlier. Composed of Four Branches of interrelated stories, which take place in what is today Wales and southwest England, and a group of seven additional stories that include the adventures of King Arthur and his knights.

megalith A large stone which has been used to construct a structure or monument, either alone or together with other stones. "Megalithic" means structures made of large stones, utilizing an interlocking system without the use of mortar or cement. They date from 4500 - 1500 BCE in Europe.

memento mori Latin for "Remember your mortality" or "Remember you will die." This genre of art, which dates back to antiquity, has as its purpose reminding the viewer that death is inevitable.

monolith Large freestanding stone.

nemeton A sacred space utilized in Celtic religion. *Nemetoi* appear to have been primarily situated in natural areas and often centered around trees; as such they are often described as sacred groves. *Nemeton* is related to the name of the Nemates tribe of what is now Germany and to the goddess Nemetona.

Neolithic The New Stone Age. A period in the development of human technology, beginning about 9500 BCE in the Middle East (5000 BCE in Brittany, 4000 BCE in Scotland and Wales, and 6000 BCE in Spain), that is traditionally considered the last part of the Stone Age. The Neolithic people were farmers who domesticated plants and animals and created pottery and woven textiles. They built numerous constructions, including dolmens, stone circles, and earthen henges and erected many standing stones. The Neolithic begins with the rise of farming, which produced the "Neolithic Revolution," and ends when metal tools became widespread in the Copper Age or Bronze Age or developed directly into the Iron Age, depending on geographical region. The Neolithic is not a specific chronological period, but rather a suite of behavioral and cultural characteristics, including the use of wild and domestic crops and the use of domesticated animals.

Nonconformist In England and Wales after the 1662 English Act of Uniformity, the term referred to non-Anglican religious groups, including Congregationalists, Baptist, Calvinists, Methodists, Unitarians, and the Salvation Army.

Ogham script An ancient form of writing, found exclusively in Ireland, Scotland, and Wales, dating around the third to sixth centuries CE.

Pantocrator Refers to Christ All-Powerful, Ruler of All, Christ All Mighty. A bearded haloed Christ is usually represented in a full frontal image, right hand raised in blessing, his left hand on a book, which may be open or closed.

passage tomb A megalithic site usually dating to the Neolithic. Some have simple single chambers, while others have sub-chambers leading off from the main chamber. They were entered via a long, covered entryway. They are called tombs but also served other ceremonial purposes.

piscine Shallow basin for holding holy water, often placed near the church altar.

puddingstone A brown sedimentary conglomerate stone composed of different kinds of rounded chunks of stone "cemented" in a matrix of very fine clay or sand.

red ochre Derived from naturally tinted earth (clay) containing mineral oxides. Ochres are some of the earliest pigments used by humankind; documented ochre use dates back at least 75,000 years.

rood screen Also known as a choir or chancel screen. An ornate divider between the chancel (space around the altar, located in the east end of the church) and the nave (main body of the church leading to the altar), popular in late medieval church architecture. Originally there would have been a rood loft above, on which was a Great Rood—a representation of the crucifixion. (Rood means cross or crucifix.) Found throughout Europe.

rhyolites A type of igneous volcanic (extrusive) rock.

sacred geometry Refers to the art or science of using geometrical forms, ratios, and relationships to embody and express sacred content. Practitioners share the underlying belief that these relationships and constants are intrinsic in nature and influence our experience of reality.

scree Also called talus. Comes from Old Norse word for landslide. Refers to broken rock that accumulates at the base of mountains, cliffs, carns, etc. Results from weathering, erosion, and deterioration of the rock face.

Sheela-na-gig Figurative carvings of (often skeletal) naked women displaying exaggerated genitalia. They are found on churches, castles, and other buildings, particularly in the British Isles, dating approximately from the 11th to 16th centuries. They have various and sometimes controversial interpretations.

simulacrum Means "likeness" or "similarity." Originally referred to a representation or copy of an original. In this guidebook, the word refers to discovering or observing a resemblance to human and animal forms in the shapes of boulders, mountain tops, trees, etc., e.g., seeing a sleeping goddess in the outline of the top of Carningli.

solstice An astronomical event that happens twice each year when the sun's apparent position in the sky reaches its northernmost or southernmost extremes. These correspond to the longest and shortest days of the year.

"squint" An angled opening resembling a window or peephole found in some churches and castles. A "squint" permitted worshippers to view the altar from a side chapel or castle owners or stewards to keep an (unseen) eye on events.

telluric Of or pertaining to the earth; terrestrial. Telluric currents are underground energy lines.

temenos A piece of land cut off and assigned as an official domain, especially to kings and chiefs, or a piece of land marked off from common uses and dedicated to a god, a sanctuary, holy grove or holy precinct.

"thin place" A place (in nature or in a human construction) where the veil between this world and other realms (faery, the Other World, etc.) is thin and passage between our normal consensual reality and a different kind of reality is more easily accomplished.

transept In medieval church architecture, the church often resembled a cross. If the nave and chancel formed the vertical piece, the transept formed the horizontal crosspiece.

vesica piscis (or pisces) Also known as a mandorla (almond shape). A geometrical shape formed by the intersection of two circles of equal diameter, so that the center of each lies on the perimeter of the other. Believed to have mystical significance, for example, representing the joining of God and Goddess and their offspring and forming the basic motif in the Flower of Life. Found in Christian art (Christ in Majesty and the Virgin Mary are sometimes represented inside a vesica piscis); in Gothic architecture; in Freemasonry; on the cover of the Chalice Well in Glastonbury; etc.

wouivre An old Gaulish name given to snakes that glide, to rivers that snake through the landscape, to telluric currents that snake underground from the depths of the terrestrial strata, bringing life that fructifies Earth and Man.

Bibliography

Atkinson, David, and Neil Wilson, *Lonely Planet – Wales.* Lonely Planet Publications: 2007.

Barber, Chris. *Mysterious Wales.* Abergavenny, Gwent: Blorenge Books, 2000.

Birch, Thomas. "The Incarceration of Wildness – Wilderness Areas as Prisons." *Environmental Ethics* 12 (1):3-26 (1990).

Blake, Steve, and Scott Lloyd. *The Keys to Avalon – The Compelling Journey to the Real Kingdom of Arthur.* London: Rider/Random House: revised and updated ed., 2003.

Boland, Eavan. "This is the noise of myth." In *The Journey and Other Poems.* Manchester: Carcanet, 1987. 322.

Bollard, John K., trans.; photography by Anthony Griffiths. *The Mabinogi – Legends and Landscape of Wales.* Llandysul, Ceredigion, Wales: Gomer Press, 2006, p. 110.

Bollard, John K., trans., photography by Anthony Griffiths. *The Companion Tales to the Mabinogi – Legends and Landscape of Wales.* Llandysul, Ceredigion, Wales: Gomer Press, 2007.

Bollard, John K., trans., photography by Anthony Griffiths. *Tales of Arthur.* Llandysul, Ceredigion, Wales: Gomer Press, 2010.

Borrow, George. *Wild Wales.* Wrexham: Bridge Books, 2002 (first published in 1862).

Brown, Elizabeth. *Dowsing – The Ultimate Guide for the 21st Century.* Carlsbad, CA: Hay House, 2010.

Brown, Joseph Epes. *Teaching Spirits: Understanding Native American Religious Traditions*. USA: Oxford University Press, 2010.

Burrow, Steve. *The Tomb Builders in Wales 4000-3000 BC*. Cardiff: National Museum Wales Books, 2006, p. 105 (pillar in Bryn Celli Ddu).

Butler, W. E. *Lords of Light – The Path of Initiation in the Western Mysteries*. Rochester, VT: Destiny Books, 1990.

Cantrell, John, and Arthur Rylance. *Sarn Helen – Walking a Roman Road through Wales*. A Cicerone Guide. Milnthorpe, Cumbria: Cicerone Press, 1992.

Calasso, Roberto. *K*. Translated by Geoffrey Brock. Vintage, 2006.

Children, George, and George Nash. *Neolithic Sites of Cardiganshire, Carmarthenshire & Pembrokeshire*. (also titled *The Anthropology of Landscape: A Guide to Neolithic Sites in Cardiganshire, Carmarthenshire & Pembrokeshire*). Monuments in the Landscape Vol. V. Herefordshire: Logaston Press, revised 2008 .

Clowes, Carl. *Nant Gwrtheyrn – Rebirth of the Lost Village*. Pwllheli, Gwynedd: Ymddiriedolaeth Nant Gwrtheyrn, 2008.

Cooper, Susan. *The Dark is Rising Sequence*. Great Britain: A Bodley Head Book, 2007. (Original copyright, 1984).

Cope, Phil. *Holy Wells: Wales – a photographic journey*. Bridgend: Seren, 2008.

Dames, Michael. *Merlin & Wales – A Magician's Landscape*. London: Thames & Hudson, 2002.

Davies, Brian. *Welsh Place-Names Unzipped.* Talybont, Ceredigion: Y Lolfa Cyf., 2001; http://www.ylolfa.com/.

Davies, Damian Walford and Anne Eastham. *Saints and Stones.* Llandysul, Ceredigion: Gomer Press, 2002.

Devereux, Paul. *The Sacred Place: The Ancient Origin of Holy and Mystical Sites.* London: Cassel & Co., 2000.

Folklore, Myths and Legends of Britain, 2nd Edition. London: Reader's Digest Association Ltd., 1997.

Gerrard, David. *The Hidden Places of Wales.* Plymouth, Devon: Travel Publishing Ltd, 2008.

Graves, Tom. *Needles of Stone Revisited.* Glastonbury: Gothic Image Publications, 1986.

Gregory, Donald. *Country Churchyards in Wales.* Llanrwst, Wales: Gwasg Carreg Gwalch, 2002.

Gwyndaf, Robin. "Welsh Folk Narrative and the Fairy Tale," In *A Companion to the Fairy Tale,* ed. Hilda Ellis Davidson and Anna Chaudhri. Cambridge: D. S. Brewer, 2003, pp. 191-202.

Hale, Susan Elizabeth. *Sacred Space, Sacred Sound – The Acoustic Mysteries of Holy Places.* Wheaton, Il: Quest Books, 2007.

Heath, Julian. *Sacred Circles – Prehistoric Stone Circles of Wales.* Pwllheli, Gwynedd: Llygad Gwalch, 2010.

Heath, Robin. *Bluestone Magic – A Guide to the Prehistoric Monuments of West Wales.* St Dogmaels, Cardigan: Bluestone Press, 2010.

Heaven, Ross. *Walking with the Sin Eater – A Celtic Pilgrimage on the Dragon Path.* Woodbury, MN: Llewellyn Publ., 2010.

Hopkins, Gerard Manley. *Poems*. Oxford University Press, 4th ed., 1967.

Hopkins, Gerard Manley. Poems. 1918. #16. "In the Valley of the Elwy." http://www.bartleby.com/122/16.html, retrieved 22 Jan. 2012.

Howard, Michael. "The Womb of Ceridwen." In *The Cauldron – Witchcraft, Paganism, and Folklore,* #98. Article available online at http://www.the-cauldron.org.uk/thewombofceridwen.htm

Hughes, T. J. *Wales's Best One Hundred Churches*. Bridgend: Seren (imprint of Poetry Wales Press Ltd.), 2006.

John, Brian. *Carningli – Land and People*. Newport, Pembs.: Greencroft Books, 2008.

John, Brian. *The Bluestone Enigma – Stonehenge, Preseli and the Ice Age*. Newport, Pembs.: Greencroft Books, 2008.

John, Brian. *Echoes and Shadows – Tales and Traditions of Newport and Nevern*. Newport, Pembs.: Greencroft Books, 2008.

Jones, Kathy. *The Ancient British Goddess*. Ariadne Publications, 1991.

Le Nevez, Catherine, Mike Parker, and Paul Whitfield. *The Rough Guide to Wales*. New York: Rough Guides, 2009.

Lieberman, Marcia. *Being still – standing stones in Wales*. Pt Reyes Station, CA: ORO editions, 2011 (www.beingstillbook.com)

Main, Laurence. *The Spirit Paths of Wales*. A Cicerone Guide. Milnthorpe, Cumbria: Cicerone Press, 2000.

Markale, Jean. *Merlin – Priest of Nature.* Rochester, VT: Inner Traditions translation, 1995 (originally published in French, 1981).

McDonald, Neil. *Anglesey – A Megalithic Journey.* London: Mutus Liber, 2010.

Miles, Dillwyn. *A Book on Nevern.* LLandysul, Ceredigion: Gomer Press, 1998.

Morton, Andrew. *Trees of the Celtic Saints – the Ancient Yews of Wales.* Llanrwst: Gwasg Carreg Gwalch, 2009.

Murphy, Julia. "Archaeology as Folklore; the literary construction of the megalith Pentre Ifan in West Wales." In *Archaeology and Folklore*, ed. by A. Gezin-Schwartz and C. F. Hortoff. Routledge, 1999.

Owen, Tefor M. *The Customs and Traditions of Wales* (A Pocket Guide). University of Wales Press: 1991 (2006 reprint).

Packer, Anthony. "Mediaeval Welsh spirituality." *Journal of Welsh Religious History*, Vol. 4 (1996), p. 1-21.

Patten, Terry. "Finding Absolute Freedom in Any Moment: The Practice of Ever-Present Awareness." Session Four in *Integral Spiritual Practice: The 8-Week Course,* 2011. Evolving Wisdom, San Rafael, CA. http://evolvingwisdom.com/integralspiritualpractice/online-course/

Pennick, Nigel. *Celtic Sacred Landscapes.* New York: Thames & Hudson Inc., 1996.

Petro, Pamela. *The Slow Breath of Stone – A Romanesque Love Story.* London and New York: Fourth Estate (HarperCollins), 2005.

Phillips, Graham. *The Marian Conspiracy – The Hidden Truth about the Holy Grail, the Real Father of Christ and the Tomb of the Virgin Mary.* London: Sidgwick & Jackson, 2000.

Prevett, Tim. *Roads & Trackways of North Wales.* Ashbourne, UK: Landmark Publ., 2008.

Redgrove, Peter. *The Black Goddess and the Sixth Sense.* London: Paladin/Collins Publ., 1989.

Rhys, John. *Celtic Folklore - Welsh and Manx.* Wildwood, 1983. First publ. by Oxford University Press, 1901.

Roberts, Tony. *Myths & Legends of Wales.* Aberteifi, Ceredigion: Abercastle Publications, 1984 (reprint 2008).

Scarre, Chris. *The Megalithic Monuments of Britain and Ireland.* London: Thames & Hudson Ltd., 2007.

_____, editor. *Monuments and Landscape in Atlantic Europe – Perception and Society During the Neolithic and Early Bronze Age.* London: Routledge, 2002.

Senior, Michael. *Cromlechs and Cairns in northern Wales.* Llanrwst, Wales: Gwasg Carreg Gwalch, 2006.

Silva, Freddy. *Common Wealth – The Origin of Sacred Sites and the Rebirth of Ancient Wisdom.* Portland, ME: Invisible Temple, 2011.

Soskin, Rupert. Standing with Stones. New York: Thames & Hudson, 2009.

Stewart, R. J. *Merlin: The Prophetic Vision and Mystic Life.* New edition. RJ Stewart Books, 2011.

Stewart, R. J., and John Matthews. *Merlin Through the Ages – A Chronological Anthology and Source Book.* London: Blandford, 1995.

Strachan, Gordon. *Jesus the Master Builder – Druid Mysteries and the Dawn of Christianity.* Edinburgh: Floris Books, 2010 (originally published1998).

Sutton, Maya Magee, and Nicholas R. Mann. *Druid Magic – The Practice of Celtic Wisdom.* Llewellyn: 2000.

Temple, Jack. *The Healer – the extraordinary story of Jack Temple.* Findhorn, Scotland: Findhorn Press edition, 2002 (original © 1998).

Tolstoy, Nikolai. *The Quest for Merlin.* London: Hodder and Stoughton, ©1985.

Watkins, Alfred. *The Old Straight Track.* Abacus Little, Brown: 1988; © 1925.

Watney, John. *Celtic Wales.* Hampshire, UK: Pitkin Guides, 1997.

Wingfield, Megan. *The Grail Journey through Wales.* Twickenham, UK: Athena Press, 2007.

Yates, M. J., and David Longley. *Anglesey – A Guide to Ancient Monuments on the Isle of Anglesey.* Cardiff: Cadw, 3rd edition 2001.

Index

A

Abercastle 104, 356
Abercych vi, 44, 152, 156
Aberdaron 22, 313, 315
Aberdovey vi, 176, 177, 187, 333
Abergavenny 161, 196, 204, 205, 210, 211, 215, 351
Aberhonddu 203, 333
Aberteifi 190, 333, 356
Aberystwyth 167, 170, 190, 217, 333
Acts of Union 31
addanc 176
Afagddu 188
Afallach 252, 309, 310
afanc 176
Afon Dyfi 41, 333
Afon Gwaun 106, 333
Afon Nyfer 139, 145
Age of Saints 29, 89, 227
Alfred Lord Tennyson 253
Aneirin 13
Anglesey vi, 16-18, 28, 66, 167, 238-240, 257-259, 264, 267, 271, 273, 275-277, 280-290, 333, 355, 357
Anglican Church 31
Anglican Society for Promoting Christian Knowledge 32
Annwn 13, 93, 120, 154, 172, 236, 333
Arbeth 13
Ardudwy Megaliths vi, 182
Ardudwy Trackway 183
Arianrhod 14, 117, 241-243, 295-297, 333
Arthur's Quoit 97, 140
Arthur's Stone 74
Athgreany Stone Circle iv
Avalon 18, 243, 252, 253, 310, 314, 351
Avebury 264
axis mundi 23, 340

B

Bala Lake 23, 188, 234
Bannau Brycheiniog 196
Baptists 31
Barclodiad y Gawres vi, 262, 267-269, 270, 333
Bardsey Island 18, 86, 144, 192, 240, 252, 293, 298, 299, 304, 306, 307, 310, 313, 314
Battle of Mynydd Carn 109
Bedd Branwen 286
Beddgelert 244, 251
Bedd Taliesin 187
Bell Rock 82
Beltane 201, 311, 340
Berwyn Mountains 235, 236, 329
Betws-y-Coed 255, 256, 333
Bishop's Palace v, 89, 90, 93
Bishop Urban 48
Blodeuedd 14
Brân vii, 13, 181, 238, 240, 246, 326-329, 334
Branwen 14, 181, 240, 243, 286, 327, 334
Brecon 203
Brecon Beacons vi, 37, 42, 59, 160, 161, 194-196, 200, 202-207
Bristol Channel 27
Brithdir Stone Circle 141, 143
Brithdir Torrent Walk 185
Broadleaf dock 37
Bronze Age 28
Brut y Tywysogyon 164
Bryn Cader Faner 183
Bryn Celli Ddu vi, 17, 38, 41, 259-263, 268-270, 334, 352
Bryn Gwyn vi, 264-267, 334
Bryn Myrddin 20, 85, 334

Bwlch-y-Saethau 252

C

Cadair Idris 19, 58, 119, 160, 171-179, 251
Cadw 36
Caerfyrddin 85, 253, 334
Caerleon 50, 51, 251
Caermeini 115
Caldey Island 18, 80
Calvinists 31, 347
Caman llan 150
Cambrian Coast vi, 160, 181, 185
Cambrian Mountain 27
Cambrian Mountains 161
Candle Center 112, 113
Capel Garmon 256
Caradoc 308, 321
Cardiff Castle 50
Cardigan 140, 157, 158, 159, 161, 173, 183, 190, 191, 314, 315, 316, 353
Cardigan Bay 161, 173, 183, 314-316
Carew Cheriton 76
Carmarthen 20, 45, 46, 65, 85, 86, 190, 200, 202, 253
Carnedd Meibion Owen 139
Carn Enoch vi, 97, 115, 119, 122-124, 341
Carn Fadrun vii, 309
Carn Ingli vi, 16, 19, 58, 97, 112, 115, 118, 119, 133, 142, 150
Carningli 118
Carn Meini 115, 116
Carn Menyn 103, 115, 118, 130, 133
Carreg Cennen v, 44, 59-64
Carreg Coetan Arthur 97, 140, 141
Carreg Samson iv, 102-104
Carregwastad Point 101
castell 152
Castell Bryn Gwyn vi, 264-267
Castell Dinas Brân vii, 238, 326-329, 334
Castell Dinefwr 59, 64
Castell Henllys 144, 152, 334
Castell-y-Bere 178
Cat Hole Cave v, 44, 68, 70, 71
Catholicism 31
Cenarth 156, 158, 159
Ceredigion Coast Path 161, 190
Ceridwen 23, 116, 117, 135-137, 147, 149, 162, 188, 189, 234, 243, 334, 354
Cerrig Marchogion 116
Chair of Idris 171-173
Chapel of Our Lady and St Non 95
Chepstow 36, 53
Chrétien de Troyes 253
Chronicle of the Princes 164
Church in Wales 31-33
Cilgerran Castle 157
Cistercian 31, 52, 80, 162, 163
Clawdd-y-Milwyr 97
Clynnog Fawr vii, 293, 299-301, 308, 334
Clywedog River 185
Coed y Brenin Forest Park 183
Coetan Arthur 38, 97, 140, 141, 182
Congregationalists 31, 347
Conwy Valley 173, 254
coracle 157
Corn Du 196
Cornel Bach Standing Stones 126
Corwen 330
Cotswold-Severn 56, 68, 256
Craflwyn Center 251
Craig Rhos-y-Felin 115
Craig yr Aderyn 180
Crearwy 188
Cwm Bychan 186
Cwm Cych vi, 13, 46, 152-154, 334
Cwm Gadair 172
Cwm Gwaun 105, 106, 112, 113, 335

Cylch y Trallwyn 130
Cymru 12, 30, 33, 86, 250, 335
Cytiau'r Gwyddelod 291

D

Dee Estuary 36
Deheubarth 30, 65-67, 163, 164
Deneb 131
Devil's Bridge 170
dinas 152
Dinas Dinlle vii, 242, 294-297, 335
Dinas Emrys vi, 238, 243-251, 303
Dinefwr Castle v, 64
Din Lligwy 272-277
Discoed vi, 160, 216, 222-224
Dolgellau 175, 176, 183-186, 235, 335
Dolmelynllyn 183
Dôn 14, 117, 173, 241
Dreaming Stone 131, 132
Druid 24, 66, 134, 135, 138, 146, 166, 224, 235, 239, 244, 257, 258, 284, 285, 303, 324, 325
Druids' Circle 324, 325
Dulas River 153
Dyfed 30, 46, 83, 91, 152
Dyffryn Ardudwy 182, 183, 335
Dyffryn Fernant 112
Dyffryn House 58
Dyfi Estuary 187
Dysynni Valley 177, 178

E

Edward I 30, 161, 164, 181, 182, 258, 278
Eglwys Gadeiriol Llandaf v, 44, 47, 335
Eglwys Gumfreston v, 75-78, 335
Eglwys Pontfaen 110
Egyptian Desert Fathers 29, 344
eisteddfodau 12, 33, 41, 335, 344

Elen Lluyddog 200, 201
Elen of the Ways 201
Elphin 189

F

Faerie Queen 67
Fairy Glen 254, 255
Felindre Farchog 152
Fferyllt 188
Fforest Fawr 194, 202
Ffwrrwm Center 51
Ffynnon Antwn 83, 335
Ffynnon Fair 22, 125, 279
Ffynnon Gwenffrewi 22, 321, 335
Ffynnon Non 93
Ffynnon Wnda v, 44, 98, 99, 102, 312, 335
Ffynone Falls 13, 46
Fionn Mac Cumhaill 188
First and Third Branches of the *Mabinogi* 83
First Branch of the *Mabinogi* 46, 106, 154
Fishguard 101, 105, 106, 107, 112, 118, 119, 123, 140
Foel Eryr 114, 117, 335
Fourth Branch of the *Mabinogi* 240, 296

G

Garnfadryn vii, 19, 309, 336
Garn Fawr 97, 103, 104, 122
Garn Fechan 97, 104, 105
Garn Wnda v, 98, 102, 103
Geoffrey of Monmouth 51, 248, 249, 253
Gerald of Wales 99, 206, 210, 213
Gerallt Cymro 99
Giraldus Cambrensis 99, 210, 226
Glamorgan v, 32, 44, 56, 68, 73, 74
Golden Dawn 182
Golden Road 114-118, 129

Goodwick 102, 105, 336
Gop vii, 19-21, 238, 239, 317-320
Gorsedd 12, 33, 344
Gors Fawr vi, 38, 114, 124, 129-132, 141, 336
Gower Heritage Center 72
Gower Peninsula v, 44, 68, 72-74
Graig Lwyd 324, 325
Great Orme 239, 323, 324
Great White Sow 149
Green Men 91
Grim Reaper 209, 210
Gumfreston church 75
Gwaun Valley v, 44, 105-118
Gwaun Valley Brewery 112
Gwenffrewi 22, 308, 321, 335
Gwion Bach 162, 188, 189
Gwydion 14, 173, 241, 242, 294, 296, 297
Gwyn ap Nudd 172, 175, 310
Gwyndaf v, 44, 67, 98, 99, 102, 198, 336, 353
Gwytherin Convent 322

H

Harddlech vi, 14, 181
Harlech vi, 14, 161, 181-183, 186, 240, 326
Harold Stones 53
Hen Capel Lligwy 276, 336
Henry III 30
Henry IV 31
Henry VII 31, 321
Henry VIII 31, 52, 165, 340
Heol Senni 202
Holyhead 259, 280, 290, 291, 310, 327
Holy Island 18, 290, 308
Holywell 144, 239, 321, 323

I

Ice Age 27, 62, 70, 71, 171, 201, 234, 345, 354

Idris ap Gwyddno 173
Irish Sea 27
Iron Age 6, 17, 45, 61, 65, 95, 97, 106, 107, 112, 114, 120, 132, 138, 144, 152, 192, 250, 266, 273, 291, 295, 302, 309, 326, 327, 345, 347
Isle of Anglesey vi, 16, 17, 28, 239, 257, 333, 357
Isle of Avalon 18, 253, 314
Isle of Iona 247
Issui 206-208, 210

J

Jack o' Kent 53
John Jones 198
Joseph of Arimathea 88, 166, 167, 243, 280
Julius Caesar 28

K

King Arthur 12, 13, 18, 20, 51, 61, 74, 86, 93, 94, 97, 116, 140, 149, 167, 173, 176, 189, 236, 242, 245-253, 314, 346
King Arthur's Round Table 51
King Tewdrig 52

L

Lady Chapel 91, 92
Lady of the Lake 20
Landranger 36
Last Invasion of Britain 101, 104
ley lines 6, 7, 133, 201, 216
Llamrai 176
Llan 346
Llanbedr 186
Llandaff Cathedral v, 44, 47-50, 126
Llandeilo v, 29, 44, 59, 64, 68, 126, 128, 336
Llandudno 29, 323-325, 336

Llanfaglan Church vii, 283, 292, 293
Llanfihangel-y-Pennant 178, 179
Llangadog 196
Llangenni 211
Llangollan vii, 326, 337
Llangolman 128, 129
Llangorse Lake 205, 206, 342
Llangybi vii, 310, 312, 337
Llanhowell 103
Llanllawer Church v, 107
Llanrhaeadr-ym-Mochanant 237
Llansteffan 83, 84, 337
Llanthony Priory vi, 160, 196, 212-215
Llanwnda Church 99
Llanychaer 106, 107, 108
Llech y Drybedd 143, 337
Llech-y-Tribedd 133, 143
Lleu Llaw Gyffes 242, 296, 337
Lligwy Complex vi, 271
Llyfr Taliesin 189
Llyn Barfog 176, 177
Llyn Carreg Bach 22
Llyn Cau Lake 173
Llyn Cerrig Bach 284, 285
Llyn Fawr 23
Llŷn Peninsula vii, 14, 19, 40, 123, 238-240, 252, 292, 295, 298, 299, 302, 306, 309-316, 345
Llyn Tegid 175, 234
Llyn y Fan Fach vi, 23, 67, 197, 200, 337
Llŷr 14, 46, 83, 240, 246, 326, 327
Llywelyn ap Gruffydd 30, 164
Llywelyn ap Iorwerth 178
Llywelyn the Great 164, 178
Loughcrew 262
Lourdes of Wales 22, 321, 322

M

Mabinogi 13

Machynlleth 31, 176
Madron 19
Madryn 309, 310
Maen Ceti 74, 75, 337
Maenclochog vi, 22, 124-129
Maenclochog Church vi, 124, 125
Maen Llia 202, 203
Maen Madoc 202, 203
Maglocunus Stone 147
Magnus Maximus 200-202
mandatum 165
Marcher Lords 30, 31
Mary Jones 178, 179
Math 14, 241, 242, 296, 297
Matholwch 14, 181, 240
Mathonwy 14, 241, 296
Meddygon Myddfai 197, 337
memento mori 47, 48, 346
Menai Strait 241, 257, 263, 277, 282, 283, 289, 292-295
Merlin 11, 12, 18-20, 38, 45, 67, 68, 85, 86, 115, 242-253, 298, 338, 352-357
Merlin's Hill 85, 86
Methodism 31
Moel Goedog 183
Moel Ty Uchaf 329, 338
Morfan 188
Morte d'Arthur 253
Mount Olympus 327
Mt Snowdon 19, 172
Mwnt 191-193, 338
Myddfai vi, 23, 41, 67, 163, 197-200, 337, 338
Mynachlog-ddu 118, 129, 338
Mynydd Dinas 106, 122, 124, 338
Mynydd Preseli vi, 19, 41, 44, 114, 118, 122, 124, 132, 143, 338
Mynydd Preseli Walk 118
Myrddin 11, 20, 85, 247-253, 314, 334, 338

N

Nanteos Cup 162, 166, 167
Nanteos House 167, 168
Nant Gwrtheyrn vii, 245, 302-304, 338, 352
Nant Mair 210
Narberth 83
Narbeth 13
national anthem 331
National Botanic Garden of Wales 45, 86
National Coracle Center 158
Neanderthal 27
nemeton 24, 346
Nennius 51, 190, 253
Neolithic 27, 45, 104, 119, 170, 182, 256, 260, 266, 267, 271, 272, 317, 318, 323, 341, 343, 347, 352, 356
Nest 157
Newport v, 27, 38, 45, 50, 51, 105, 112, 113, 118, 121, 122, 124, 133, 137-141, 144, 354
Newton House 64, 65, 68
Nonconformist 12, 31, 32, 347
Nos Galan Gaeaf 117

O

Offa's Dyke 30, 196, 213, 215
Ogham 24, 80, 124, 125, 146, 147, 347
Old Lligwy Chapel 276
Old Priory 80
Old Radnor 226
Oriel Ynys Môn 288, 289
OS Explorer 36, 175
Otherworld 22, 24, 120, 135, 154, 175, 236, 309, 310, 315
Owain ap Gruffydd 30
Owain Glyndwr 30
Owain of Powys 157
Owen Glendower 30, 139

P

Paleolithic 27, 62
Pantocrator 100, 347
Parc le Breos v, 44, 68-72
Parc y Merw v, 109, 338
Parkmill 72
Partrishow vi, 17, 160, 206, 207
Parys Mountain 289
Pass of the Arrows 252
Patrisio vi, 17, 160, 206-211, 226
Paviland Cave 73
Pembrokeshire Coast National Park 82, 89, 114
Pembrokeshire Coast Path 89, 133, 190
Penlan Uchaf Gardens 112
Penmaenmawr 324, 325
Penmon Priory vi, 277-280, 312
Pennant Melangell vi, 160, 227-233, 338
Pentre Ifan vi, 16, 113, 115, 124, 132-139, 144, 150, 188, 355
Pen y Fan 196
Physicians of Myddfai 23, 197, 198
Pilgrim's Cross 151
Pistyll Rhaeadr 235-339
Plaid Cymru 33
Plas Glyn-y-Weddw 315, 316, 339
Plas Newydd 289, 327
Plas yn Rhiw 316, 339
Plysgos 157
Pontfaen v, 106, 110-112
Pontnewydd Cave 27
Pontrhydfendigaid 169
Pont Saeson 115
Porthclais 88
Powys vi, 17, 30, 157, 160, 161, 203, 206, 216, 217, 222, 225-228, 235
Preseli Hills vi, 19, 41, 44, 46, 106, 109, 113-116, 122, 124, 132
Prestatyn 320
Presteigne 222-226

Prince Brochwel 228, 229
Prince of Wales 30, 31
Protestantism 31
puddingstone 53, 348
Pwyll 13, 41, 46, 83, 152-154, 241, 339

Q

Queen Elizabeth II 92

R

Radnor Forest vi, 160, 216, 217, 226
Ramsey Island 98
Rhaeadr Ddu 184, 339
Rheidol River 170
Rhiannon 13-15, 46, 83, 106, 117, 171, 241, 243, 339
Rhiwallon of Myddfai 163
Rhos-y-gilwen 154-157, 240, 242
Rhys ap Gruffydd 61, 65, 163
Rita Gawr 19, 251
Ritec Valley 76
River Dovey 187, 333
River Glaslyn 250
River Gwaun 105, 106
River Mynach 170
Robert de Boron 166
Roman Legion Museum 51
Roman Steps 186
Romantic Movement 33
Rosebush 118, 126

S

Sarn Helen 200, 202, 203, 352
Second Branch of the *Mabinogi* 181, 240, 326
Sennybridge 202
Siambr Gladdu Tinkinswood 56, 339
Simulacrum 121
Sir Benfro 45

Skirrid Mountain 53, 215
Snowdonia vi, 14, 19, 160, 161, 171-173, 194, 202, 239-246, 250-252, 255, 277, 316, 324
Snowdonia National Park vi, 19, 161, 171-173, 239, 243, 244, 251, 252, 255
St Anne's Well 53
St Anthony's Well 83, 84
St Beuno vii, 299-301, 306-308, 321, 322
St Beuno's Church vii, 299-301, 306-308
St Bride 41, 45, 89, 96, 97
St Brynach v, vi, 19, 44, 96, 110, 111, 119, 120, 128, 144-146, 149, 150
St Brynach's Church v, vi, 44, 110, 111, 144
St Brynach's Day 146
St Cybi's Well vii, 310-312
St Davids v, 41, 44, 46, 76, 80, 87-92, 96-98, 105, 115, 119, 123, 140, 144, 192
St Davids Cathedral v, 90, 91
St David's Head 96-98
St Davids Parish Church 80
St Dogmael's 190
St Dyfrig 47
St Govan's Chapel 81, 82
St Illtud's Church 80
St Illtyd's Chapel 49
stinging nettles 37, 222
St Lythan's Cromlech 58
St Mary's Church 124, 204, 223
St Mary's Well 22, 125
St Melangell vi, 160, 227-233
St Michael's Church vi, 198, 199, 216-218, 222, 223, 227
St Nicholas 58, 59
St Non's Well v, 87, 89, 93, 94, 96
Strata Florida vi, 31, 144, 160, 162-170, 198
Strumble Head 102, 103

St Seiriol's Holy Well vi, 277, 281
St Teilo vi, 22, 47, 59, 124-129
St Teilo's Well vi, 22, 124-129
St Tysilio Church 282
St Winifred 96, 321
St Winifred's Well 22, 239, 321, 322
Swansea Museum 73

T

Taliesin vi, 13, 162, 187-190
Tal-y-Llyn 175
TalyLlyn Lake 175
TalyLlyn Railway 176
Tanat Valley 227, 228, 233
Teifi Marshes Nature Reserve 157
Teifi River 157
Tenby 77-80, 128
Third Branch of the *Mabinogi* 46
Thomas Malory 253
Tinkinswood Burial Chamber v, 44, 56, 57, 119
Tintern Abbey 52-55
Trefdraeth 139
Treffynnon 103, 321
Treffynon 22
Tregaron 169, 171
Tregaron Bog 171
Trellech 53, 55
Tre Taliesin vi, 187, 189
Tudor Acts of Union 31
Twrch Trwyth 116, 117, 149, 253
Tŷ Canol vi, 138
Tycanol Wood 132, 138, 139
Ty Canol Woods 113
Tylwyth Teg 134, 138, 254
Tyn-y-ddol 179
Ty Talcen 199, 200
Tywn Wharf 176

U

Underworld 13, 20, 46, 152-155, 172
Upper Paleolithic 27, 62

Urban of Llandaf 29
Ursa Major 253
Usk Valley 196

V

Vale of Rheidol Railway 170
Valle Crucis 31
Virgin Mary 22, 167, 191, 280, 350, 356
Virtuous Well 53-55
Vitalianus Stone 146
Vortigern 11, 243-250, 303-305, 310

W

Wales Coast Path 36
Wales Millennium Centre 56
Warrior's Dyke 97
Welsh Not 33
Welsh Regimental Chapel 47
White Horse 103
White Lady 109, 117
White Park cattle 65, 66
Whitesands Bay 97, 115
Whitland Abbey 162
William de Lacy 213
William Morgan 31
William the Conqueror 30, 92, 226
Witches Cauldron 133

Y

Y Fenni 204
Yggdrasil 23
Ynys Dewi 98, 339
Ynys Enlli 18, 298, 306, 313, 314, 339
Ynys Gybi 290, 339
Ynys Môn vi, 18, 239, 243, 257, 258, 267, 275, 277, 280, 288, 289, 298, 310, 339
Ystradfellte 195, 202
Ystrad Fflur vi, 162

www.ingramcontent.com/pod-product-compliance
Lightning Source LLC
Chambersburg PA
CBHW022100150426
43195CB00008B/210